NH

T5-ASN-626

PUBLIC ENTERPRISE

By Professor Ramanadham — A Select List

Public Enterprise in Britain (Frank Cass, London, 1959)

Problems of Public Enterprise (Quadrangle, Chicago)

The Structure of Public Enterprise in India
(Asia Publishing House, New York, 1961)

The Finances of Public Enterprises
(Asia Publishing House, New York, 1963)

Control of Public Enterprises in India
(Asia Publishing House, New York, 1964)

The Structure of the British Electricity Supply Industry
(Kamath, Mangalore, 1954)

The Yugoslav Enterprise (ICPE, Ljubljana, 1982)

Parliament and Public Enterprise (ICPE, Ljubljana, 1982)
(With Professor Yash Ghai)

*Organization, Management and Supervision of Public
Enterprise in Developing Countries* (United Nations, 1974)

The Nature of Public Enterprise
(Croom Helm, London, 1984)

Studies in Public Enterprise (Frank Cass, London, 1986)

Books edited

Pricing and Investment in Public Enterprise
(Oxford IBH, 1974)

Joint Ventures and Public Enterprises in Developing Countries
(ICPE, Ljubljana, 1980)

Public Enterprise and the Developing World
(Croom Helm, London, 1984)

Public Enterprise: Studies in Organisational Structure
(Frank Cass, London, 1986)

PUBLIC ENTERPRISE

STUDIES IN ORGANISATIONAL STRUCTURE

Edited by
V. V. RAMANADHAM
London Business School

FRANK CASS
LONDON

350.009
P976

First published 1986 in Great Britain by
FRANK CASS & CO. LTD.
Gainsborough House, Gainsborough Road,
London, E11 1RS, England

and in the United States of America by
FRANK CASS & CO. LTD.
c/o Biblio Distribution Centre
81 Adams Drive, P.O. Box 327, Totowa, N.J. 07511

This Collection Copyright © 1986 Frank Cass & Co. Ltd.

British Library Cataloguing in Publication Data

Ramanadham, V. V.
Public enterprise: studies in organisational
structure.
1. Government business enterprises—Management
I. Title
338.7   HD62.36
ISBN 0-7146-3248-1

*All rights reserved. No part of this publication may be reproduced in
any form or by any means, electronic, mechanical, photocopying,
recording or otherwise, without the prior permission of Frank Cass
and Company Limited.*

Typeset by Williams Graphics, Abergele, North Wales
Printed and bound in Great Britain by A. Wheaton & Co. Ltd., Exeter

TO CHANDRAVATI

UNIVERSITY LIBRARIES
CARNEGIE MELLON UNIVERSITY
PITTSBURGH, PA   15213-3890

CONTENTS

PREFACE

This volume brings together papers on the organisational structure of select public enterprises from nine countries, developed and developing. They are set in different forms, work in different sectors and have diverse experiences, often on similar issues. The papers are written by top executives of the respective enterprises and, therefore, contain an authentic presentation of the problems and processes of organisation.

I have included, at the beginning, an analytical review on certain fundamental aspects of organisational structure which, for the purpose of this volume, has been conceived of in wide terms. Every one of these aspects is not exactly covered by every empirical paper. At the end I have provided a comparative review, trying to keep to a minimum repetition of material from the papers.

The Yugoslav enterprise, reputed for self-management, deserves notice in a volume of this kind. Hence I have provided a paper on its organisational structure, common to all enterprises in Yugoslavia, on the basis of my close study of many Yugoslav enterprises over the years.

The preparation of the volume has involved arduous work. In several cases a great deal of discussion, personal or through correspondence, took place. The authors have all been most generous in their co-operation with me in responding to my queries and demands for additional information or explanation. I gratefully admire their cordiality, competent presentation and generous indulgence in the face of editorial compulsions. I fondly hope that the multiple inputs that have gone into the volume, probably the first of its kind, will be of some value in promoting an understanding of the organisational structures (including diversities) of public enterprises in different countries.

London Business School   V. V. RAMANADHAM
December 1983

NOTES ON CONTRIBUTORS
(at the time of writing)

Mr R.W. Roseveare, Secretary and Managing Director, Policy Co-ordination, British Steel Corporation, London

Mr J.R. Baxter, Secretary, The Post Office, London

Mr Jean Virole, Senior official, Electricité de France, Paris

Dr V. Ajmone Marsan, Head, Department of Long-range Planning and Economic Studies, Istituto per la Ricostruzione Industriale, Rome

Mr Ernst Pieper, Chairman, Salzgitter AG, West Germany

Mr Louis L.J. Gambaccini, Assistant Executive Director, Port Authority of New York and New Jersey, New York (who made this paper available)

Mr Enrique Viloria, Manager, Industrial Development Division, Corporación Venezolana de Guayana

Mr Riyaz H. Bokhari, Chairman, National Fertilizer Corporation of Pakistan Ltd., Lahore

Dr B.L. Wadehra, Chairman, Coal India Ltd., Ranchi

Mr A.K.M. Yusof, Director General, Urban Development Authority, Kuala Lumpur

Professor V.V. Ramanadham, Visiting Fellow, London Business School, London

6140

1

THE ORGANISATIONAL STRUCTURE OF A PUBLIC ENTERPRISE: AN ANALYSIS

V. V. Ramanadham

The aim of the opening chapter is to analyse certain major issues of relevance to the organisational structure of a public enterprise. The term is employed in this book in a comprehensive sense so as to cover the legal basis of the enterprise, the economies of size, the decision-making and managerial structures, and the impacts of the functions assigned to it. Many of these aspects will be covered in the individual enterprise studies that follow and in the concluding chapter. The present analysis is devoted to two aspects in the main, viz., the size of the enterprise and the organisational impact of its functions; a third, the legal structure, comes in for a brief treatment at the end.

1. THE SIZE OF THE ENTERPRISE

The size of the enterprise has basic significance in the evolution of its organisational structure. As a first step in analysing this issue we need to be clear about the connotation of the term 'enterprise' as employed here.

A close look at public enterprises in several parts of the world suggests that, while there is great organisational variety, the bases of diversity stem from four considerations: (i) whether the organisation produces a single product or multiple products within a given sector; (ii) whether it operates in one sector or more than one sector; (iii) whether it has a single location and plant or is spatially dispersed; and (iv) whether its parts have, from the legal standpoint, a fairly independent status vis-à-vis the apex and one another.

The following is an illustrative description of the variety:

(a) An organisation with a more-or-less single product and in a single location: e.g. (the former) Heavy Electricals Ltd. in Bhopal (India), and Mumias Sugar Company Ltd. (in Kenya).

(b) An organisation with dispersed plants but operating in a more-or-less single sector: e.g., British Steel Corporation, Bharat Heavy Electricals Ltd. (in India), and Steel Authority of India Ltd. (in India).

(c) An organisation with diversified plants and operating in different sectors: e.g., Hindustan Machine Tools (in India), and Ghana Industrial Holding Company (in Ghana).

(d) An organisation with legally separate parts engaged
  (i) either in a more-or-less single sector − e.g., National Textile Corporation Ltd. (in India), Mineral Development Corporation (in Zambia) and Kenya Tourist Development Corporation;
  (ii) or in different sectors, of which the most well-known example is IRI of Italy. Other examples are National Development Corporation (Tanzania), Pernas (Malaysia), Temasek (Singapore), National Enterprise Board (UK), Industrial and Commercial Development Corporation (Kenya), and Guystac (Guyana).

(e) An organisation with almost all public enterprises in its fold. There are not many examples of this structure. ZIMCO in Zambia is a conspicuous one, having under it such large holding companies as INDECO (for industry), MINDECO (for mining), FINDECO (for finance) and so on. A nearly similar organisation was set up in Argentina, Corporación de Empresas Nacionales, which covered all public enterprises with the exception of banks, provincial and municipal, and armed forces enterprises.[1] GUYSTAC is another near example (in Guyana), though the big DEMBA (Bauxite) enterprise stands outside it.

While the last category is exceptional, ZIMCO probably representing the government policy level, with the President as its Chairman, there are large numbers under all the other categories. Perhaps the very first is also not too important on the whole, except in small countries or at the provincial level in big countries. Besides, there is a tendency for that category to attract some kind of managerial or administrative apex arrangement, as illustrated by the creation of the Board of Industrial Management[2] in Pakistan to take care of the many enterprises suddenly nationalised under the Economic Reforms Order of 1972.

For the present analysis we shall consider as an enterprise the top-most statutory level. Some of its sub-units may themselves have an independent legal status. It will be a part of our analysis to examine the interface between the apex and the sub-units.

The 'size' aspects of a public enterprise will be analysed here under three heads: largeness, excessiveness and sectoral dominance.

A. Largeness

The term 'large', to be meaningful, is relative in its connotation. That many public enterprises are larger than private enterprises, is a simple version of largeness, true in many developing countries.[3] This does not necessarily constitute an unfavourable feature of organisation, assuming that the required kind and quantum of managerial ability is available, and that the large sizes happen to be the most economical under the cost and demand conditions concerned. Largeness causes problems when the claims of economies of scale are exaggerated and when the requisite managerial capacity does not exist. It is generally assumed that an enterprise expands up to the point of minimum unit cost or maximum net revenue. Whether it clearly reaches either point is not easy to demonstrate; but such is the direction of its size expansion, ordinarily.

This is qualified by several considerations in the case of a public enterprise. First, there prevails a tendency to over-internalise the market processes, such that the decisions of the enterprise management operate as a substitute for the market. This is sought to be justified on the ground that markets are too imperfect in developing countries. Specific arguments for size enlargements tend to be built as follows:

(a) That skills and capital, being scarce, can be more economically used within a large enterprise than through the imperfect market forces. (It is common to meet this contention in favour of a large size in airline business.)
(b) That investment planning and technology development can be consciously undertaken, with an eye on eventual economy in the long run.
(c) That strength can be gained in international markets.

Second, there prevails a strong preference for internalising government−enterprise relationships through the creation of large enterprises. The point is generally argued on the following lines.

(a) That co-ordination can be effected easily between the supply of outputs and the demands in a whole sector, if one large enterprise or a small number exist.
(b) That co-ordination of enterprise activities with national plan strategies will be easy if the enterprises to be dealt with are few rather than many.
(c) That it will be convenient for the parent ministry, the Treasury and Parliament to have to contact a few large enterprises rather than a multitude of smaller ones.
(d) That governmental wishes as regards prices, closures, etc., will be relatively smooth, whether openly or disguisedly, if it is a few large enterprises that the government has to direct or arm-twist.

Besides, where public enterprises are looked at as media of power and patronage, both the ministers and the enterprise executives may be inclined towards creating large-sized units.

The proneness of public enterprises to largeness derives from two roots. For one thing, an enterprise goes on expanding – e.g., Hindustan Machine Tools Ltd. in India; for another, the very measures of nationalisation envisage the creation of large unifications of what once used to be independent units, as in British coal and steel, fertilisers in Pakistan, and coal and road transport in India.

The major problems caused by over-largeness are as follows.

(a) The average cost per unit of output rises, partly because the production activity goes beyond the optimum point, and partly because errors become common in decision-making, in monitoring the totality of operations and in co-ordinating them. Besides, a great deal of the management's energies get diverted to meeting criticisms of high cost and to explaining it away with tact.
(b) In general, complex structures of organisation accompany the largeness, creating serious problems in non-cost terms as well. Decisional inefficiencies build up, the more perceptibly the more severely centralised the decisional process; friction develops among the management levels; and a sense of inadequate or ineffective participation develops at the levels below the apex and hampers initiative. In the specific area of labour, serious disadvantages can arise in that any local unrest tends to spread over the entire breadth of the large organisation.
(c) An over-large enterprise entails some suppression of competition in the production and marketing activities, with detrimental consequences for the consumers. No doubt, attempts at decentralisation are made and 'profit centres' established. However, the

view develops that, while authority can be decentralised, responsibility cannot, in the case of a public enterprise so organised as to internalise government–enterprise relationships. The topmost levels of management feel compelled constantly to overlook the managerial shoulders below.

Herein lies an element of asymmetry between public and private enterprises. The top level in a private enterprise which bears ultimate responsibility and accountability, has the advantage of the criteria being compressed, even if crudely, into the realisation of a set financial return consistent with the shareholders' satisfaction and the long-term well-being of the enterprise. In the case of most public enterprises the criteria are not so neatly inferable; even the quantifiable part, e.g., the financial target, is not (clearly) set in every case; and then there are numerous elements of non-financial (or 'social') returns that are vague both in identity and in quantum. Hence the bias for managerial centralisation in public enterprise is the more pronounced the larger the enterprise.

(d) A large enterprise possibly entails cross-subsidisations among the markets, sometimes in a disguised way. These may be the result of managerial indifference to the issue, or of a governmental preference communicated to it in some way, or a determination by the management itself of what is 'socially good'. Herein lies an internalisation of decisions that ought to be external in source and transparent in remit to the enterprise.

(e) Large public enterprises attract vigilant intervention from the government; for, the size of its investments, outputs and employment would be considered as too important to be left to the managements.[4]

Let us consider the policy options available in dealing with the problem of uneconomically large public enterprises. First, they may be cut to size (whenever a convenient opportunity arises). For instance, several parts of the National Development Corporation in Tanzania have, from time to time, been hived off into independent and homogeneous enterprises. Likewise the Industrial Development Corporation in Zambia has been pruned by separating out certain sectors that can be easily disaggregated, from time to time.

While these illustrate attempts at sectoral disintegration, there are not many examples of disintegration of a large public enterprise operating in a given product line into independent units. (In fact there have been integrations, e.g., Steel Authority of India Ltd. absorbing most steel plants, and Coal India Ltd. absorbing almost all coal fields.) This is where organisational reform may prove helpful.

Second, the operating sub-units may be so organised as to represent optimal sizes as far as possible, and effective managerial decentralisation effected on the basis of clear criteria and targets. This can minimise the degree of intervention by higher levels of management in the working of the operating units, the more surely if the sub-units are given a status of legal autonomy.

Third, any extra-enterprise considerations to be imposed on the enterprise may be uncoupled from the level of board decision and transmitted to it openly and across the market. In other words, the practice of internalising external decisions has to be substantially mellowed.

If the above measures do not prove possible or effective, the only option we are left with is to expose the enterprise to institutionalised systems of public scrutiny, e.g., by a monopolies commission, a consumer's council or a management audit board. The effect of these will be, not to render an uneconomically large enterprise economical, but to induce it to evolve economical size changes and, more probably, to highlight the nature and extent of diseconomies that mark the enterprise; appropriate methods of meeting them can then be explored.

In a country where none of the preceding measures is implemented, society will almost permanently be under the impact of the cost of over-large organisations in public enterprise.

A concluding observation: several of the problems associated with public enterprises are really problems of large sizes: e.g., poor decision, inadequate monitoring, ineffective internal control and low managerial initiative and participation. These apply to large private enterprises as well but do not stand out equally prominently in their case, since profit, their overriding thrust, keeps these from the public gaze. On the other hand, with public enterprises whose major object has not been profit-making by whatever means and whose cross-sectional performance has not yet been one of satisfactory profit, the problems of largeness − along with any others − come in for public comment, and rightly so.

B. Excess capacity

Another major aspect of the size problem of several public enterprises is excess capacity. The term is used here to connote a structural excessiveness, in relation to current demands or foreseeable demands in the near future, and not in terms of seasonal, cyclical or any other short-run declines in demand. Conceptually it is over and above the reserve capacity ordinarily needed in such businesses as electricity supply. (Excess capacity is not the same as large size. It represents excessiveness in relation to demand, whereas the latter represents the mere fact of largeness or over-largeness by some criterion.)

Evidence on the existence of excess capacities in the public enterprise sector is fairly ubiquitous; e.g., in Tanzania,[5] India,[6] and the U.K.[7] While not totally absent in the private sector, excess capacity as a feature is unique in public enterprise in both cause and consequence.

First there are four principal causes.

(a) In a large number of cases adequate demand surveys are not made before setting up public enterprises.

(b) The anxiety to err on the side of idle capacity rather than be exposed to the contingency of even an occasional under-supply, leading to public, if not parliamentary, criticism, is a potent consideration in the minds of those that prepare project reports and help in decision-making on capacity in the public sector.

(c) There is a relative ease in the procurement of capital – especially in the sixties and early seventies when the first generation of public enterprise capacities were set up in many countries. Where a foreign aid is offered at governmental level (and not through the World Bank), considerations (a) and (b) tend to gain in significance.

(d) Basically, capacity decisions in public enterprise in several developing countries with development plans – and most of them have these – are a reflection of the long spans of perspective that characterise the plans. 'Eventually', it is contended, the demands will be there; hence the large capacities, which can turn out to be economical in the end. (The gestation may actually prove to be so long that the costs of under-utilization over a long period raise serious questions of justification.)

Private enterprises, by and large, are constrained in their capacity decisions by considerations of the costs of capital, rates of growth in demand, balance between current costs of excess capacity and eventual costs of full utilisation, if and when it occurs, and the need for a satisfactory dividend rate, commencing not too late from inception. It is doubtful that these criteria weigh adequately on civil servants who happen to be the main decision makers in the case of (new) public enterprises, and in developing countries.

Let us proceed to look at the organisational problems traceable to capacity. Basically, excess capacity complicates pricing and places the enterprise in a position of confrontation with three sides: the consumers, price commissions, and the government.

(a) The consumers protest at being asked to pay for costs of maintaining capacity that is unnecessary in the context of demands, current and immediately foreseeable. In fact full-cost pricing may even cause a contraction of demand below the levels that smaller, 'necessary' capacities might find at prices based on their own costs.

(b) Price commissions, if empowered to examine public enterprise matters, will constantly require the management to proceed in terms of the costs of capacity reasonably required by the state of demands met, i.e., in terms of, not resources sunk, but resources required to be used.

(c) The most complicated tussle is with the government and on such serious issues as the following:

 (i) First, the enterprise has to streamline its organisation so as to present to the government a convincing estimate of what the costs of excess capacity are. This is not too easy an accounting exercise involving assumptions on the probable costs of a smaller (needed) capacity and the cost economies currently experienced because of the existence of the large, though excess, capacity. Technical questions of cost centres and their organisation arise, the more seriously when the under-utilisation cannot be significantly attributed to a given product line or to a given plant or to a given sub-unit of the organisation.

 (ii) Second, the energies of the enterprise tend to be substantially drawn into negotiations (and public relations) with the government on the questions of closing excess capacities and of compensations, if closures are not permitted. In fact the closure proposals entail labour unrest. Negotiations in the area of industrial relations, redundancies, retraining, creation of new jobs, etc., will be necessary; and labour satisfaction in the enterprise should be maintained at a satisfactory level.

 (iii) Third, there will be need for evolving a decisional apparatus that takes into account the benefits of capacity contraction in a given case compositely with the potential benefits of shifting the resources into a better-yielding use. Even if the closure entails certain costs (e.g., payments for labour redundancy), the returns from the shifted resources in new uses can be of a compensatory nature. Amicable decisions in this regard presuppose an organisational interface between the enterprise and the government.

(iv) Fourth, the enterprise experiences an uphill task in rendering its accountability to the public and to Parliament, especially where the accounts are in the red. Over a period, the managers tend to lose job satisfaction and get frustrated.

To sum up: excess capacity in public enterprises is, in many cases, a problem of development planning in developing countries and of structural changes in developed countries;[8] and appropriate changes in the enterprise sizes and composition are slow in coming, unlike in the private sector.

C. Sectoral dominance

The extent of dominance associated wtih a public enterprise in the sector of activity concerned constitutes another issue of substantial relevance in our organisational analysis.

The higher its sectoral dominance, the greater the government's concern with the affairs of the enterprise on the ground that it has monopoly power. In fact several instances of government participation in industrial ownership, are the result of the monopoly organisation of the enterprises not only in the case of public utilities like electricity but, in some countries, even in relation to small-sized production which 'simply cannot sustain more than one factory' – as in Zambia.[9]

Besides, overlaps of involvement begin to develop as between the government and the enterprise with regard to current operations and growth, which seem to the former to be sectoral matters of policy and to the latter to be intra-enterprise matters of business. While most of the technical expertise rests with the enterprise, power lies with the government on questions of investment, expansion and location of activity; and second-guessing becomes its pastime much to the annoyance of the enterprise management. The fear of parliamentary committees faulting the parent ministry for passivity or errors in sectoral policy-formulation strengthens its desire to intervene in board decisions. Thus the decision structure becomes blurred.

Decisional overlaps as between the government and the enterprise are certain to develop where the enterprise's functions include items that smack of governmental responsibilities. For instance, the Liberian Development Corporation has, among its functions, 'statistical collection, pricing of competitive imports and encouragement of merchants to use locally manufactured products'.[10] Further it was made the secretariat for the Investment Incentive Committee whose members consisted of the Secretaries of Commerce and Industry, Treasury, Planning and Economic Affairs, and Agriculture. Several clashes between the Corporation as the secretariat and the Committee composed of government officers occurred.[11]

The net outcome of such government–enterprise relationships is a loss of autonomy on the part of the enterprise, through official dominance on the board and through approval processes that make the enterprise over-dependent on the will of the government.

There are two ways in which the organisational problems of a sectorally dominant enterprise may be dealt with. First, the monitoring of its operations may be left to national structures of price control, monopoly control, capital issues control and so on, without any attempt to internalise these at the board level or abridge them into informal government relationships with the enterprise. Second, a sectoral policy level may be distinctly set up under the auspices of or within the government, even if mainly dependent for its technical work on the enterprise, and the decisions emanating from that level openly transmitted to the enterprise. Care has to be taken to keep that policy level from making merry excursions into the realm of management.

An important organisational question relates to how a sectorally dominant enterprise is sub-divided. Broadly there can be three ways: (a) the Act (or the government) may lay down the major structure of the sub-units under the apex-board (as under the original Transport Act, the Electricity Act and the Gas Act in the UK);[12] (b) the task may be left to the board of the enterprise itself (as under the Coal Nationalisation Act in the UK); or (c) the Act may stipulate that the board should design the structure, on any principles indicated, and perhaps seek the approval of the government; by implication major changes effected from time to time call for government approval. The British Steel Corporation illustrates this method.

Appropriate subdivisions, economy-wise and management-wise, are a matter of serious concern to the enterprise, and, in a special way, to the government. Where it has aims other than mere commercial viability, which the board has to realise, e.g., to subserve rather than let decay certain relatively poor ports or coal pits or canals, the government may feel inclined to influence the process of designing the organisation structure. Probably the most useful way will be for the

Act (a) to lay down any broad lines of division the government wants at the minimum, (b) to require the board to design an organisational structure appropriate to the economics of the industry, subject to (a); and (c) to seek the government's approval for a proposed structure or for any subsequent modifications of a major kind.[13]

Another aspect which has relevance to the organisation of a sectorally dominant public enterprise is the consumer interest. It is but appropriate that the government which has a material role in evolving such a monopoly organisation responds to the situation, as in the UK, by creating consumer councils parallel to the enterprise management and by conferring on them certain rights of information, recommendation and access not only to the board but to the minister. Their effectiveness as an organisational tool parallel to the enterprise organisation depends on their powers and modus operandi. For the management, however, it can raise two major problems: (a) the councils may so function as to step on its toes and disrupt its own managerial prerogatives and responsibilities; and (b) by virtue of their access to the minister they may provide 'one more' occasion for ministerial intervention in enterprise management, the more so if Parliament begins to be supportively concerned wtih the councils' activities and actively watchful of what the minister does, or does not do, on the findings of the consumer councils.

The device of consumer councils as an institution accompanying sectoral monopolies in the public sector has not been employed, exceptions apart, elsewhere in the world.[14] (A distant version is illustrated by the 'Advisory Committee' that the National Irrigation Board (in Kenya) '*shall* appoint' 'in respect of *each* national irrigation scheme'.)[15] This device will be fruitful (a) if the councils' terms are broadly limited to second-order, though not unimportant, matters such as local complaints, terms of supply, quality of output, and particular grievances, leaving such first-order matters as price levels, cross-subsidisations, expansions, and monopoly practices, to other agencies like a monopoly commission; and (b) if public attention to, and action on, the councils' findings are limited to the usual channels available in the case of other matters of enterprise operations, for example, through statutory references in the annual report of the enterprise, parliamentary notice of the report tabled in the House, and scrutinies by parliamentary committees, monopolies commissions, audit committees, and the Comptroller and Auditor-General. In this way it will be possible to defuse the organisational anomalies that consumer councils may raise for the enterprise boards.

3. THE 'SOCIAL' CONTENT IN ENTERPRISE FUNCTIONS

The term 'social' content is used here as a shorthand expression signifying that part of the functions of a public enterprise that derives its main justification from considerations other than its long-term financial viability. (Thus the economic versions of marginal cost pricing are outside the purview of the term.) Certain public enterprises are exposed to non-viable decisions on location, technology, product-mix, rate of growth, choice of markets, price concessions and discriminations, and factor combination, as they are considered as instruments of government policy or as too important to be left alone. What impact does this have on the organisational structure of the enterprise?

The simplest measure of appropriate organisation would be to bifurcate the enterprise, just below the level of the board, into two parts, one entrusted with the commercial functions and the other with the non-commercial or social functions. The assumption, here as elsewhere in this section, is that there can be some public agreement, even if approximate, on what the two segments are (for example, the functions of the National Small Industries Corporation Ltd. (in India) are clearly demarcated under two broad categories, viz.: (a) promotional and developmental and (b) commercial; and the former are financed by the Government of India by way of grants to the Corporation).[16]

Second, a two-tier system of top decision-making may be adopted, consisting of a policy council and a board of directors. The former takes care of all 'policy' matters inclusive of social functions, and can be so constituted as to provide for effective participation by the government. It can offer the board, which turns out to be an inflated management committee, guidelines on the non-commercial functions to be undertaken by the enterprise. This system was recommended by the National Economic Development Office in the UK in 1976;[17] but it has not been implemented.[18]

Third, where the social content in function is significant, the board of directors may be so composed as to include ministers, members of Parliament, other politicians, and senior civil servants (who can carry out the ministers' wishes).[19]

Fourth, the capital structure of the enterprise may be so designed as to cushion the incidence of its social functions. The 'endowment fund' method of Italy in respect of IRI's investments in non-viable locations of activity is a well-known illustration. Grants and conversion of loans into equity are among the usual financing methods adopted in several countries, for example, in Pakistan.[20] Interest-free loans or long moratoria on interest and loan repayments are yet another method. Or, a special fund may be set up — from government sources — to finance certain activities that the ministries might themselves have undertaken but preferred a public enterprise to take up.[21] All these are ways in which the capital structure of the enterprise is sought to be relieved of the impacts of its social functions.

Fifth, it is important to keep an enterprise from practising cross-subsidisations through management decisions while discharging its social functions. One of the ways in which this can be controlled is by stipulating diverse financial targets in respect of the social and the commercial functions, for example on British Railways in respect of the inter-city and freight traffic as against the provincial passenger services in respect of which a public-service-obligation subsidy is offered by the government.[22]

What is basic to all the preceding techniques is that the government should agree with the enterprise on the nature and size of its social functions: for example, how much of a 'social railway' in the UK context,[23] how much of rural electrification, or what extent of kiosks and call boxes, etc. Short of this no satisfactory arrangements regarding the financial and decisional structures of the enterprises are possible.

Empirically these measures seem to be an exception rather than the rule. Hence the organisational dilemma and unpleasantness for the enterprise in that ad hoc interventions are experienced from the government on such issues as extension of outputs, closure of plants, price concessions and cross-subsidisations. The less formal the interventions, the more problematic for the enterprise, for it has no way of proving its own organisational mettle before the public and of demonstrating the limited extent of its own responsibility for a given set of results.

One has to conclude, vis-à-vis the social content of public enterprise functions, that on the whole the right organisational measures are yet to be devised.

4. THE LEGAL FORM

The legal form in which a public enterprise is organised is of inherent significance, in that it demarcates the bounds of autonomous behaviour of the management from those of intervention by the government or other external agencies. In the early years of public enterprise organisation emphasis was placed on the virtues of the public corporation form 'clothed with the power of government, but possessed with the flexibility and initiative of private enterprise'.[24] Practice has moved so far away from this description as well as the Morrisonian concept of a public corporation that even the British corporations set up after 1945 entailed 'a considerable increase in the powers of the ministers to control and to interfere in the working of the corporation',[25] as compared with the pre-1945 corporations.

So much has been written on the merits of the public corporation form over the departmental form that we shall limit the present discussion to certain subtle points. In theory, it can have the following organisational merits.

(a) The Act setting up a corporation can deal satisfactorily with its broad substantive issues, e.g., electricity pricing.

(b) The minister derives powers from what is stated in the Act; and it can be presumed that he does not otherwise have specific powers vis-à-vis the corporation.

(c) The Act may specify the composition of the board in such a way that it may prove difficult for the minister to fill it as he likes; and the kind of persons meant to occupy the top decisional layer can be clear to all from the Act.

(d) There is unlikely to be any shareholder control by the government; its powers of control are akin to those that it wishes to have as government. In this way a public corporation can represent an advanced step in the divorce between ownership and management.

In many countries today these merits sound like a chorus of fiction. Most Acts resemble one another and the claims of an Act dealing with the industry concerned are invalid.[26] The minister acts under the most convenient interpretation of whatever powers are provided in the statute.

Most Acts describe those eligible for nomination to boards in such permissive terms that the minister has wide latitude in making the appointments.[27] It is only an ex-officio appointment that is beyond his discretion.

Broadly there have been five ways in which the organisational autonomy of a public corporation has been severely diluted.

(a) By availing of a permissive provision of the Act to introduce governmental controls that truncate the decisional range of the enterprise board. A conspicuous example is provided by the UK where, having nearly monopolised the powers of supplying finance to the nationalised industries, the government has brought them within the rigorous discipline of external financial limits. That these have affected the boards' decisional behaviour is on record.[28]

(b) By bringing public enterprises under the impact of 'other' Acts subsequently passed, involving substantial ministerial or other kinds of external control on their organisational prerogatives such as recruitment and purchasing.[29]

(c) By parliamentary enthusiasm in the use of the question hour, in the course of debates, and in enquiries by select committees.[30] This prompts the ministers to develop close control over the enterprises.

(d) By filling the boards of directors with civil servants.[31]

(e) By the sheer exercise of unfair pressures over the enterprise boards by ministers and other politicians.[32]

It is difficult to see how the situation can be effectively reversed into the original model of public corporation organisation. As long as the situation continues unabated, unintended costs of public enterprise organisation arise, both in the positive sense of departures from managerial canons of efficiency and in the indirect sense of politicians benefiting at the expense of the producers and the consumers concerned.

The best hope of improving the situation lies in Parliament, through its committees, establishing the extent and consequences of ministerial extrastatutory interferences and calling the ministers and the departments to account. This is by no means easy to expect, for an examination of what passes between the minister and the civil servant or the enterprise is difficult on grounds of confidentiality. Moreover in several political systems in the world today many members of Parliament may not be willing or heroic enough to engage in exercises of this kind. Similarly enterprise executives themselves may keep from exposing the minister or the civil servants and courting the risk of losing their jobs.

A few observations may be added on government companies which share in the general slant of comments made on public corporations in the preceding paragraphs. They are not governed by specific Acts, unlike the corporations, and thus lack even the merits that the Acts may be able to confer on the organisation and operations of the enterprises. The question of whether the minister's interventions are ultra vires does not arise as there exists no statutory basis – one way or the other – in the first place.

On the other hand, they are governed by the Companies Act; and the articles of association that govern the minister's 'dos' and 'don'ts' are an internal document which does not go to Parliament either for first formulation or for subsequent revisions. There is, on the whole, little scope for the public to spot out cases of governmental involvement in the managerial decisions of the companies; and the problem of their accountability gets complicated. No wonder the literature provides an extensive body of opinion unfavourable to the company form as against the corporation form.[33]

One of the serious shortcomings of the government company form is that the law that governs it requires it merely to present an overall set of financial accounts; neither are any subdivisions of these called for nor is a well-designed narrative on operations necessary. In this way the sources of information needed for accountability reviews turn out to be too inadequate; whereas in the case of a public corporation the Act can be so designed as to cover all such issues explicitly.

But the government company has come to stay in both the developed and the developing countries.[34] And the status of public corporations seems to be but marginally superior to that of government companies from the standpoint of enterprise autonomy and government involvement in enterprise management. The conclusion, therefore, follows, viz., that irrespective of the legal form of organisation all public enterprises call for a well-designed substantive framework codifying the enterprise—government relationships in such matters as investment, pricing, technology, productivity, consumer interest, wage levels, etc. The form of the organisation, no doubt, influences the channels of implementation of the relationships and the corporation form may help in keeping these somewhat more transparent.

We shall close this section by raising an interesting empirical question. What is the nature of shareholder interest that governments have evinced in autonomously organised public enterprises, by and large? Their counterparts in the private sector are active in trying to ensure the following: (a) a high enough dividend, (b) long-term stability of the enterprise and security of investments, (c) appreciation in share values, (d) capital restructuring, when necessary and (e) a board that is capable of producing the (a) to (d) results. Experience with public enterprises in several parts of the world suggests that as a cross-section they have attracted a great deal of control attention from the government rather than the kind of shareholder interest as described above. Even in the U.K., which seems to provide one of the best cases, this has been the situation until financial targets were introduced a few years ago; the shareholder interest was then temporarily under the impact of inflation controls in the early seventies; and today the swing is broadly towards the shareholder interest of returns. Certain schemes of privatisation are accompanied by open announcements against government interventions in enterprise management.[35]

NOTES

1. This was set up in 1973 under Law 26558, but was abolished under Law 21800 a few years later.
2. This was abolished in 1979.
3. For example, during 1977–78 51 public enterprises accounted for 80% of the total assets and 70% of the total net sales of the 101 corporate giants in India. The first twelve biggest enterprises (in terms of assets) were public enterprises. Of the first 25 large enterprises 22 were public enterprises. *The Economic Times*, 30 April 1979.
4. National Economic Development Office, *A Study of UK Nationalised Industries: Their role in the economy and control in the future* (London, 1976), p. 7.
5. 'Capacity utilisation often amounts to 35% only of the actual production capacity.' Hans G. Klaus, 'Analysis and Summary of the Workshop' on *The Role of Public Enterprises in Development in Eastern Africa*, Occasional Paper No. 39, Institute for Development Studies, Nairobi (1980).
6. Heavy Engineering Corporation Ltd., Praga Tools Ltd., and Neyveli Lignite Corporation Ltd. are particular examples of under-utilization. Bureau of Public Enterprises, Government of India, *Annual Report on the Working of Industrial and Commercial Undertakings of Central Government (1976–77)*, Volume I, Statement XXIV. Also see Report of the Comptroller and Auditor General of India, Union Government (Commercial), 1976, Part VI, *Praga Tools Ltd.* (p. 140), which refers to 'under-utilisation of capacity' as a cause of the chronic losses of the enterprise. See the CAG's Report, 1975, on *Hindustan Teleprinters Ltd.* (p. 65), which states that the percentage of under-utilization varied between 29.44 and 43.76 in the workshop and between 28.92 and 43.78 in the assembly shop during 1970–74.
7. For example, British Steel Corporation and National Coal Board.
8. For example, in British Steel Corporation in the UK and in the textile enterprises of ENI in Italy.
9. K. D. Kaunda, *Zambia's Economic Revolution* (Lusaka, 1968) pp. 65, 22.
10. *Annual Report of Liberian Development Corporation* (1971–72) p. 8.
11. Another instance of governmental functions being entrusted to an autonomous enterprise may be cited from Venezuela. The National Agricultural Institute has, among others, the functions of transformation of the land tenure system by incorporating the peasantry within the process of national production, promotion of productivity of crop-growing and livestock-raising, equitable distribution of land, better organisation of agricultural credit system and improvement of rural living conditions.
12. Of course there were differences even in these cases.
13. A helpful technique in this regard is illustrated by the Organisation Committee set up in the UK at the time of the second reading of the Steel Bill, under the

Chairmanship of one who, by design or otherwise, eventually became the first Chairman of the British Steel Corporation. An incidental point (which the British Steel technique substantiates) is that importance attaches to the preparation made, at the time of nationalising or creating a public enterprise, with regard to its organisational structure.

14. Nor are consumer councils universal in Britain itself today. For instance British Steel Corporation has none now, possibly because of its lack of monopoly power, thanks to (cheaper) imports and because of the controvertibility of ministerial interventions a council may eventually entail, within the spirit of the European Community's rules.

15. *The Irrigation Act* (Nairobi, 1967) Section 24(i). Italics mine.

16. *Annual Report on the Working of Industrial and Commercial Undertakings of the Central Government 1976–77* (Vol. II) p. 173.

17. 'The Policy Council is to carry out the functions of agreeing corporate aims and objectives, agreeing strategic policies needed to achieve these aims and objectives, establishing performance criteria, endorsing corporate plans, including annual budgets and related pricing and cost assumptions, and monitoring performance, at appropriate intervals, against pre-determined policies and criteria.' National Economic Development Office, *A Study of U.K. Nationalised Industries: Their Role in the Economy and Control in the Future* (H.M.S.O., London, 1976) p. 46.

18. The White Paper, *The Nationalised Industries*, did not respond favourably to the 'Policy Council' idea. (Cmnd. 7141, London, 1978).

19. For example, the Industrial Development Bank (in Kenya) had two prominent political personalities in the positions of the chairman and the managing director in 1982.

20. As with Utility Stores Corporation of Pakistan Ltd. whose 'main objective' is 'to protect real income of the consumers, particularly of the poorer sections of the society'. *Government Sponsored Corporations, 1980–81* (Islamabad, 1982) p. 244.

21. This method is widely followed in Mexico. For instance, Nacional Financiera has many 'earmarked funds': e.g., Fondo de Garantia y Fomento a la Industria Mediana y Pequena; Fondo de Garantia y Fomento del Turismo; Programa Nacional Frontevizo; Frideicomiso de Minerales no Metalicos; Plan Lerma Asistancia Tecnica; Frideicomisco de Inginios Azucareros; Fondo de Garantia y Fomento a la Pequena y Mediana Mineria; Fondo de Estudios de Preinvasion; Fondo Nacional de Fomento para Plantas Industriales; and Fondo Nacional de Fomento Industrial. The funds are administered by special technical committees, which include government and Nacional Financiera representatives; and the finances of the funds are kept separate from those of Nacional Financiera itself.

22. For example, inter-city business should aim at contribution to indirect costs, of £159m. by 1982; and freight should cover 66 per cent of CCA depreciation after all costs by 1982.

23. For example, the Serpell Committee on *The Review of Railway Finances* (1983) suggested that 'whenever a PSO Direction is made, a Command Paper should be published setting out the Government's policies and strategies covering the role of the railway in public transport, objectives for the business sectors, the extent of the network to be supported or excluded from the support, and guidance on closure policy' (p. 55).

And the Transport Committee of the House of Commons, Session 1982–83, believed that 'a clear statement of Government policy towards the railways, including the financial and operational targets, is urgently required'. In *Serpell Committee Report on the Review of Railway Finances*, (H.M.S.O., 240, 1983) p. xv.

24. Franklin D. Roosevelt's words ascribed to the Tennessee Valley Authority. David E. Lilienthal, *Tennessee Valley Authority: Democracy on the March* (New York, 1944) p. 50.
25. D. N. Chester, *The Nationalised Industries, A Statutory Analysis* (London, 1948) p. 19.
26. To cite an example: the Korean corporation Acts present 'excessive uniformity and mutual similarity, rather than specialisation according to the characteristics of the individual enterprises'. Korea Industrial Development Research Institute, *Survey of Government Enterprises in Korea* (Seoul, 1972) p. 25.
27. The clauses usually incorporate such wording as the following: 'who', in the minister's opinion, 'have qualities of benefit to the Board'. *The Irrigation Act* (Kenya, 1967):
    'being persons who in his opinion possess special knowledge of housing development or housing finance'. *The Housing Act* (Kenya, 1972).
    How effectively the powers of board appointments can be abused may be seen from the Nigerian experience: 'boards of corporations and institutions were a means of distributing political patronage in the First Republic'. *Report of the Nigerian Railway Corporation Tribunal of Inquiry* (Lagos, 1967) p. 154.
28. For instance, referring to 'the persistent application of negative EFLs' to the Post Office, the Industry and Trade Committee of the House of Commons (Session 1981–82) observed with concern 'the impact on the Corporation's activities'. 'The EFL will tend to encourage the Post Office to raise its tariffs more frequently and by larger amounts than would otherwise be the case.' Or the Post Office may 'attempt to contain increases in operating costs or reduce capital spending'. 'The EFL system is a crude and indiscriminate method of financial control.' (H.M.S.O. 343; 241-i-iv, 1982, London) p. ix.
29. Evidence is available from Nigeria where the Corporations Standing Tenders Board decree No. 54 was passed in 1968 bringing many public enterprises under external control in respect of their purchases.
    The Statutory Authorities Act 1966 of Trinidad and Tobago is another example in the area of personnel.
30. An extreme example of strong criticism comes from the reports of the Committee on Public Undertakings (in India) during the 1970s.
31. Evidence is available of civil servant dominance on public enterprise boards in all regions of the world. In Mexico, for example, all eleven directors of Aeropuertos y Servicios Auxilieres were secretaries and other government officials, five out of seven in Comision Federal de Electricidad, all seven in Productos Forestales Mexicanos, seven out of nine in Ferrocarriles Nacionales de Mexico, and all three of CONASUPO (in 1973).
32. Many illustrations are available from the Reports of the Inquiry Tribunals set up in Nigeria in the late sixties on the Electricity, Ports, Railway, and Air Corporations; and as regards Ghana, from R. C. Pozen, *Legal Choices for State Enterprises in the Third World* (New York, 1976) Chapter 6.
33. W. A. Robson, *Nationalised Industry and Public Ownership* (London, 1960): 'The public corporation ... is far better than the joint stock company owned and controlled by the State; or than government departments engaged in business activity' (p. 493).
    The Estimates Committee of Parliament (in India), 1959–60, *Eightieth Report* (New Delhi): 'All wholly state-owned public undertakings should generally be in the form of statutory corporations or, when required for special reasons, in the form of departmental undertakings; and the company form should be an exception to be resorted to only for organisations of a specific nature' (p. 5).
    V. V. Ramanadham, *Organisation, Management and Supervision of Public*

Enterprises in Developing Countries (United Nations, New York, 1974) Chapter V.

34. For instance there are many companies presenting varying degrees of public ownership in the UK; most of the public enterprises covered by the Bureau of Public Enterprise annual reports on the commercial and industrial enterprises of the central government have the company form; and in several countries like Kenya and Tanzania, many but not all of the holding companies are set up as public corporations and most of the subsidiaries have the company form.

35. For example: 'HM Government does not henceforth intend to exercise its rights as a shareholder to elect directors to the Board, to intervene in the commercial decisions of the Group, or to vote in opposition to a resolution supported by a majority of Directors.' Letter dated 1 February 1983 from the Secretary of State to the Chairman of the Associated British Ports Holding plc.

6312
6140
5732 6110
UK

21-50

2

BRITISH STEEL CORPORATION

R. W. Roseveare, CBE

INTRODUCTION

The British Steel Corporation (BSC) came into existence in 1967 when the largest steel companies in the UK were taken into public ownership, or nationalised, and their securities were vested in the Corporation. The Corporation is a public body, whose Board Members are appointed by the Government, but it has an independent statutory existence and its employees are not civil servants.

BSC's organisational structure has been through several phases since 1967. The phases of organisation adopted help to demonstrate the many changing factors that must be taken into account in determining the structure of a public (or indeed a private) enterprise. These factors may change in relative importance over the years, according to the external economic or statutory environment, the size of the enterprise, its expanding or contracting nature at any one period, the patterns of its facilities, and even the changing personalities. A manufacturing public enterprise such as BSC, trading in a competitive international market, will also need to ensure that its form of organisation is that best fitted to meet the character and intensity of the commercial competition, which can change over the years.

This paper begins by surveying briefly the historical background to the formation of BSC and its initial composition, and the way in which the external economic environment has changed since BSC was established and has impinged on the form of organisation needed for the Corporation. It then goes on to describe in more detail the features of each of the successive phases of organisational structure which the Corporation has adopted, against that wider economic background.

HISTORICAL SURVEY

Formation of British Steel Corporation

The steel industry in Britain was in private ownership just over fifteen years ago, with about 250 separate companies carrying on their operations in some 300 separate works.

The industry had been nationalised in 1949, by the then Labour Government which also nationalised the coal, gas, electricity, transport and other industries. However, before the 1949 measure could be fully implemented, a Conservative Government was returned which restored the industry to private ownership in 1953, albeit under the general supervision of a statutory Iron and Steel Board.

In 1967, a later Labour Government once again nationalised the industry – or rather the major part of it. The fourteen largest companies, accounting for 90% of British crude steel production and about two-thirds of product sales, were taken into public ownership, with their securities vested in the newly created British Steel Corporation (BSC).

The fourteen companies had between them 148 subsidiaries registered in the United Kingdom and 48 overseas subsidiaries. So all these 210 companies became subsidiaries of BSC. The capital employed by the fourteen companies in 1966 amounted to £1409 million, their total turnover was estimated at over £1000 million, and together they employed 270,000 people. Thus BSC, on its formation, became the largest steel enterprise, and among the largest six undertakings of any kind, in the non-Communist world outside the USA.

BSC as a result inherited the assets of thirty-nine crude steel-producing works, of which twenty-one were fully integrated. It also became the owner of many other works, producing either finished iron and steel products, or other products such as structural and general engineering goods, chemicals, bricks and plastics. The works were spread over many different locations, in the North and Midlands of England, in Scotland and in Wales. For most of the fourteen companies it was true to say that the company owned works confined to a reasonably compact geographical area; and some of the companies had concentrated mainly on a single broad type of steel product. But a few of them had a wide geographical or product spread.

This is the background – massive 'statutory merger' – against which the BSC's initial organisational task must be seen.

Before the act of nationalisation, the Chairman-designate of the BSC was put in charge of an 'Organising Committee' to make preparations. This Committee considered it of great importance for BSC to be in a position, on the date it was to take over, to assume effective control of the fourteen separate companies as one manageable single business entity. This meant that a new organisation had to be devised and introduced quickly. BSC therefore adopted an interim structure in 1967 as an immediate step; but it replaced this in 1970 as soon as the BSC Board had gained the necessary experience of running the new, very large, Corporation and had had time to work out a more radically changed and longer-lasting organisational structure.

Influence of Economic Factors

Even this more lasting form of organisation could not take account of the likely future pattern of BSC's production facilities as it was not until rather later that BSC was able to plan, and secure Government agreement to, the major plant modernisation and expansion strategy needed to rationalise and bring up to date its diverse pattern of inherited assets. This strategy, besides rationalising and modernising the plant inheritance, had also to plan to meet BSC's share of the steady growth in UK steel demand, and world demand, then in prospect. This strategy was published in 1973. Since very large steelworks take some six or seven years to complete, from the planning stage to final commissioning, BSC put in hand in the early 1970s (under the strategy) a major plant building programme to meet the large demand foreseen for the end of the decade. It was to involve investment of £3000 million, at 1972 prices, over ten years, and it was clear that it would change radically the size and pattern of the plant facilities. The programme involved not only expanding total capacity but also concentrating it in a few large and to some extent multi-product coastal works, so as to minimise production costs. This greatly changed pattern of facilities in prospect naturally had direct implications for BSC's organisational structure, and a new structure was approved, for final introduction in 1976.

Not long after this major development strategy was agreed and put in hand, the world saw far-reaching economic changes following the Middle East oil crisis. No leading Government or industry or other forecasters had foreseen this tremendous check to economic growth. The resulting recession affected UK and world steel demand greatly. From around that date also, the competitiveness of much of UK industry, including the large steel-using industries, began to decline, and an increasing proportion of steel-containing goods used in Britain has since then been imported rather than made in the UK (mostly from UK steel).

The UK's overall demand for steel was 15.6 million tonnes in 1967. It had grown to 19.9 million by 1973 and it then seemed likely to all informed observers to continue to grow steadily. But in fact the trend was sharply and unexpectedly reversed by the world and UK recession caused by the oil crisis, and UK demand had fallen right back to 11.8 million tonnes by 1981 − its lowest level since 1951. UK motor vehicle manufacture and shipbuilding provide particularly clear examples: the former's use of steel fell by 33% between 1975 and 1981, and the latter's by 60%.

BSC is dependent on home sales to the extent of about three-quarters of its total sales, and this course followed by UK steel demand was, of course, mirrored in the size and pattern of production capacity needed by BSC and hence in its organisational structure.

When it became clear, in the later 1970s, that the reduction in demand was to be long lasting, the need for BSC's massive capital investment plan had to be radically re-assessed. This implied major changes in the pattern as well as the size of BSC's production capacity. The reduced world demand had also thrown up surplus steel-making capacity in other countries, giving rise to sharply increased international competition among steelmakers. The emergence of important third world producers exacerbated the situation. The new pattern of BSC's plant, and the strenuous competitive conditions meant that BSC's organisation had to be restructured once again to reflect the changed need. Some organisation changes were progressively introduced in the late 1970s, and in 1980 a completely revised structure came into being.

It could be said that in the days of BSC's expansion the planning emphasis was on the facility pattern, but when demand fell steeply and world competition became even more intense, the planning emphasis moved away from capital investment to the marketing side.

Other Factors

It can be argued that a further factor relevant to the development of BSC's organisation over its comparatively young life has been the mere process of 'getting off the ground'. At the start, when fourteen separate companies with separate and differing policies and philosophies had to be welded into a single business, it was necessary to draw authority into the centre, at least to some extent. The newly created Corporation resulting from the massive statutory merger had to formulate its policies, its capital development plan, its relationships with the trade unions and other interests, its operating procedures and a host of other arrangements covering all business aspects. Perhaps it was only after having done this that BSC could sensibly and progressively decentralise as fully as the economic considerations dictated.

BSC's organisational pattern is also greatly affected by the fact that it produces a wide variety of products, each serving different market sectors and each needing to be sold against a different set of competing companies at home and overseas. It is in no sense a monopoly or public utility producing a broadly homogeneous product. There is a competing private steel sector in the UK, which was not nationalised, and there are of course many foreign competitors in both BSC's home and overseas markets. BSC is not a 'price maker'. It has to be a 'price taker'. For much the same reasons there is no statutory steel consumers' council. It can be argued too that its exposure to strenuous international competition makes it less necessary for its efficiency to be audited by the Monopolies and Mergers Commission, the Comptroller and Auditor-General, etc. The strong competition it faces should be a sufficient spur to efficiency.

Likewise, its form of organisation at the various stages through which it has passed has hardly if at all been influenced by its status as a public enterprise but rather by the economic situation in which it has found itself.

Its public enterprise status does mean, however, that it is subject to the set of provisions relating to organisation that appear in the specific statute under which BSC, unlike commercial companies, has to conduct itself. Like war and the generals, the subject of organisation has been considered, by successive British governments, to be too important a matter to be left to the discretion of the Corporation alone. It may be asked why a Corporation which is in many respects left to operate in a commercial, competitive way − and is not a public utility − should be subject to any more control by the Government as regards its internal organisation than is a private company operating in a similar competitive manner. A company is subject only to the Companies Acts, which in fact do not trouble themselves to regulate the matter of internal organisation. And why should the BSC be subject to statutory control on the matter of its internal organisation when it is left free of statutory control on many matters of wider public interest, including large individual investment projects, steel prices, purchasing policies, and employees' wages?

The reason appears to be partly that Governments see the question of organisation as capable of having regional political implications, impinging on Scottish and Welsh devolution, for example; and partly because they fear that at some future date a Board of BSC might wish to adopt a highly centralised – or continue with its present highly decentralised – form of organisation which might run directly counter to the general philosophy of the Government of the day.

But the main reason is probably historical: the original national-isation statute had, for pressure of time, been drafted without the benefit of a thorough prior examination of, among other matters, the desirable form of organisation to be adopted once the fourteen private companies were 'merged' together under public ownership. There was only a fairly brief Government White Paper, published in 1965. This was in contrast to what happened for some, but not all, other nationalised measures in the UK, e.g. the nationalisation of the gas industry was preceded by the inquiry carried out by the Heyworth Committee. Therefore, the steel nationalisation measure – the Iron and Steel Act 1967 – did not prescribe at all the form of internal organisation; in this respect, the Iron and Steel Act differed from other nationalisation Acts – for example for gas, or electricity, which prescribed in detail the number, extent and powers of the 'next layer down' in the organisation, in these cases Area Boards.

But the subject was, as stated earlier, considered too important to leave entirely at large. Therefore, as foreshadowed in the 1965 White Paper, the Act required the Corporation to propose a form of organisation, within a prescribed time limit, for the Minister's approval. There were other provisions on organisation also, for example that the Minister could at any time in the future require BSC to review its organisation, that BSC must not change it substantially without the Minister's consent, that it must consult the unions on the matter, etc. These provisions have since been modified, notably in the Iron and Steel Act 1981, but they have not been repealed altogether and thus the remaining provisions for some Government control over organisation may be seen as a residuum from the content of the initial Act of Parliament.

PHASES OF ORGANISATION STRUCTURE

Against this background, let us now consider the characteristics of the successive phases of organisational structure which the Corporation has introduced, and the reasons which have underlain its decisions on each occasion.

A. 1967–70: Multi-Product Groups

When the Corporation was formed in 1967, as a result of the fourteen largest British steel companies being nationalised, it had to devise a single coherent organisation for managing the resulting very large steel business of fourteen major companies and several dozen works. As explained earlier, it could not hope to design and introduce a permanent form of organisation in the very short time available to it, particularly as the Chairman and some other Board Members of the new Corporation were new to the affairs of the steel industry. It therefore concluded, as a result of a study carried out mainly by the Organising Committee (or 'shadow Board') set up a few months before the date of nationalisation itself, that certain fairly limited changes in organisation at the company level should be introduced as from that date, but enough to enable the Corporation to assume immediate and effective control of a 'unified business entity', with a single management organisation replacing the fourteen independent companies. The organisation had to take account of the inherited patterns of facilities.

The organisation was described in BSC's first statutory report on organisation, published in August 1967. The Corporation did not say that this initial organisation was regarded as only temporary – morale would have suffered seriously if the upheaval of a second reorganisation had been in prospect – but a much more prolonged and deep study was in fact needed (and began to be put in hand late in 1967) before the Board could decide upon the radical changes that had to be made in order to form a longer-lasting organisational structure.

This first phase of organisation was therefore confined to setting up the Head Office structure, with responsibilities defined for the main BSC Board Members, and to placing the fourteen companies into four multi-product operating Groups, four being considered a manageable number and corresponding to a logical grouping of the steel facilities of the companies, largely on a geographical basis. Each Group was placed under a Group Managing Director who was responsible to the Chairman of the Corporation (who served as Chief Executive also). Each Group Managing Director was advised by a group 'Board' (advisory and non-statutory). The fourteen companies and their statutory Boards remained legally in existence, but their functions were now purely formal. For a few weeks, their chief executives became accountable for management purposes to the relevant Group Managing Director, but from the autumn of 1967 the Groups were split into Divisions, with ultimately between three and six

Divisions within each Group, and the Director-in-charge of the Division replaced the chief executive of the company as the individual responsible to the Group MD.

The Groups

The four Groups were Midland; Northern & Tubes; Scottish & Northwest; and South Wales. As the names indicate, they were mainly but not entirely multi-product, being drawn up on a geographical rather than on a product basis; but the main determinant was the desire to avoid breaking up strong company managements. This also determined exactly how the largely geographical boundaries should be drawn. One strong company (Stewarts & Lloyds Ltd.) had for many years concentrated on tube making and was fairly widespread geographically: it had also been merged, shortly before nationalisation, with two other companies and this newly merged company was kept intact within one part-geographical, part-product group (Northern & Tubes). Two of the companies were widespread geographically but, unlike Stewarts & Lloyds, were not confined to a single product line. They were therefore split up between two or more Groups. With these exceptions, each of the fourteen companies' set of works was left intact and placed in the Group appropriate to its geographical location. However, as stated earlier, the companies were no longer used as the management units within the Groups.

Another reason for rejecting a product-based grouping at that stage, in favour of multi-product Groups, was that the scope for competition between the Groups would have been lessened. However, this was of limited importance as competition on price (as opposed to costs, quality, service and delivery, and technical rivalry) was ruled out anyway within a single Corporation in a small market the size of the UK. BSC could not afford to compete against itself when it was subjected to such strong international competition in all its markets. Indeed it was appreciated from the start that there must be some central Corporation policies and mechanisms for co-ordinating the commercial activities of different Groups making the same products, and this was effected.

The Head Office

The Corporation needed to decide, at the start, not only how the works should be grouped, but how the Head Office should be structured, including the Board itself. The Board Members are appointed by the Minister under the statute, but the allocation of responsibilities among them, though clearly connected with their particular qualifications for appointment by the Minister, is strictly a matter for the Corporation. That is to say, the Minister appoints Mr A. to be a Board Member, but BSC decides to appoint him Finance Member or whatever. The BSC in fact decided:

(a) that, at least in this formative period, the Chairman should also be Chief Executive;

(b) that the 'line' responsibility for operations should come up to him through the four Group MDs (all of whom were Board Members). Some measure of co-ordination was secured by a Group Managing Directors' Committee chaired by the senior of the four who also ranked as a Deputy Chairman of the BSC;

(c) that other Board Members should assume functional responsibilities: for Finance; Commercial matters; Personnel & Social Policy; Technical matters (comprising Engineering and R&D); and Administration. A system of functional advisory committees provided a forum for each functional Member (e.g. for Finance, or Personnel) to discuss the policy for his function across the Corporation, with the Group executives responsible for the same function at that level;

(d) that, with the Minister's agreement, there should be three Deputy Chairmen. They were respectively in charge of Operations (the senior Group MD mentioned earlier), Administration, and Technical matters.

The Board

The Board itself, appointed by the Minister, comprised five non-executive Members from outside BSC as well as the three Deputy Chairmen and the nine other line or functional executive Members whose roles have been described above. The Board is the ultimate authority in the Corporation. Its main responsibilities were (and remain) to set overall policy objectives for the BSC, to approve strategies and policies to achieve those objectives, to approve corporate plans and major organisational changes, to approve major acquisitions and disposals, and to approve (or delegate the approval of) capital expenditure projects and senior appointments. To help it to exercise effective and speedy conduct of its business it formed three committees – Finance, Planning (to deal with development planning and capital expenditure), and Appointments. The formal membership of each was confined to Board Members, and (unlike any other Committee in BSC) each exercised a corporate responsibility on the Board's behalf with defined limits of authority. At this stage there was no provision for an Audit Committee.

Employee Involvement at Board Level

Even in these very early days of the Corporation, it wished to reinforce the ordinary trade union consultative processes by a more
dramatic change in the arrangements for employee participation and
involvement. Accordingly, the Minister appointed (on the Chairman's
advice) a shopfloor employee to be a non-executive Member of the
main BSC Board from the start, and in 1968 the Corporation appointed about four 'Employee Directors' to serve on each of the
Group 'Boards'. These Group Boards, as stated earlier, were advisory
and non-statutory. They were not true boards but were in effect
Management Committees with the role of advising the Group MDs
who chaired them. Besides the Employee Directors, they comprised
the Directors-in-charge of the constituent Divisions and also the Group
Finance Director, Group Personnel Director, etc. The Employee
Directors, who were shopfloor employees of BSC and who carried
on doing their normal jobs for most of the time, had the same status
when serving on the Boards as did the executive Directors.

While the BSC did not publish in definite form its reasons for
introducing the scheme, they were identified as follows by the authors
of a research study published in 1976: that it would symbolise a new
departure in industrial relations in the newly nationalised industry;
that it would provide the Group Boards with a new dimension in their
discussions; and that it was part of a serious effort on the part of the
Corporation to involve its very numerous employees in working out
the future policies of the industry.

The system has been continued and developed over the years, and
the appointment of 'Employee Members' to the main Board in 1978
is described later in this paper.

Management Control

Several main principles of management control were enunciated and
followed by BSC in these early days, and they have survived to the
present day. These were that:

(i) Maximum operating autonomy and profit accountability should
     be accorded to the Groups, within the concept of a unified Cor-
     poration (which required substantial planning and policy-making
     authority to be retained by the Head Office).

(ii) An Annual Operating Plan should be prepared by each Group
     and, after approval by the BSC Chairman, should represent a
     firm commitment for the Group.

(iii) The principle of 'line' and 'functional' authority should apply throughout BSC.
(iv) Individual accountability should apply. That is to say, the Group MDs, the Directors-in-Charge of the Divisions and other managers should be held individually responsible for the results of their units. In other words, the Group 'Boards', the Divisional Management Committees and any other Committees (except the three Board Committees) would be purely advisory and have no corporate responsibility.
(v) BSC's policies and those procedures determined centrally should be clearly formulated in writing and promulgated throughout BSC.

Dissolution of the Companies

The former company structure had become irrelevant in 1967 as explained earlier. It did not interfere with the new system of management control but was unnecessary, and the statutory formalities involved a certain expense, to no purpose. The Corporation recommended in 1969, therefore, that the 'assets and undertakings' of the companies should be transferred to itself and that some of the companies or their subsidiaries should thereafter be dissolved where appropriate. The Iron and Steel Act 1969 was passed partly to facilitate this process. The transfer took effect from March 1970, and the Corporation thenceforth operated as a single legal entity, owning all the assets direct and not simply the securities of the fourteen main companies.

Some company names continued to be used, wherever appropriate, with the object of retaining the goodwill attaching to names, particularly in export markets.

Capital Structure

A very important change took place in this era affecting the BSC's capital structure. On its creation in 1967 BSC's capital had been on an all-debt, interest-bearing basis. This followed the precedents for all previous British nationalised industries (with the sole exception of British Airways) but the new Corporation regarded it as wholly inappropriate for a manufacturing concern trading against strenuous competition in its home and overseas markets and therefore (like British Airways) subject to cyclical fluctuations in its sales volume, prices, and results. The Government agreed with this view and as a result the Iron and Steel Act 1969 reconstituted the Corporation's capital on the basis partly of debt and partly of 'Public Dividend Capital'. The latter is held by the Government and BSC pays a dividend on it, or not, as trading results permit each year (it did so in 1974 and again in 1975, after its capital reconstruction had been completed in 1972/73, but the major recession and losses since then have ruled out any further payments and indeed the liability to pay dividends was suspended in 1978).

Although this change in capital structure did not affect the matter of BSC's organisation, it is worth mentioning in this paper as another reflection of the impact of BSC's commercial nature on its affairs.

B. 1970–76: Product Divisions

As stated earlier in this paper the initial organisation structure of the BSC was changed in 1970, when the Board had gained experience of running the major new Corporation and had had time to work out a longer-lasting form of organisation. In fact, the Board had begun to consider this change as early as the end of 1967, within a few months of vesting date when the first interim organisation took effect, but progress was delayed by a serious illness of the Chairman. This new and second main phase of organisation was heralded in two statutory organisation reports published in 1969, and it was introduced in March 1970 after a deep study chaired by one of the Deputy Chairmen.

The introduction of this new organisation was accompanied by the transfer to BSC of the assets and undertakings of the companies (and the dissolution of some of them) which was facilitated by the Iron and Steel Act 1969, as explained earlier.

The main change made in this second phase of organisation was the replacement of the multi-product Groups by Product Divisions. There was no opportunity to organise the BSC in this way in its first phase (1967–70) because of the need for the newly created Corporation to take immediate control of the formerly independent companies without the long delay and disruption of a thoroughgoing reorganisation. Also, a large upheaval in those early days, while controversy over the fact of nationalisation itself was still warm, might have seen the loss of several valued members of the senior management. But it became clear and generally accepted as early as 1968 that a system of multi-product Groups impeded the rationalisation of BSC's assets and their optimum utilisation and also the best planning of future development. Steel, after all, falls into several distinct products, which have to be sold separately, in different market sectors, and indeed produced separately albeit from a common crude source. A system of Product Divisions would enable the heads of each Division to be given the responsibility for both the manufacture and the sale of a product (or group of related products) and thus bring together, at a level below the centre, the responsibility for what are the two main streams of any industrial process. This would facilitate the decentralisation which BSC had always advocated, and would provide valuable training grounds in general management for BSC's future top managers.

All this was recognised as desirable in BSC's second statutory report on organisation, published in March 1969, and with the Government's agreement the BSC's review committee set about devising how it could and should be done. BSC's conclusions, again agreed by the Government, were set out in the third statutory report, in December 1969, and implemented as from March 1970.

The Divisions

The Product Divisions were six in number: four for the main groups of iron and steel products (General Steels, Strip Mills, Special Steels and Tubes) and two for the main 'diversified activities' of constructional engineering and chemicals. The latter were constituted as limited companies, instead of Divisions, in the early 1970s. This made no difference whatever to the management control of them but was done in order to facilitate the introduction of private capital – in line with the policy of the Conservative Government which had then been returned – though both companies in the event remained 100% owned by BSC throughout the 1970s.

The four iron and steel Divisions could not be quite 'clean', in that some works produced products falling within more than one product group. But the works were allocated to the Division with the main product interest, and rules were devised for dealing with the 'overlap' areas. The Divisions continued to have Management Committees and these still included Employee Directors as well as executive Directors.

The Head Office

While considerable authority was delegated to the Divisional heads ('Divisional Managing Directors'), and the Divisions were clearly constituted as profit centres, there had to be constraints on their autonomy so as to optimise results for BSC overall. The constraints were defined in some detail: those matters reserved to the centre included the development of financial systems, borrowing, assessment of capital investment proposals above certain limits, developing planning, raw materials procurement, acquisitions and disposals of interests in companies, overall personnel and industrial relations policies, overseas interests, and main pricing and sales policies. Economic forecasting, legal services and certain R&D activities were also provided centrally. Arrangements were also made for co-ordinating the activities of different Product Divisions located in the same region and two main Board Members were given the specific role of advising on Scottish and Welsh questions respectively.

The range of functional Divisions at the Head Office remained broadly unchanged, and the heads (Managing Directors) of them were in some cases, but not all, Members of the main Board. The Managing Directors in charge of the Product Divisions were not on the main Board but were left to concentrate on their business responsibilities. Until 1971, all the MDs reported to the Chief Executive, who was still the BSC Chairman acting in both roles; but this arrangement was then changed and the two top roles – each of which was very onerous – were separated. One of the Deputy Chairmen became Chief Executive and took charge of those Divisions, both in the field and at Head Office, concerned with direct operations, whether in the production, sales, finance, purchasing, personnel or technical areas. All the MDs reporting to the Chief Executive met under him once a month in the Chief Executive's Advisory Committee to ensure full co-ordination and monitoring of the executive activities.

The Chairman, while remaining responsible for the 'external' role of contact with Government, Parliament, press, public and others (a particularly demanding role in a nationalised industry), and while of course continuing to be responsible for BSC overall, retained direct responsibility for 'corporate' functions. The latter were grouped in a 'Corporate Office' covering main Board policy matters, Corporate Strategy and Planning, Administration, the Treasurer function, International Affairs, Acquisitions, etc. At this stage, all the Corporation's overseas interests, which comprised assets of over £50 million mainly inherited from the fourteen pre-nationalisation companies, were set up under a separate wholly owned subsidiary company – BSC (International) Ltd. They comprised sales companies, ore mining companies and some steel-processing concerns and many were in Commonwealth countries.

Other Factors

Two aspects of this period, though not directly impinging on BSC's organisation, should be mentioned as of considerable importance. First, the Iron and Steel Act of 1972 brought about a major capital reconstruction in BSC, to reduce its capital into line with the earning power of its assets: the reduction affected both the interest-bearing debt and the 'Public Dividend Capital'. It was designed to restore BSC to profit after the losses it had suffered in the early 1970s and was successful in that the Corporation was profitable in the three years up to 1975.

The second feature of this era was the first major inquiry into BSC's affairs by the House of Commons Select Committee on Nationalised Industries (in 1972). The report contained no very dramatic conclusions but it did underline the importance of improved working relations between BSC and the Government: this question had loomed fairly large in BSC's first five years and in some ways it dominated the Committee's inquiry. The report also drew attention to the need for BSC — so distinct from many other public enterprises in being a manufacturing and international trading concern — to be left free from excessive Government interference in its commercial affairs, though it recognised that BSC was far too important to the UK economy for its affairs to be left entirely to the Board of the Corporation.

The Committee's report was soon to be overtaken by two major events. The UK joined the Common Market in 1973 and this meant that BSC became an enterprise subject to the rules of the European Coal and Steel Community set up by the Treaty of Paris. Specifically, the UK Government was no longer permitted to exercise control over BSC's selling prices, and its powers over finance and investment were to become rather more limited also.

That event, again, did not impinge on BSC's organisation but the other major event was to have a considerable impact. This was the publication of BSC's *Ten Year Development Strategy*, also in 1973. It was the culmination of two to three years' work by BSC, latterly in close conjunction with the Government. As soon as it had been established in 1967, BSC had recognised the need for major modernisation and rationalisation of its production facilities — there had been a dearth of steel investment in the UK in the 1960s — and capital expenditure by BSC increased sharply up to the early 1970s. But the creation of the Product Division organisation in 1970 enabled the planning for the end of the decade to go ahead fully. At the time the strategy was published (1973), all the major steel-making nations in the world were planning to increase their capacity markedly in the face of an expected increase in world steel demand of 4–5% per annum. A similar, though rather slower, rate of growth was expected (by all concerned, in both BSC and Government) to be in prospect in the UK, and the world steel surplus capacity problem of the 1960s was considered to be a thing of the past.

Thus the strategy was for BSC to increase its capacity (then 27 million tonnes p.a.) to 33—35 mt by the late 1970s and to 36—38 mt during the first half of the 1980s. This was to involve bringing its five major coastal or near-coastal sites up to their optimum capacity, concentrating bulk steelmaking there, and beginning a major new steel complex.

Some of the smaller inland works would have to close, and the social problems were recognised. BSC co-operated with the Government and the European Commission in re-training and re-adaptation aid programmes and developed its own scheme for individual counselling of redundant employees. It also established a subsidiary company, BSC (Industry) Ltd., in 1975 to attract alternative employment to steel closure areas.

The new development strategy was recognised as bold, and was to cost some £3000 million over ten years (at 1972 prices). Some of the major works would be multi-product and this had direct implications for the future form of BSC's organisation.

The Corporation therefore began to review its form of organisation again at the end of 1973 and set up an internal Committee for this purpose in 1974. It published its conclusions in its *Organisation Review 1975* in August 1975. Some of the changes were implemented in 1975 but the new organisation did not formally take effect until March 1976. It is with that new structure that the next part of this paper now deals.

C. 1976—80: Manufacturing Divisions and Product Units

Towards the end of the period just described, there had been disturbing signs of economic recession following the international oil crisis of the mid-1970s, but this, while recognised as the worst downturn for forty years, was at the time regarded as temporary. The rationale of BSC's new organisation, designed to cope with the planned major expansion and concentration of its facilities, therefore seemed to be unaffected, and it seemed important to bring the new structure into being before the development programme was too far advanced.

Production and Sales Activities

The virtues and attractions of product-based profit centres, outlined earlier, were still recognised, and BSC's approach was to preserve this structure wherever possible. This was done, for example, for tubes, tinplate, stainless steel, forges, foundries, electrical steels, stockholding, constructional engineering, chemicals and overseas affairs.

But these areas all lay outside BSC's main iron and steel activities. In that 'bulk' area the prospect of progressively fewer and progressively larger works – with some of them being multi-product – appeared to BSC to call for a new organisation to replace the Product Divisions. These five major geographical production complexes – of which three were in one of the still-existing Product Divisions – were to be given a more direct reporting relationship to the Corporation's Chief Executive. At the same time it remained true, of course, that steel still had to be sold as separate products into separate market sectors and that therefore a product-based selling organisation should continue. For the main iron and steel business, therefore, the new structure was deliberately designed as a hybrid.

The main production complexes were formed as five geographical Manufacturing Divisions (Scottish, Welsh, Teesside, Sheffield and Scunthorpe), acting as cost or performance centres and not profit centres. The Managing Director in charge of each reported direct to the Chief Executive (and he, of course, to the Chairman). Orders and sales, on the other hand, were made the responsibility of four main Product Units, each dealing with a group of products (Billet, Bar and Rod; Plates; Sections; and Strip Mills) and each situated near to the most relevant Manufacturing Division. The Product Units allocated orders to the works. The Directors in charge of these Units reported to the Commercial Managing Director at BSC's Head Office who thus exchanged his former functional responsibility for a direct line responsibility. He in turn reported to the Chief Executive who integrated the production and sales activities. Both activities had also to be integrated by the Chief Executive with the supporting Head Office functions (Personnel, Finance, etc.) and a top-level monthly meeting of the Chief Executive's Committee was still a crucial element in the process.

This more centralised commercial organisation was not only considered necessary but was also made more feasible by the development of BSC's computer programme which could now deal with order handling and production planning.

It was clear that the production and commercial activities must not be integrated at the top only. Accordingly, the Director of each Product Unit served as a member of the Management Committee of the adjacent Manufacturing Division. He also chaired a business team for his product of which production and other staff were members in addition to sales staff. This was seen as essential for customer service and other reasons. Finally, the manufacturing and the commercial functions (as well as others) were jointly involved in planning

activities − both for the annual operating plans and also longer-term
development plans.

The geographically based Manufacturing Divisions of course made
it far easier to cater for regional policy matters, e.g. affecting Scotland
and Wales, though there was a fear in some quarters that the removal
of a profit or general management responsibility from senior managers
situated in the steelmaking areas would militate against the interests
of devolution in the broader political sense.

The Head Office

Apart from the far-reaching change in commercial responsibilities,
the effect of the new organisation in BSC's Head Office structure was
not great. The opportunity was taken, however, largely to eliminate
the concept of a 'Corporate Office' distinct from the Chief Executive's
Office and to remove some of the duplication and illogicalities which
had resulted from it. Another broad distinction began to be drawn,
however, through the explicit recognition that many of the Head
Office staff directly supported the works activities, and needed no
longer to be located in the same headquarters as the central 'policy'
staff.

Changing Economic Factors

By an irony, it was not long after this new organisation fully came
into existence that it began to be generally realised (in 1977) that the
'temporary' economic recession following the world oil crisis was in
fact a sea change of the greatest significance, and that as a result the
collapse of steel demand in the UK and the rest of the world was a
more permanent feature. A serious decline in the competitiveness of
British steel-using (and other) industries also set in from about the
mid-1970s and again reduced severely the UK demand for steel. By
another irony, these developments coincided with the fact that BSC
(like some foreign steel industries) had really got into its stride with
its major capital expenditure programme, spending no less than £579
million in 1976/77 alone.

UK steel demand fell further, and the pace of world competition
increased sharply in the face of the surplus capacity problem in most
steelmaking countries.

It became clear therefore that BSC's major development strategy
would need to be unwound and the greatly expanded multi-product
works became less and less likely to come into existence.

This fall in the volume of sales in the late 1970s was accompanied
by very weak steel prices because of the world surplus, and in the UK

by high inflation. Thus BSC's prices were unable to keep pace with its costs which rose sharply. This was a classic prescription for financial losses and BSC's losses rose alarmingly. The only cure was massive cost reduction through plant closures, reduced manning and in other ways.

At this stage, in the 1977–78 Parliamentary session, the Select Committee on Nationalised Industries mounted another inquiry into BSC, five years having elapsed since the last. Apart from raising certain constitutional questions about the provision of information, its reports concentrated on the need for improved efficiency and productivity, and criticised BSC's forecasting. The Government, in its reply, stressed the effect of the recession in adding to the difficulty of forecasting. The Committee was indeed conducting its inquiry at the same time as BSC and the Government were engaged in a very fundamental reconsideration of the whole strategy for steel. A Government White Paper published in March 1978 (*The Road to Viability*) stressed the need, fully recognised by BSC, for capacity to be reduced, some new investment plans to be abandoned and productivity to be increased. The need for a substantial capital reconstruction was also foreseen, and the inability of BSC to pay dividends meanwhile was recognised.

Audit Committee

These far-reaching financial and economic developments had little direct effect on BSC's form of organisation, at least for a little time. It is true that BSC established an Audit Committee in 1977 (being one of the first UK nationalised industries to do so), and the genesis of this was certainly the desire to monitor internal financial controls. At first, incidentally, the Committee endeavoured to cover not only financial aspects but also efficiency aspects, through discussing BSC's 'performance indicators' which are regularly published and which cover physical as well as financial measures. But later this element was abandoned as it involved technical steelmaking factors which the non-executive BSC Board Members who constituted the Committee felt were best left to the BSC's Chief Executive to monitor. The Committee remains active in the financial field, however. Essentially, it satisfies itself that BSC's external auditors are receiving all the assistance and co-operation they need from the BSC executive, on the Annual Accounts and other matters, and it also regularly reviews the work of BSC's Internal Audit Department.

Re-Structuring of the Board

An organisation change of considerable interest that fell in this period was the restructuring of BSC's main Board, in 1978. While it continued to comprise some top BSC executives, and also some outside businessmen as non-executives, two new elements of membership were added. There had been a BSC shopfloor employee on the Board since its inception, and Employee Directors on the Management Committees of its subsidiary Divisions, but this arrangement was greatly expanded by the appointment of six 'Employee Members' to the main Board in August 1978, as part of the (by now) Labour Government's policy of 'industrial democracy'. The six Members were BSC paid employees, not full-time trade union officials. They were individually acceptable to the unions (as well as to BSC) but were not appointees, nor formal nominees, of the unions: like all other Board Members they were appointed by the Minister. Their status (and salary as Board Members) is the same as that of any other non-executive Member of the Board, and they participate fully in the Board's business.

The arrangement clearly poses difficult 'conflict of interest' situations for the individuals (especially with closures and manpower reductions rife) but an appraisal of the system lies outside the scope of this paper. It should be emphasised that the system is in no sense a substitute for the consultative arrangements between BSC and the trade unions (let alone the negotiating machinery), but is a supplement to those processes of consultation.

The other change in Board membership arrangements saw the appointment to it of two serving civil servants – one from H.M. Treasury and the other from the Department of Industry (BSC's 'sponsoring' department). Perhaps this can be seen as connected with BSC's serious financial losses which escalated in the late 1970s. Again the arrangement poses potential conflict of interest situations – at least in theory – but it clearly has the advantage of increasing the knowledge by the Government of BSC's problems and of the reasons for its responses, and *vice versa*. However, this paper does not in any sense purport to appraise the scheme.

A Crisis of Survival

The worsening economic and financial situation afflicting BSC reached proportions which seemed likely to threaten the Corporation's very survival and gave rise to very far-reaching remedial measures in 1979. In December of that year BSC announced a massive reduction in its manned capacity – from 21½ million tonnes p.a. to 15 million tonnes p.a. – to match the drastically reduced market. This involved major plant closures. Manpower at ongoing works was also greatly reduced to increase BSC's competitiveness in an increasingly serious international market situation. By March 1980 BSC had reduced its manning to 166,000 – or over 60,000 less than five years earlier.

The abandonment of the ambitious development strategy, now that the expected burgeoning market had been replaced by a much smaller and highly competitive prospect, meant that the case for the Manufacturing Division/Product Unit organisation introduced in 1976 was weakening rapidly. The commercial case for greater decentralisation and fuller profit responsibility 'down the line' was, by the same token, becoming much stronger again. Two of BSC's regional Manufacturing Divisions (Sheffield and Scunthorpe) were particularly active in making steel billets and billet-derived products, and they were joined up in 1979 with the related Product Unit to form a major decentralised product-based profit centre for billet products. (Despite its product basis it had the geographical name of BSC Yorkshire and Humberside.)

This was a precursor for a complete move in 1980 to a highly decentralised system of product-based profit centres or 'businesses', designed to face the extremely competitive market situation, as described in the next section of this paper.

D. 1980 to Date: Businesses

Following the appointment of a new Chairman of BSC in mid-1980, an urgent and thorough review of the organisation was undertaken in response to the need to restore the Corporation's financial and competitive strength. The conclusions were embodied in BSC's *Report on Organisation, 1980*, and the new structure took effect from September 1980. It is shown on the annexed Organisation Chart.

Production and Sales Activities

The report emphasised that the very highly competitive steel market conditions – more so than ever before – demanded competitive costs, quality and service to an unprecedented extent. This was seen to call for all BSC's activities to be organised into a series of discrete 'Businesses', each oriented towards separate product markets, and acting as a profit centre linking the production and commercial responsibilities. In other words the main iron and steel 'core' of BSC was now to be organised in rather the same way as in the Product Division structure adopted in 1970 before the massive development strategy was mounted in the mid-1970s, and as the more diversified parts of BSC (tubes, tinplate, stainless steel, chemicals, etc.) had continued to be organised all along.

The market outlook, competitors and customers of each iron and steel product Business differed considerably, as always, and this called for different strategies and priorities. But a new factor was that the widespread closures of works and progressive rationalisation had by now greatly reduced the 'overlap' problem and meant that each Business's discrete range of products was now manufactured in relatively discrete production facilities.

This devolution into separate 'Businesses' has also enabled employees to identify with the success of their own Business – more important than ever in the 'survival' climate now prevailing – and has greatly increased their motivation and that of the management of each Business.

The main iron and steel Businesses (for Sections, Strip Mill Products, Plates, Special Steels, Tinplate, etc.) are gathered under two main Groups – General Steels and Strip Products – each under a Group Chairman who reports to BSC's Chief Operating Officer. Each Business incorporates the production facilities from the former Manufacturing Divisions relevant to its product, and the relevant commercial activities from the former Product Units. The central commercial 'line' control by BSC's Head Office has therefore ceased to exist. Customer contacts have been largely unaffected as the same individuals, albeit under new 'hats', deal with the same customers as before.

The Managing Directors of all the Businesses are still advised by Management Committees, which typically meet monthly and comprise that Business's line and functional Directors (plus some Employee Directors still).

While the degree of decentralisation – or more accurately 'delegation of authority' – has been greatly increased, the Businesses do not have complete profit centre autonomy. BSC must still be managed as a total corporate entity and not simply as a financial holding company. It must take a corporate view of the extent of integration from basic steelmaking through to distribution, and thus of the degree to which the individual Businesses should import their semi-finished steel – so as to ensure proper remuneration of BSC's heavy investment in basic steelmaking capacity. Large customers dealing with more than one BSC business also continue to call for some co-ordination on BSC's part, as do pricing and international affairs, and therefore a small 'Commercial Services' Department remains at Head Office.

It might be added here that BSC is steadily forming some of its 'non-mainstream' Businesses into limited companies — as it did for its construction engineering division in 1972 (now disposed of, as Redpath Dorman Long Ltd.) and as regards BSC (Chemicals) Ltd. in 1973. The reason is partly the same as it was then — to facilitate the introduction of private capital into these Businesses, or even their complete sale in line with the 'privatisation' policy of the present Conservative Government in regard to the nationalised industries generally. Another, connected, reason is that this change of status makes a Business more 'transparent' as it must publish its own separate accounts under the Companies Act.

This change of status does not, however, materially affect the degree of control which BSC exercises over these Businesses so long as they remain wholly owned subsidiaries. The same was true (in reverse) in the early life of BSC when it exercised its management control through a structure of Groups and Divisions notwithstanding the continuation of all the former companies, as legal entities, until 1969. Limited companies must, of course, have statutory Boards for largely formal purposes but the Corporation's management control in such cases is exercised through the Managing Director of the Business as in the case of those Businesses which have not been converted to limited company status.

In addition to its wholly owned subsidiaries, BSC either inherited or has since acquired substantial interests in other companies. In some cases these are 'joint venture' companies in which BSC's interest is 50%. This has usually been arranged for commercial reasons, often with BSC providing the input material for the company (e.g. semi-finished steel or slag) and the other partner contributing the means of enabling the sale product to be sold in a market rather different from the main steel product markets. In other cases, raw material supply is involved. And more recently, with shrinking markets, a motivation has been to rationalise BSC-owned and privately owned steelmaking facilities serving the same product sector, into a single and much stronger UK company. Some earlier joint ventures have ceased but current examples include Allied Steel & Wire Ltd., Sheffield Forgemasters Ltd., Templeborough Rolling Mills Ltd., Darlington & Simpson Rolling Mills Ltd., Air Products Llanwern Ltd. and several slag disposal companies.

Head Office Functions

Aside from its overall concern for production and commercial matters, BSC's Head Office must also still be responsible (under the Chief

Operating Officer) for several central activities. These include both raising funds and allocating them according to a corporate view of priorities, raw material purchasing, and several policy matters, such as pricing policy, personnel policy, international relations (particularly with EEC), accounting procedures, some R&D activities, co-ordination of development and financial planning, etc. And, as well as giving overall supervision and leadership, the Chairman must as always represent BSC externally, with Government, Parliament, the press and the public, and many other interests. Therefore, there are still Head Office staff functions for Finance, Personnel, Supplies, Technical matters and some Administrative matters, serving the Chairman and the Chief Operating Officer. BSC's interests in overseas subsidiaries are now looked after by the Business most relevant to each overseas activity (indeed many of these interests have been disposed of to raise cash) and therefore the former subsidiary BSC (International) Ltd. has effectively disappeared. Corporate strategy no longer calls for a separate function.

The Chief Operating Officer (whose title has been re-styled from Chief Executive, since the executive Chairman is now styled as Chairman and Chief Executive Officer) convenes his Operations Committee each month to assist him in integrating all the matters for which he is responsible, to advise him on current and future problems and to monitor results. These meetings take place two weeks before the monthly meetings of the BSC main Board, to which the Chief Operating Officer (who is also Deputy Chairman of the Corporation) reports on the month's operations.

The Board still delegates certain authority to a Finance Committee, comprising some executive and non-executive Board Members; and the Audit Committee (confined to certain non-executive Members) is still in existence but now concentrates on financial auditing matters. In addition, the Board has recently set up a Salaries Committee, again confined to certain non-executive Board Members, which is responsible for considering salary policy and actual salaries for the executive Members and for making recommendations on these to the Minister who is responsible for determining them under the statute.

Corporate Plans

BSC's response to the still extremely difficult market situation was set out in a Corporate Plan in 1981 (covering 1981/82) and another in 1982 (covering mainly 1982/83 but looking forward also to 1985). These have been addressed not so much to recovery as to survival, as BSC's increasing losses up to 1980 had posed real threats to its continuation if it could not achieve a major increase in competitiveness. While broadly maintaining the present level of manned capacity (at about 14½ million tonnes p.a.) the Plans have concentrated on ensuring that sales are sufficient to utilise the capacity efficiently; on securing additional cost reduction through further reduced manning, increased productivity, pay restraint, economies in energy consumption, etc; and on the maintenance or increase of prices insofar as the very competitive international market permits. As a result, BSC's manning has (as at end-June 1982) been reduced to 97,000 – less than half its level only four years earlier – and productivity at several of its works is comparable to the best in Europe. Its losses have been reduced from £668 million in 1980/81 to £358 million in 1981/82. It has lived within the greatly reduced external financing limit set for it by the Government in 1981/82, and is pledged to comply with a very large further reduction in 1982/83: this external financing by the Government has also had to cover the major redundancy and closure costs incurred by the Corporation.

This big reduction in losses can partly be attributed to the new motivation springing from the new organisational structure described in this section. The change in organisational structure has also been accompanied, deliberately, by a change in management style consonant with the greatly reduced manning and thinning out of staffs (as well as manual operatives). There is now less reliance on paper, more insistence on face-to-face contacts and less bureaucracy. There are great dividends in efficiency to be derived from this.

The Corporate Plan published in 1981 was the subject of an inquiry by the House of Commons Industry and Trade Committee in the 1980/81 Parliamentary session (and a follow-up enquiry in the next session). The reports of the Committee, which has replaced the former Select Committee on Nationalised Industries as the Parliamentary Committee concerned with BSC's affairs, were cautious in expressing views on BSC's prospects but concentrated on the problems of ensuring fair international trading in steel and on the high UK energy prices which affect BSC's international competitiveness.

Statutory Changes

In conclusion, attention should be drawn to certain statutory changes affecting BSC's freedom to reorganise its internal structure. The Iron and Steel Act 1981 leaves BSC completely free now to consider changes at will – with no statutory duty to do so and no statutory power for the Minister to order it to do so. It is still required to ensure that its organisation is efficient but the subject is now treated under the statute more like other commercial subjects. BSC no longer has to produce formal statutory reports to the Government on organisation and its consultations with the trade unions on any changes are now non-statutory, like consultations on all other topics. Any substantial changes it makes in its organisation, however, still require the Government's consent (perhaps to ensure that they are not in a direction completely opposed to general Government policies). Acquisitions and disposals – i.e. the constitution of BSC's business as opposed to its organisation – remain subject to various controls by Government. The Act also made an interesting change in the Corporation's status, removing its general statutory duties and giving it greater freedom to act as a commercial organisation. This may be seen as a step to facilitate privatisation, as there no longer *has* to be a British Steel Corporation to carry out stated statutory duties.

SOME CONCLUSIONS

This essay has been more in the nature of a historical survey and a description of the phases of organisation which the British Steel Corporation has adopted since its formation in 1967, rather than a critique of those different structures. Few specific conclusions therefore emerge but the following may be worth identifying:

(1) BSC, unlike many public enterprises which are public utilities, is a non-monopoly manufacturing concern trading internationally against strenuous competition. The increasing intensity of this competition has directly affected the choice of the most effective management organisation structure for the Corporation. In particular, it has underlined the advantages of a decentralised system of profit centres in motivating both management and shopfloor.

(2) Radically changed economic factors, both domestic and international, have affected the size and pattern of BSC's production facilities over the years and hence its organisation structure.

(3) Profit centres within BSC must necessarily be on a product basis, rather than geographical, in a country as small as the UK where distance and freight costs are insufficient to insulate the selling operations of one area from those of another.

(4) Whether subsidiary units are constituted as Divisions or as limited companies makes virtually no difference to their management control by the Corporation (though there may be other good reasons for making the change – in either direction).

(5) Even in a public enterprise, the motivation of subsidiary units is considerably strengthened by a suitable management style which relies more on face-to-face contacts than on paperwork, elaborate Committee structures, and complicated reporting and control mechanisms.

(6) The need for a commercial concern of the character of BSC to change its organisation to respond to changing market conditions strengthens the case for it to be free of too many statutory constraints on its organisation structure.

August 1982

BIBLIOGRAPHY

British Steel Corporation: Report on Organisation 1967, HMSO Her Majesty's Stationery Office, August 1967 (Cmnd. 3362).
British Steel Corporation: Second Report on Organisation, HMSO, March 1969 (House of Commons Paper No. 163).
British Steel Corporation: Third Report on Organisation, HMSO, December 1969 (House of Commons Paper No. 60).
British Steel Corporation: Organisation Review 1975, HMSO, August 1975 (House of Commons Paper No. 604).
Report on Organisation, 1980, BSC, September 1980.
British Steel Corporation Organisation Guides, BSC, 1971, 1973, 1976, 1977, 1980 and 1981.

British Steel Corporation: Annual Reports and Accounts, 1967–81.
BSC Annual Statistics, 1968–81/82.
Iron and Steel Industry Annual Statistics, Iron and Steel Statistics Bureau.

Steel Nationalisation, HMSO, April 1965 (Cmnd. 2651).
Memorandum on Iron and Steel Bill, HMSO, April 1969 (Cmnd. 4022).
Memorandum on Iron and Steel Bill, 1971, HMSO, December 1971 (Cmnd. 4839).
Steel: British Steel Corporation: Ten Year Development Strategy, HMSO, February 1973 (Cmnd. 5226).
British Steel Corporation: The Road to Viability, HMSO, March 1978 (Cmnd. 7149).

Finance for Steel, BSC, May 1969.
Prospects for Steel, BSC, April 1978.
The Background of the Corporate Plan [for 1981/82], BSC, February 1981.
The Background to the Corporation Plan 1982–85, BSC, June 1982.

Iron and Steel Act 1949.
Iron and Steel Act 1953.
Iron and Steel Act 1967.
Iron and Steel Act 1969.
Iron and Steel Act 1972.
Iron and Steel Act 1975 (consolidation measure).

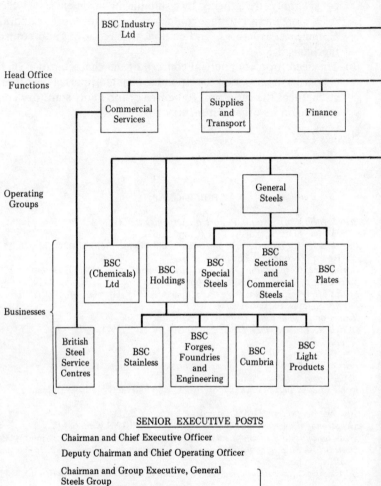

SENIOR EXECUTIVE POSTS

Chairman and Chief Executive Officer

Deputy Chairman and Chief Operating Officer

Chairman and Group Executive, General
Steels Group

— MD, BSC Special Steels
— MD, BSC Sections and Commercial Steels
— MD, BSC Plates

Chairman and Group Executive, Strip Products
Group and MD, BSC Strip Mill Products

— MD, Operations, BSC Strip Mill Products

— MD, BSC Holdings

— BSC Tubes

Businesses

BSC MANAGEMENT ORGANISATION CHART, AUGUST 1982

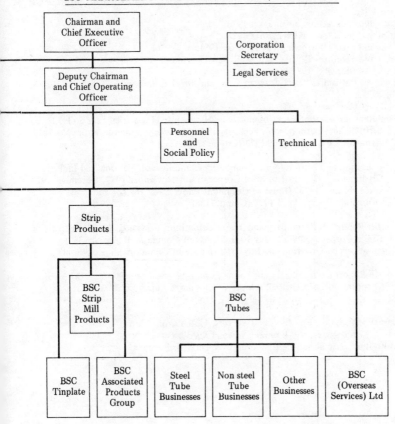

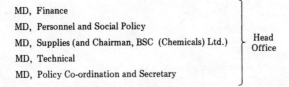

MD, Finance

MD, Personnel and Social Policy

MD, Supplies (and Chairman, BSC (Chemicals) Ltd.)

MD, Technical

MD, Policy Co-ordination and Secretary

Head Office

Iron and Steel (Amendment) Act 1976.
Iron and Steel (Amendment) Act 1978.
Iron and Steel (Borrowing Powers) Act 1981.
Iron and Steel Act 1981.
Iron and Steel Act 1982 (consolidation measure).
Treaty Establishing the European Coal and Steel Community (Treaty of Paris), 1951.

First Report from the Select Committee on Nationalised Industries, Session 1972–73, 'British Steel Corporation', February 1973 (House of Commons Paper No. 141).
Government's Reply, August 1973 (Cmnd. 5399).

First, Second and Fifth Reports from Select Committee on Nationalised Industries, Session 1977–78, 'British Steel Corporation', November 1977, December 1977 and February 1978 (House of Commons Papers Nos. 26, 127 and 238).
Government's Reply, April 1978 (Cmnd. 7188).

Fourth Report from Industry and Trade Committee, Session 1980–81, 'Effects of BSC's Corporate Plan', May 1981 (House of Commons Paper No. 336).
Observations by Government, July 1981 (House of Commons Paper No. 444).

Fourth Report from Industry and Trade Committee, Session 1981–82, 'British Steel Corporation', March 1982 (House of Commons Paper No. 308).
Observations by Government, July 1982 (House of Commons Paper No. 491).

Brannen, P., et al, *The Worker Directors*, Hutchinson, 1976.
Bank, J. and Jones, K., *Worker Directors Speak*, Gower Press, 1977.
[Both books are about the BSC Employee Director Scheme.]

3

THE POST OFFICE

J. R. Baxter

1. HISTORICAL BACKGROUND

The Bridgeman Report and After

The suggestion that the Post Office should be converted from a Government Department into a public corporation was first considered in the early 1930s. A committee was set up at that time under the chairmanship of Viscount Bridgeman 'to enquire and report as to whether any changes in the constitution, status or system of organisation of the Post Office would be in the public interest'. The Committee's report, published in August 1932, considered the possibility of transferring the functions of the Post Office to an independent public authority but rejected it in favour of more limited reforms.

The Committee's main recommendations were that:

(i) Treasury intervention in the financial arrangements of the Post Office should be reduced to the minimum in recognition of the fact that it was essentially a commercial organisation, and

(ii) There should be a devolution of powers and responsibilities from Headquarters to a new regional organisation.

The Government implemented the Bridgeman recommendation that the Post Office should pay a fixed annual contribution to the Exchequer and that any profits remaining should be available to the Post Office for improvements in service. This arrangement continued from 1933 until 1940 when it was suspended because of the exceptional circumstances of the war. The arrangement was, however, revived with the publication in 1955 of the Government White Paper *Report on Post Office Development and Finance* (Cmnd. 9576) and introduced experimentally in 1956, when the level of the Post Office's contribution to the Exchequer was fixed at £5m a year, but despite these accounting arrangements, all revenue was still paid into the Exchequer and all expenditure voted by Parliament.

In 1961 the final links with the Exchequer were broken by the Post Office Act 1961. The Post Office was still a Government Department directly represented by a Minister of Parliament but in its financial arrangements it closely resembled a public corporation.

The Act set up the Post Office Fund and all receipts (with a few exceptions) and payments were made into and out of it. The Fund replaced provisions in the Budget for the Post Office's self-balancing revenue and expenditure and the Post Office ceased to present annual estimates to Parliament, and was required to produce accounts showing the trading position for each year together with a balance sheet. In addition the Post Office had to ensure that its revenues were sufficient to meet its expenditure on revenue account, including allocations to a general reserve − a requirement in effect to do rather better than break even. Over the period 1963/64 to 1967/68 the Post Office had a financial objective of a net return of 8% on net assets, net return being defined as profit before interest, tax and supplementary depreciation, but after historical depreciation. This objective was for the organisation as a whole and had the disadvantage of allowing one business to operate at a level below the objectives so long as the shortfall was covered by the other. Thus, although there was no cross subsidy in cash terms, the postal service was in effect cushioned by the high achievement of the telecommunications service.

McKinsey

The regional structure set up following the Bridgeman Report, comprised 8 provincial regions, headed by a Regional Director responsible for both Postal and Telecommunications services, and in London separate Regional Directorates for Post and Telecommunications.

In the 1960s the Post Office engaged consultants, McKinseys, to carry out a fundamental examination of its organisation and management practices. One result of the McKinsey study was that a radical reorganisation of Headquarters was undertaken in 1967 to separate the functions of the two main Businesses, Posts and Telecommunications. Certain functions which had formerly been centralised were grouped under these Businesses. At the same time the combined organisations in the Regions were (apart from Northern Ireland) split into separate organisations for the two main services, each under a separate Regional Director. Below regional headquarters level, the organisations were already divided into separate Postal and Telephone Areas, headed respectively by Head or District Postmasters and by Telephone Managers (now General Managers).

Decision to make the Post Office a corporation

In 1965 the Parliamentary Select Committee on Nationalised Industries carried out an inquiry into the Post Office. During the course of that inquiry the Government announced its intention of changing the Post Office into a public corporation. The Government's proposals were published in the 1967 White Paper *Reorganisation of the Post Office* (Cmnd. 3233). In that paper the Government stated that it 'had carried out a fundamental review of the Post Office, set against the challenging future of change and expansion which faces many of its services. Its present structure and methods are those of a Department of State. These have been evolved primarily for the formulation and execution of Government policy, and are geared to the discharge of ministerial responsibility to Parliament. They are unsuited to the running of the postal, telecommunications and remittance services, and the new Giro service. The Government concluded that the process begun in 1932 should be carried to its logical conclusion. A public corporation should be created to run these great businesses with a structure and methods designed directly to meet their needs, drawing on the best modern practice'.

The Government's stated objective was to create an authority which would:

- be responsible for developing the most efficient services possible, at the lowest charges consistent with sound financial policies;
- carry on in a worthy manner the tradition of service to the public;
- develop relations with its staff in a forward looking and progressive way.

Discussions were held with Post Office trade unions on all aspects of the change affecting them and the Government gave assurances relating to the security of jobs and the conditions of service of Post Office staff. The Government's decision was given effect in the Post Office Act 1969 and the Post Office acquired its new status on 1 October 1969.

PE–C

II. THE POST OFFICE ACT 1969

The Post Office Act 1969 provided for the following changes. The office of Postmaster General was abolished and responsibility for running postal, telecommunications and related services (including National Girobank, established in 1968 as a money transmission service) was transferred to a new public authority known as the Post Office. The Post Office was given monopolies of letter carrying and telecommunications (except public broadcasting).

A new Government Department, the Ministry of Posts and Telecommunications, was established with responsibilities for (i) the functions of the Postmaster General in relation to wireless telegraphy and broadcasting, and (ii) the general control and supervision of the Post Office.

A separate Department for National Savings (a Government Department responsible to Treasury Ministers) was set up to administer the former Post Office savings services.

The Act followed the general pattern of earlier legislation such as that nationalising the coal and electricity industries; it provided for an independent corporation and for a Minister with powers to appoint its Members and to exercise certain general controls over it. There were, however, some features unique to the Post Office as these examples show.

International Relations

Because the Post Office runs international services and is closely involved in the work of certain international organisations (e.g. Universal Postal Union), it was appropriate to give the Minister a power to issue specific directions on international matters.

Work for the Government

As the Post Office acts as an agent for the Government and for local authorities in paying pensions, issuing licences etc. over post office counters, it was appropriate to give the Minister power to direct the Post Office to continue to do this work.

Telecommunications licensing

Under the division of functions, control of telecommunications went to the Post Office and regulation of broadcasting and use of the radio spectrum to the Minister. Where a telecommunications system used radio, or a broadcasting system used cables, licences were needed from both authorities.

III. ORGANISATION OF THE POST OFFICE AFTER THE 1969 ACT

From 1 October 1969 the Post Office consisted of three separate financially independent businesses – Posts, National Girobank and Telecommunications, with which the previously independent Data Processing Service was subsequently merged. Posts was set a financial target of earning a surplus of 2% on expenditure over the five years from 1968/69 to 1972/73, while the telecommunications target was set at 10% on mean net assets. Under the 1969 Act management of the Post Office was vested in a Board consisting, in accordance with the Act, of a Chairman and up to twelve other Members, all appointed by the Minister of Posts and Telecommunications (since 1974, by the Secretary of State for Industry – see IV below).

IV. MINISTRY OF POSTS AND TELECOMMUNICATIONS – TRANSFER OF FUNCTIONS

The Ministry of Posts and Telecommunications was abolished in 1974. Responsibility for wireless telegraphy and broadcasting policy was transferred to the Home Office. Responsibility for Post Office affairs (postal, telecommunications, data processing and National Girobank services) was transferred to the Department of Industry.

The Secretary of State for Industry is assisted in his Department by two Ministers of State and two Parliamentary Under Secretaries of State. One of the Ministers of State has the specified task of exercising responsibility for Post Office affairs.

An Industrial Democracy experiment was instigated in the mid-seventies by the Minister of State for Industry. A Joint Study Group comprising PO and union representatives formulated arrangements which were introduced at National, Regional and local levels early in 1978. The Post Office Act was amended for a period of two years to permit the Post Office Board to be expanded to include seven employee representatives and five independent outside Members. This arrangement was mirrored in six Postal regions which had advisory boards. At local level, Area Policy Committees were set up to provide an advisory forum to positively influence policy decisions without impinging on the existing negotiating arrangements.

The Board level arrangements ceased after two years on 31 December 1979 and those at regional and local levels on separation of the Post Office from BT. The experiment was not deemed a success at Board level mainly due to manifestations of conflicts of interests. At regional and local levels some duplication arose with the existing well-developed consultative/negotiating machinery which already gave unions a high level of participation in business affairs. However, certain aspects of the experiment remained, particularly more open union–management relationships and improved communication with the staff.

In November 1975 the Secretary of State appointed a Committee under the chairmanship of Mr C. F. Carter FBS, Hon. D. Econ. Sc., to review the Post Office with the following terms of reference.

> To examine the performance and main features of the organisation of the Post Office and its use of its resources and assets; and to consider whether any changes would better enable it to perform its functions under the Post Office Act 1969; to assess the policies, prospects and social significance of the Postal Business, including methods of financing it as a self-supporting public service; to consider whether the Post Office Act 1969 places undue restrictions on the activities of the Post Office; and to make recommendations.

The Committee reported in July 1977 and made recommendations concerned primarily with structure and general management principles, but also touching on operational and financial matters.

The prime recommendation was the proposal that the Post Office should be divided into two new authorities, one consisting of Posts and National Girobank and the other of the Telecommunications, including the Data Processing service.

Following upon that recommendation of the Carter Committee, the Government announced in September 1979 its intention of removing the Telecommunications Business from the Post Office and establishing it as a separate Corporation. The main reason for effecting the separation was the recognition of the fundamental differences between the two principal Businesses; on the one hand, Posts, labour intensive, with relatively low demands for capital investment, and on the other, the highly capital intensive Telecommunications business. For Posts, the key factors were the efficient use of labour and control of staff related costs, while for Telecommunications efficiency in the use of capital and technical development was equally important. The necessary legislation for this change, the British Telecommunications Act 1981, took effect on 1 October 1981, when responsibility for operating telecommunications and data processing services was transferred from the Post Office to a new public authority known as British Telecommunications. Postal (including counter) services and National Girobank remained under the control of the Post Office Board (whose current composition is shown in the Annex). Such common links as remained from 1969 were severed and dealings between the two Corporations put on normal commercial terms. In organisational terms, the main changes were:

(i) the separating of former common functions such as legal services, public relations, catering, health and welfare and their assimilation within the independent Businesses;
(ii) the division of common assets;
(iii) the establishment of a separate purchasing organisation for Posts and National Girobank (previously Telecommunications had dealt with all purchasing matters).

Structure below Board level

Postal and Counter Services (Posts)

Below Post Office Board level, there are Headquarters Directors of the various policy functions and Regional Directors to whom the running of the postal and counter services is delegated and who have wide devolved powers, including powers for capital expenditure within agreed programmes. Control of their areas is exercised through Head Postmasters (in Inner London, District Postmasters).

National Girobank

National Girobank has a Headquarters in London but its main operational centre is at Bootle, near Liverpool. Business with customers is transacted via the network of Post Office counters. Regional offices are being established to improve direct contact with customers.

V. POWERS OF THE POST OFFICE

The Post Office Act 1969 (as amended by the British Telecommunications Act 1981) gives the Post Office powers to provide:

(i) postal, banking and other remittance services, and telepost services;
(ii) services for British Telecommunications and its subsidiaries;
(iii) services for the Government, other Governments, local authorities and with the consent of the Secretary of State, for other public authorities.

It also has powers to carry out certain activities, as defined in the Act, in connection with these services. The powers are wide enough to permit expansion of services and activities such as developing sites to the maximum extent and letting surplus space.

The Post Office's powers are considerably wider than its monopoly, confined to the basic letter service only. Important areas of Post Office activity, e.g. parcels and premium services are entirely outside the sphere of the monopoly. Competition takes a number of forms — competing communications media include telephones, telex, TV, newspaper advertising, bank transfer, micro-computers and on-line systems, plus activities allowed under exceptions to the letter monopoly. It is therefore essential that the Post Office offers a comprehensive range of letter, parcel and premium services, tailored to meet customer needs, along with price stability and a variety of contract options for large users of the Royal Mail.

The British Telecommunications Act, in line with the Government's policy of liberalising public sector monopolies, made relaxations in both the letter and telecommunications monopolies. In the case of the letter monopoly, the range of exceptions was extended. Before the BT Act, the main exception was that the sender of a letter might himself carry and deliver it or send it by private friend or by a special messenger employed by him for the purpose. To this has now been added the conveyance of an overseas letter by a messenger sent for the purpose to an aircraft which will take the letter out of the UK, and the bulk transportation of mail for onward transmission in the postal service. Additionally, the term 'letter' was for the first time defined.

The Act also gave powers to the Secretary of State to license people to do things which would otherwise fall within the monopoly and transferred power to suspend the monopoly (wholly or in part) from the Post Office to the Secretary of State (after consultation with the Post Office). Since the passing of the Act two general licences have been granted by the Secretary of State: the first to allow charities to deliver Christmas cards and the second to license document exchanges — centres where business customers deposit and collect mail for each other — and allow the transfer of mail between exchanges. Both licences had a twenty-five year validity. The monopoly has been suspended for time-sensitive, valuable mail, i.e. 'express' mail, providing that a minimum fee, initially £1 per item, is charged. The Post Office response to this competition has been to engage in extensive product development in all its main areas of activity.

VI. DUTIES OF THE POST OFFICE

The main duties laid on the Post Office are to provide services for the conveyance of letter throughout the UK and in exercising its powers, to have regard to efficiency and economy, the social, industrial and commercial needs of the nation, the desirability of improving and developing operating systems and developments in the fields of communication and banking. Thus, the Post Office is committed to the maintenance of an efficient mails and counter network nationwide and to the 'Rowland Hill' principle of a common rate of charge for letters irrespective of distance.

New services, such as facsimile transmission, have been introduced as technology has developed and National Girobank's wide range of services offered through post office counters, the largest retail network in the country.

VII. USERS' COUNCILS

The Post Office Act 1969 established independent Post Office Users' Councils set up to look after the interests of consumers. It provided for

(i)   the Post Office Users National Council (POUNC)
(ii) 'Country Councils' for Scotland, Wales and Northern Ireland.

In addition the Secretary of State was empowered to give financial assistance to any body, such as local non-statutory Post Office Advisory Committees (POACs) recognised by him as assisting the National Council.

The Chairman of POUNC and up to thirty-two other members, including the three Chairmen of the Country Councils, are appointed by the Secretary of State for Trade, with the advice of the National Consumer Council and after consultation with the Secretary of State for Industry. The Government provides POUNC with staff, office accommodation, equipment etc. and is empowered to pay allowances to the Members. Thus the Council is completely independent of the Post Office.

Either the Post Office or Government, jointly through the Secretaries of State for Industry and Trade, may refer to the Council any matters relating to Post Office services. Furthermore, the Council has a statutory duty to consider matters so referred, as well as those referred to it by users of Post Office services or by a Country Council, or any other matter to which it thinks consideration ought to be given.

At local level many areas have non-statutory Post Office Advisory Committees made up of representatives of local businesses and other interests; these Committees consider and discuss with the Head Postmaster (or his representatives) all aspects of Post Office services within that local area.

Under the powers conferred on him by the British Telecommunications Act, the Secretary of State for Industry can relax the relevant provisions of the 1969 Act so as to exclude services which the Post Office does not have the exclusive privilege of providing (and has done so in respect of banking services and other services for the transmission of money (except postal orders), and services for the conveyance of letters where not less than £1 is paid (excluding inland and overseas registered/insured letters)).

The Post Office is not bound to follow POUNC's recommendations on its proposals, but it is responsive to its representations, and re-inforces the formal consultation required of it by statute with regular informal contacts which allows two way flows of views and information to be established.

VIII. TRADE UNION REPRESENTATION IN THE POST OFFICE

The Post Office recognises several union organisations, each with representative responsibility or a discrete body of staff. By far the largest of these is the Union of Communication Workers (formerly the Union of Post Workers) representing some 155,000 basic grades postal and counter staff. Other unions represent supervision and management grades in Posts and National Girobank, engineering grades, and approximately 20,000 subpostmasters who are not Post Office employees. The Post Office negotiates direct with each union on matters of individual concern, e.g. pay, but when proposals have an impact on members of more than one union, they are channelled through the Post Office Unions' Committee, a co-ordinating body for the unions representing staff in the Post Office.

IX. THE POST OFFICE IN 1983

Every working day the Post Office collects over 30 million letters and over half a million parcels from 100,000 posting boxes and post offices and delivers them to more than 22 million addresses. In parallel, 5 million customers visit the network of post offices which, at over 21,500 is the largest retail network in the country, to transact a wide range of business. The Post Office is thus a major force in the economy.

In common with other public corporations (nationalised industries) the Post Office operates to a series of targets agreed with Government, and primarily related to financial performance. Currently, these are the following.

Posts

Profit

A 2% per annum profit on turnover, after charging interest and historic and supplementary depreciation, for the three year period 1980/81 to 1982/83. (Posts has made a profit since 1976/77.) The target was amended by Government to 2.8% for 1982/83 to reflect reductions in the rate of National Insurance surcharge.

External Financing Limit

A target which can be defined as a gap between a nationalised industry's expected total outlays on capital account (including the value of leased assets) and its expected total internal financial resources. In the case of a profitable industry such as the Post Office, the concept of a 'negative' External Financing Limit has been introduced. In this case, the definition relates to the amount which an industry is called on to pass over to Government after meeting all normal obligations and fully financing its total capital outlays from internal resources. Posts had for the 1982/83 year a negative EFL of £56m.

Real Unit Costs

In simple terms, these are calculated by adjusting for inflation, as measured by the Retail Prices Index, the cost of producing one unit of output. Posts had as an objective that, taking 1981/82 as a base, real unit costs should be reduced by 5% over the period 1982/83 to 1984/85 with 2% reduction in 1982/83 (which was achieved).

National Girobank

The National Girobank has been set a three year target from 1982/83 to 1984/85, of 19% a year annual average return, before interest on long term loans, on mean net assets, this being calculated in historical cost accounting terms.

In addition to the financial targets, the Post Office has agreed with Government performance aims for the quality of service given to letters. The targets are that 90% of letters posted under the first class service should be delivered the day after collection and 96% of second class letters should be delivered by the third working day after collection.

Monitoring by the Government (through the Secretary of State for Industry) of the industry's financial position and prospects is undertaken by a variety of means including:

(i)   the submission by the Post Office of monthly and more detailed quarterly financial returns and regular meetings to discuss them;
(ii) examination of the Post Office's investment Review, covering a period of five years ahead and including fairly detailed forecasts of the Post Office's investment plans;
(iii) discussion of the Corporate plan covering a ten-year period in which the Post Office sets out how it sees its longer term prospects.

In addition to these procedures, National Girobank is also subject to prudential supervision on the same basis as other banks.

CONCLUSION

The Post Office has made the transition from a Government Department to a profitable commercial organisation still mindful of its social role. It has extended the scope of its services as opportunities have arisen, in many cases in direct response to a perceived customer need. In terms of the future there is optimism; mails volume has been maintained in the face of severe recession, and although technological and economic developments may be expected to encroach on some of the traditional sources of work, in particular, correspondence posted by businesses, the evidence of the last few years suggests that this challenge may take longer to materialise than is often supposed.

May 1983

BIBLIOGRAPHY

Report on Post Office Development and Finance (Cmnd. 9576).
Reorganisation of the Post Office (Cmnd. 3233).
The Post Office Act 1969, ISBN 10 S44869 9.
Report of the Post Office Review Committee (Cmnd. 6850).
The British Telecommunications Act 1981, ISBN 10 543881 2.

ANNEXE: MEMBERS OF THE POST OFFICE BOARD (MAY 1983)

Full time members

Chairman
Deputy Chairman and Managing Director, National Girobank
Board Member for Mails Operations and Estates
Board Member for Finance, Counters and Planning
Board Member for Postal Marketing
Board Member for Personnel and Industrial Relations

Part time members (five)

Secretary

4

ELECTRICITÉ DE FRANCE

Jean L. Virole

Electricité de France – usually known by its initials, 'EDF' – is, in Anglo-Saxon terms, a public corporation, incorporated by law on 8 April 1946, having the task of undertaking the generation, bulk transmission, and distribution of electricity for the whole of Metropolitan France. It is, but only de facto and not de jure, a monopoly controlling 85 per cent of French electricity output, 100 per cent of transmission, and 96 per cent of distribution. The absence of a complete monopoly is due to some self-generation of electricity by industry,[1] to the exemption of low capacity producers (i.e. those producing under 8,000 KVA or 12,000 Kwh per year) as well as small local distributors (the *régies communales*), and to history (the existence, for example, of the Compagnie nationale du Rhone).[2] EDF thus ranks as one of the largest electricity enterprises in the world, similar to the electricity organisation in the United Kingdom. EDF is not merely an outstanding electricity undertaking, it is also a representative French public enterprise. In the mixed economy of the European Community and of France in particular, such enterprises have a special function, namely, the fulfilment of missions of general economic interest, such as helping the State and other public authorities to achieve full employment, raise living standards, promote regional development, and so forth.

This second function is often of considerable significance and may sometimes impinge on the performance of the primary function. This is the reason why more and more, especially in countries with socialist governments, as is today the case in France, it is difficult to arrive at a single, comprehensive judgement upon the enterprise. The Treaty of the European Economic Community (EEC) recognises this possible duality of functions and allows the enterprises and their governments some flexibility so long as there is respect for the rules of competition and the general interest of the EEC does not suffer.

This study has as its object to show how EDF, whilst conforming to Common Market rules, fulfils its dual roles as public undertaking and purveyor of electricity.

I. EDF, A NATIONALISED ENTERPRISE

EDF was created by the Nationalisation Act of 8 April 1946 under which it acquired the assets and liabilities of the privately owned electricity undertakings. There were several reasons for this nationalisation.

The first reason was economic: the industrial fabric of the country had been destroyed by allied bombardment and battles with the enemy. It had to be rebuilt, with electricity as one of the priorities; but, after five years of war and no profits, the electricity companies lacked the finance needed.

The second reason was technical: the electricity industry was excessively fragmented – eighty hydro-electricity generating companies, ten transmission companies but no national grid, and 3000 distributing companies. There was a need to centralise the system and concentrate technology.

The third reason was political: in conformity with the views of the 'Conseil national de la Résistance', the trade unions, and the majority of the political parties, it seemed necessary that the productive apparatus should be answerable to the interests of 'the Nation', not 'Capital'. This was especially so in the case of electricity on which the entire economy rested.

So was born EDF, a public enterprise responsible for the supply of electricity.

EDF – a public enterprise

In terms of Marxist analysis, a distinction is drawn between the superstructure, namely the State, and the infrastructure, namely the Nation. The intention of the law of 8 April 1946 was to place the electricity industry in the hands of the Nation; but the chosen instrument was not some new type of organisation but the *'établissement public à caractère industriel et commercial'*, the public corporation of classic type, which is in the hands of the State.

EDF, moreover, was not an entity established with novel rights and obligations but was the heir to all the rights and obligations of the many private companies previously responsible for the supply of electricity. These rights and obligations, affecting land, goods, titles, stocks, installations, were transferred without any change in their legal status; they continued as rights and obligations under private law; and all contracts (subject to only limited exceptions) continued in force without modification.

EDF was heir, too, to all the concessions granted by the State for hydro-electricity generation and for transmission and by local authorities (both departments and communes) for distribution, a total number of concessions in excess of 15,000. These concessions continue to this day, despite a twenty year study of the possibility of their revision. To obtain new concessions from the State or local authorities, the pre-1946 rules still apply. Thus the pre-existing legal framework remains with but few modifications. In the case of distribution, now only EDF can apply for concessions and they can only be granted to EDF; in the case of transmission, since 1960, there is now only one general concession to EDF, the concession entitled the *Réseau d'Alimentation générale*; but, in the case of hydro-electric generation, the State grants concessions to EDF for eventual transmission and distribution as it would previously have done to the private companies and to industries for their own consumption, and similarly in the case of thermal generation, whether nuclear or conventional.

Thus, it is plain that the creation of EDF left the legal framework for the supply of electricity virtually intact; nevertheless, though it was the legal successor to the private companies, EDF emerged not just as a private utility but as a public body.

EDF, as has been stated, was constituted by the nationalisation act as an *établissement public à caractère industriel et commercial*. Such a body, by definition, is a public body. It has separate legal personality. It is under the control of the State, if its activities are on the national plane, as with electricity, or of a regional authority when the activities are localised.

Such a body reflects an attempt at decentralisation. The *établissement public* has rights similar to those of a company under private law, in particular, the right of legal action against the State and other public authorities. There are, nevertheless, some differences as between the *établissement public* and a company. The *établissement public* is not permitted to resile from any of its statutory functions, whatever its financial situation; if funds are lacking, the State (or local authority) must come to the rescue. Similarly, the assets that an *établissement public* requires for the performance of its statutory duties cannot be seized or impounded.

As an *établissement public*, EDF is also subject to a range of controls by the Ministry of Economy and Finance and by the Ministry of Research and Industry. Amongst the most important of these are the requirements for government approval of investment programmes, long-term plans, changes in tariffs, acquisition or construction of plants and other facilities, and acquisition or disposal of interests in other enterprises. Furthermore, the accounts of EDF are subject to scrutiny by a minimum of two *commissaires aux comptes* (statutory auditors), appointed for three-year terms by the Ministry of Economy and Finance, and its annual financial statements, together with the reports of the statutory auditors, are required to be submitted to the Cour des Comptes (France's supreme, quasi-judicial institution responsible for the audit of public accounts) which issues an opinion on the accounts before they are laid before the French Parliament, together with the responses of the Ministries of Research and Industry and Economy and Finance to the Court's observations.

The remit of the Cour des Comptes is not confined to financial audit but extends to an audit of efficiency and effectiveness. Reports of the Court on individual enterprises are made available to the Ministries concerned and, on a confidential footing, to the Finance Commissions of the Senate and the Chamber of Deputies, but are not published. There is, however, a published general report about once every two years, reviewing the Court's work in the field of public enterprise. Given the considerable influence exerted by government over the strategic direction of the major public enterprises, criticisms by the Court of enterprise management must often imply, if they do not actually express, criticisms of government.

Nevertheless, outside the range of controls exercised by government over its operations and management, EDF functions like a private enterprise. This is the reflection of its *caractère industriel et commercial*. In its relations with customers, suppliers, creditors, and other parties, it acts like a private company: and it pays taxes like other commercial undertakings.

EDF's organisation, at national, headquarters, and local level is as follows.

(i) At the national level

The central organ of direction is the Conseil d'Administration (the supervisory Board) comprising fifteen members. Five of these represent the Government (they are usually top rank civil servants); five are chosen for their business or professional qualifications or ability to represent regional or local interests (they include mayors of communes and towns, large or small); and five represent the employees of EDF (they are nominated by the trade unions in rough proportion to their memberships in EDF). They are appointed by a decree of the Council of Ministers on the recommendation of the Minister of Research and Industry for a term of five years; but they may be removed at any time 'for cause'. The Chairman of the Board is also appointed by a decree of the Council of Ministers on the nomination of the Board from amongst their own number.

The Director-General of EDF is similarly appointed by decree of the Council of Ministers, in this case on the recommendation of the Chairman of the Board. Although there is no legal requirement, the appointment has always been made from amongst the top executives of the undertaking.

The foregoing – that is to say, the Chairman and Members of the Conseil d'Administration and the Director-General – and only these have the status of *Agent public*. They are charged with responsibility to the State for EDF and do not have the status of employees of EDF.

Two civil service institutions are juxtaposed to the Conseil d'Administration. These are the Commissaire du Gouvernement and the Mission de Contrôle économique et financier (or Contrôleur d'État).

Ordinarily, the Commissaire du Gouvernement is the Director of Electricity in the Ministry of Research and Industry and, as such, a high ranking civil servant. He is the lineal descendant of the Commissaire du Gouvernement appointed to the former private electricity companies when they had the advantage, and responsibility, of loans from private sources; he then had the function of ensuring that the loans were indeed applied to their advertised purposes and also that the enterprise conformed to the government's regulations for the industry. There has been no change in his statutory functions but now he is only concerned with compliance with government policies and regulations for electricity.

The Chef de la Mission de Contrôle (he is known as Contrôleur d'État in the case of some of the public enterprises smaller than EDF) represents the Ministry of Economy and Finance. He had no equivalent in the case of the former private companies. His function is to ensure EDF's compliance with all financial policies and regulations of the government and to keep his Ministry posted on the enterprise's financial situation and prospects, as well as observing the quality of its general financial administration.

Both these officers have the power to impose a suspensory veto on decisions of the Board, its Chairman, and the Director-General. This power, however, has been exercised but rarely. The explanation is as follows. That there should be some control over EDF follows from the fact that it was intended that EDF should replace, and take over from, the private companies and that it should be a public body, though without becoming part of the State. However, as EDF's prime function is public service and not profit, as was the case with the private companies, there is now less occasion for governmental control. Moreover, the community of outlook of the Chairman and Director-General and of the top civil servants diminishes the need for dependence on legal forms of control. Frequently, all concerned will have had a common education, either at the École Polytechnique or the École Nationale d'Administration, and some individuals may have served together in the same Ministry; despite their currently differing responsibilities, they are, therefore, likely to have a common approach to problems, a common understanding of the difficulties, and a common appreciation of the possible solutions.

It is appropriate to note at this point that the close relationship between EDF and the government is not replicated in the relationship with Parliament. Members of Parliament are not allowed to be members of the Conseils d'Administration and the only regular control over public enterprises available to Parliament is its control over the annual budget law (to the extent it contains any provision for funds for public enterprises). In general terms, the government stands between Parliament and the enterprises and this is regarded as a means of preventing Parliament from substituting its control for that of the Executive. Admittedly, there is provision for Parliament to set up Commissions to undertake particular investigations but this occurs only rarely.

(ii) The headquarters' organisation

(1) The *Direction Générale* is the policy-making division which prepares the strategic decisions taken by the enterprise. The Director-General is its head and he is supported by one or two Deputy Directors-General, by two directors for long-term planning and industrial relations, and by heads of specialist services such as the Service des Études économiques générales, the Service d'Information et des Relations publiques, the Service des Marchés et Contrats, and the Service d'Étude et de Promotion de l'Action commerciale (the consumer service department). Directly responsible to the Director-General, there is, too, the Inspection Générale, charged with the duty of checking any aspect of performance by any unit or branch of the enterprise with a view to the improvement of efficiency.

(2) *The Research and Development Division* (2400 employees)[3] is responsible for the improvement of equipment and techniques with a view to maximising efficiency in meeting demand.

(3) *The Construction Division* (5000 employees) is responsible for the design of all new generating capacity and facilities for transmission and for supervision of the construction by private companies of new generating capacity to those designs.

(4) *The Generation and Transmission Divison* (30,000 employees) is responsible for operating the power stations and transmission system and for the construction, using private companies, of the new lines and transformer stations made necessary by the growth of the system. It is also responsible for dealing with those customers who take supplies direct from the high voltage system (the Réseau d'Alimentation générale).

(5) *The Distribution Division* (65,000 employees) is responsible for the maintenance and development of the medium and low voltage systems and for customer service to nearly all the 24 million customers of EDF.

(6) *The General Affairs Division* is responsible for questions affecting property, insurance, pension funds for employees and dependents, regulations regarding staff safety, and accident prevention.[4]

(7) *The Personnel and Social Relations Division* is responsible for the development and implementation of EDF's policy towards its employees. The Division thus handles, inter alia, recruitment, basic training, and advanced training for engineers, technicians, and executives. In addition to EDF's total staff of 125,000, the Division is also responsible within its field for the personnel of Gaz de France.[5]

(8) *The Finance and Legal Divison* is responsible for EDF budgets, cash flow, capital investment programmes, accounts and accounting practices, and legal policy. Each Division has its own legal branch but these branches are subordinate to the Finance and Legal Division's legal service which also acts as the legal adviser to the Direction Générale and thus to EDF as a whole.

(9) *The EDF – International Division* is the channel for relations between EDF and countries abroad, affecting such matters as international co-operation, the provision of consultants, the promotion of joint economic, tariff, or technical studies, and liaison with French overseas territories (T.O.M.). It has responsibilities towards some EDF subsidiaries.

Finally, there is *SAPAR* (*Société anonyme de Participations*), a company whose shares are held by EDF and which, in its turn, holds the EDF stake in its numerous subsidiary companies and services and co-ordinates them.

(iii) At the local level

The organisation does not conform to the prescription in the Act of 8 April 1946. It was originally intended that distribution should be entrusted to enterprises − public enterprises − that would buy their supplies from EDF and be at arm's length from it; the intention has been regarded so far as unrealistic and the relevant provisions in the Act have not been implemented. As a result, each of the Technical Divisions has its own regional and local units, centres, and organisation. In practice, the head of the Distribution Division's local or regional office is regarded as the appropriate point of contact between EDF and the relevant external agencies, authorities, and members of the public; but this is a matter of practice and confers no authority on the Distribution Division over other Divisions.

EDF − the French electricity supplier

As has been observed, certain bodies other than EDF are permitted to generate electricity; but any production surplus over their own consumption has to be fed into the EDF Réseau d'Alimentation générale. Certain other bodies similarly retain their concessions for local distribution of electricity; but they have to draw their supplies from the EDF Réseau. Today, the generating capacity available to EDF is more than adequate to meet French requirements, so supplies of electricity are available for export. In these circumstances, EDF can be regarded as effectively the source of electricity for the whole of France and for all classes of consumers.

The generation, transmission, and distribution of electricity has given rise in France to a complex structure.

(a) *Hydro-electricity*. EDF has about 520 hydro-electric power stations (of which 260 have a capacity of 10 MW or more) giving a total installed capacity of 18,000 MW and an average generating potential of over 60,000 Kwh, equivalent to 92 per cent of the average total for French hydro-electric production.

EDF inland hydro-electric installations comprise all possible types to suit heads of water ranging from a few metres at run-of-river plants or on slow-moving rivers to heads of over 1,000 metres at high, mountain sites. Storage capacity is around 6,000 million cubic metres, equivalent to nearly 10,000 million Kwh. Storage is seasonal. It contributes about one-third of total hydro-electricity generation; the balance comes from run-of-river schemes without pondage. Pumped storage schemes are also in course of development as a contribution to peak loads; they are based on the use of cheap, off-peak electricity.

EDF also generates hydro-electricity from the River Rance tidal power station in Brittany, the only commercial station in the world of this class. It consists of twenty-four 10 MW sets that can operate as pumps and turbines in both directions of flow of the water. Annual output is around 500 million Kwh. A project has been prepared for a tidal station for the Bay of St. Michel between Brittany and Cotentin. It would require the use of rocks and islands in the Bay, some French and some British. A decision by the International Court on the use of these 'pedestals' has been held up by local interests, conservationists, and doubts about the project's financial viability as compared with a thermal station of one kind or another.

(b) *Thermal generation* is also of two main kinds — conventional and nuclear.

In 1982, conventional generating plant in France produced 95,300 million Kwh, 68,100 million Kwh from EDF plants and 27,200 Kwh from the electricity plants of other producers, mainly in the coal, steel, and chemical industries. EDF adopted the policy in 1974 of standardising the size and design of new generating sets. The standard capacity increased between 1955 and 1980 from 125 MW to 800 MW. As the result of this policy, design and construction costs have been reduced, construction time shortened, capital costs per capacity Kw cut, and running costs per Kwh brought down. Now, however, as the result of the rise in the cost of oil during the seventies and the fall in the relative cost of nuclear power, there has been a shift from conventional to nuclear generation and, in particular, a reduction in the use of oil. Only 15 per cent of EDF output is now generated from oil, as opposed to 40 per cent in 1973. This is of great advantage to France because of the relief it affords to the balance of payments.

In 1982, nuclear plant in France supplied 99,600 million Kwh. The types of plant in service were:

(i)   gas-graphite-natural uranium (French type): 6 sets of individual maximum capacity 400 MW.

(ii) heavy water: 1 set, maximum capacity 70 MW.
(iii) PWR and enriched uranium: 26 sets, including 13 of individual maximum capacity of 900 MW and 13 of individual maximum capacity of 1300 MW.
(iv) fast breeder: 1 set, maximum capacity 233 MW.

The nuclear share of output has increased rapidly and a programme for the construction of 6 new sets per annum up to 1989 is being implemented, by which year France will be provided with a nuclear generating capacity of 55,000 MW. Of special interest is the internationally financed programme of fast breeder construction.

One fast breeder set of 1300 MW is being built in France (the financial participation being EDF, 51 per cent, R.W.E. (West Germany), 33 per cent, and ENEL (Italy), 16 per cent) and one similar set in West Germany (financial participation being EDF, 33 per cent, R.W.E., 51 per cent, and ENEL (and other interests), 16 per cent). When these projects are complete, France, through EDF and the Commissariat à l'Energie atomique (the Atomic Energy Commission) and their subsidiaries, will have all phases of the nuclear cycle in full production; and, already, one nuclear power site, at Bugey, is capable of an output greater than the entire French consumption of electricity in 1946.

(c) *The transmission system* is comparatively straightforward.

Power is transmitted at 'extra high voltage' (that is to say, at 400 KV and 150 KV) and at 'high voltage' (that is to say, at 90 KV and 63 KV). The capacity of the former was 18,000 GWKm at 31 December 1982 and of the latter 3500 GWKm, whilst the total length of the system approached 76,000 kilometres. Total transformer capacity for reducing the transmission voltages down to the distribution voltages was 65,000 MVA.

EDF is committed to alleviating the impact of the power lines on the landscape. Thorough studies are accordingly made to find the best routes for new lines and new types of towers and pylons have been designed to adapt to the countryside as unobtrusively as possible.

There are more than 600 customers — they take about 30 per cent of total electricity sales — who draw their supplies direct from the transmission system under individual contracts. They normally benefit from low charges reflecting their proximity to generating stations and points of supply and the local density of distribution.

(d) Through its *distribution system*, EDF delivers to 24 million consumers. The distribution system comprises about 500,000 kilometres of low voltage line (of which 9 per cent is underground) and an aggregate transformer capacity of about 48,000 MVA. Power enters the distribution system at either 15 KV or 20 KV. The latter is now standard and other voltage levels, ranging from 5 KV to 30 KV, are in course of being phased out. The standard voltage level for supply to ordinary consumers is 220/380V. There is an accelerating trend towards the remote control of substations in the interests of increasing operating efficiency and speeding the clearance of faults.

EDF, as has been noted, is responsible for supplying 96 per cent of all French consumers of electricity. They fall into two categories. The first comprises about 130,000 consumers, mostly industrial and commercial, who take about 30 per cent of total production and are connected to the high voltage network. The second is constituted by the bulk of consumers − 23 million and more − who are supplied at low voltage. Among these are 440,000 public services and authorities.

Worthy of special note is the difference in the legal relationships of EDF as between certain of the groups with which it has dealings, essentially, on the one hand its customers, employees, and others contracting with EDF and, on the other hand, those having non-contractual relationships, including claimants for damage, trespass, and so on. The differences require some elaboration.

As has been noted, there is always a contractual relationship between EDF and the consumer, even though many of the obligations between the parties are expressed in regulations. Consequently, in the event of dispute, judgement is given in the civil courts under the civil law.

This is so, despite the fact that the charges are established by EDF within limits set from time to time by the government. The charges conform to the principle that each customer, so far as possible, shall pay according to the cost of supply to him and not by reference to the use to which the supply is put. Customers are billed, therefore, on the basis of an annual charge for their maximum indicated consumption, plus a charge varying with their actual usage and the time of consumption. (For bulk consumers, the arrangements, as noted above, are slightly different.)

In the case of contractual relations between EDF and its suppliers, the civil law again applies except, however, where the contract affects operations classed as public works in which case administrative law is applicable.

In the case of disputes between EDF and third parties, the relevant law is administrative law and an administrative tribunal is the appropriate court. In the event of injury to a member of the public attributable to an EDF installation or to EDF equipment, the claimant has only to prove damage and not wrongdoing by EDF. There are, however, two exceptions to the applicability of administrative law:

(i) compensation for the compulsory concession to EDF of rights in land is a matter for the civil law and the civil court;
(ii) by special legislative provision applicable to all vehicles in France, compensation for damage done by an EDF motor vehicle is a matter for the civil law and the civil court.

Apart from their legal relationships with EDF, several of the groups, as will have been noticed, have a participatory relationship through their representation on the supervisory board. Despite the fact that the interests of the different parties are, to some extent, conflicting − consumers, for example, naturally wish to see charges lower than the rates established and employees wish to see pay and working conditions bettered − the experience to date has been that the different interests are able to collaborate in promoting the public interest in an economic and efficient electricity service. No doubt the fact that disputes over wages and working conditions are handled for the most part at management level has been helpful, as has been the recognition that charges are heavily influenced by government policy.

In concluding this section, we may observe that the authority and strength of EDF derives from its technical competence and administrative capacity. It is not derived from advantages not available to the private enterprises prior to the law of 8 April 1946. But there is another side to the medal − the weakness of EDF. This weakness is the liability to use by the State for purposes other than the production and supply of electricity. EDF is part of the public sector. It is a public enterprise that can thus be used by the State as an instrument of general economic policy, even though this may conflict with its primary function, the supply of electricity on commercial principles. This is the central issue of Section II.

II. EDF, A FRENCH PUBLIC ENTERPRISE WITHIN THE EEC

A characteristic common to the *établissement public* and the public corporation is the absence of share capital. EDF, therefore, has no share capital and the effective owner is the State (or the People). The owner, as such, has obligations towards its enterprise but the State is also, and pre-eminently, sovereign so that it is bound to take the EDF into consideration, not merely as the purveyor of electricity but from the point of view of its impact on the finances and economy of the country. Such consideration, however, cannot be untrammelled in the EEC, as public enterprises are the object of special provisions of the Treaty and the EEC Commission has comparatively recently (25 June 1980) issued a directive on the subject of the transparency of financial relations between States and their public enterprises. Admittedly, public enterprises in the field of electricity are at present outside the scope of this directive but a further directive embracing electricity will certainly follow before long, as has already occurred in the case of one other of the exclusions (namely, the field of credit); so the Common Market context of the financial and economic relations between the State and EDF must be kept constantly in mind.

The financial relations between the State and EDF

EDF expects the State correctly to discharge both its roles in relation to the undertaking, namely, as owner and sovereign. That EDF has to look to the State in this way is, nevertheless, a measure of its dependence and special position. EDF is not just an enterprise; it is a public enterprise.

Every year as the need arises, EDF is in touch with Ministries and Directorates to secure governmental agreement on matters such as changes in tariffs, *dotations* of capital, the issue of loans from the State, or access to the capital market. The *tableau carré* (i.e. square) provides the framework for these discussions. There are four sides to this square whose size is determined by the investment requirement; the sides are: internal financing, additional State capital, additional State loans, loans from other sources.

This *tableau carré* is no mere theoretical concept but the expression of the EDF's real relations with the Government.

First, EDF submits to the Ministry of Research and Industry its programmes of development and investment. The Ministry approves the programmes if the Administration is satisfied that they conform to the government's energy policy and to the National Plan. As a result of the nuclear programme, EDF's financial needs have risen to a new dimension, making it necessary for the State to ensure that they do not overstrain the economy. Expressed in constant (1979) francs so as to eliminate the influence of inflation and devaluation, the overall level of EDF's investment has risen from 10 billion francs in 1973 to 30 billion francs in 1979 and is expected to total 40 billion francs in 1985.

This increase is attributable to three main factors, of varying importance over time. At the beginning, the traditional requirements for investment, namely generation, transmission, and distribution predominated and there was a gradual increase from 8 to 12 billion francs. In 1973, expenditure on nuclear generation (including both construction and the constitution of a stock of nuclear fuel) totalled only 1 billion francs; but, by 1979, this had risen to 15 billion francs and to 20 billion francs by 1980 when the nuclear programme attained its intended steady pace during the eighties, allowing for the modification adopted by the Government in 1981 following the drop in the rate of growth of demand for electricity consequent upon the economic crisis. Traditionally, this demand has doubled in France every ten years; today, it is increasing at only 2 per cent per annum.

Its investment programme approved, EDF enters into discussion with the Ministry of the Economy and Finance over the level of tariffs appropriate to the financing of the programme. From EDF's point of view, a high level of self-financing is regarded as desirable, as well as contributing to the policy of energy conservation. A 5 per cent increase in tariffs would, for example, reduce the borrowing requirement by about 20 billion francs over the years from 1980 to 1985. Electricity tariffs, however, have to be fixed in consideration of the prices of other forms of energy (coal, gas, and oil) and of the price index generally. Consequently, tariffs are never settled as EDF would wish. In March 1983, for example, when beginning talks with the Minister, the EDF Chairman told the press that if, to make up for the inadequate price increase authorised in 1982, prices were increased by 20 per cent, EDF would make a profit of 20 billion francs instead of making a loss, as at present, of 8 billion francs; but permission was given for an increase of only 8 per cent, the current rate of inflation. So much for the EDF's relations with the State as sovereign; now for its relations with the State as owner.

There are several ways in which the State can channel funds to a public enterprise; it can provide a *dotation* of capital;[6] it can provide loans from State funds and cancel or consolidate former loans; at the least, it can grant a moratorium on the payment of interest on these loans. The State, however, is in practice a reluctant capitalist and tends to shirk its role as owner. This is true in France in relation to public enterprises generally; so, for some years, EDF has not secured the increases in capital desired and other means of financing have been necessary.

In the circumstances described, EDF has been obliged to seek governmental approval for borrowing in the capital market. The Ministry of the Economy and Finance, however, has to weigh the consequences for other industries and activities which could find themselves crowded out of the capital market by EDF, given that its borrowing requirements are so large. The Ministry has often resolved the problem by inviting EDF to place its loans in the international market. For the State this is an attractive option as the foreign currency goes into France's central holdings of foreign exchange (against francs issued to EDF) and, as there is no exchange guarantee, the risks in respect of the payment of interest and redemption of capital in foreign currency are shouldered by EDF. For public enterprises, therefore, the solutions of financing problems are, essentially, not technical but political – and they rest in the hands of government.

In French administrative parlance, the financing solution adopted is known as 'the diagonal of the square'.

EDF, of course, has its ideas as to the preferred diagonal; but it understands that considerations and interests wider than its own must be taken into account. Once informed of the propositions of the corporation, the Government must take its own decisions on tariff changes and the level of its capital contributions and thus on the degree of external borrowing by EDF, whether in France or abroad. However, placing these loans to the best advantage of EDF remains the responsibility of the corporation's financial management.

The financial problem of EDF is not simply the result of the State's shortage of finance. There are two further special reasons.

First, the French State has a tradition of exerting its role of sovereign in relation to the economy by reliance upon economic policies rather than the provision of finance. This has been particularly marked in the case of its own enterprises.

Second, from the point of view of administrative science, it is possible to see the State's practice as a means of going beyond the control given to it by such institutions as the Commissaire du Gouvernement and Contrôleur d'État and thus of extending and consolidating its control over its most important public enterprises, particularly in the field of energy. The technical competence of the management of these enterprises generally leaves little scope for governmental intervention but the financial power of the State can be used to deprive management of their autonomy and so make the enterprises available as instruments of the State's economic policies.

The economic relations between the State and EDF

Like all members of the European Economic Community, France has a mixed economy, that is to say that the economy is made up of enterprises, some public and some private, and the State's policy for the economy is to a large extent exercised by way of influence on the enterprises through taxes and financial incentives and, notably so in France, through indicative economic planning.

Since 1946, there has been a series of five-year plans in France, aimed at the expansion and modernisation of the economy. They operate, not by specific instructions or legal directions, but by establishing a general framework within which it is hoped public and private enterprises will draw up their investment programmes; they also indicate priorities for expenditure in the public sector and try to provide some guidance as to the direction of economic development in the medium term. The situation today (1983) is that the Government has adopted an interim plan of eighteen months' duration, to allow time for the preparation of the Ninth Plan which is intended to cover the years 1984 to 1989. For EDF, the planning process within a mixed economy poses in explicit form the issue of reconciling the broad national interest with the particular interest of the electricity industry.

The broad national interest, in particular the demands it presents in regard to industrial policy and regional development, may generate serious burdens for EDF.

From the point of view of the State, electricity can appear as an excellent means of promoting industrial development by way of low prices. This is a factor in EDF's difficulties in getting agreement to significant increases in its tariffs. EDF understands the reasons but the policy of low tariffs creates for it serious difficulties.

As an enterprise operating in all parts of the country, electricity can similarly appear to the authorities as a convenient instrument of regional policy, providing opportunities for creating employment or providing orders for small or medium-size businesses. The supply of electricity may even enable departments and communes to enlarge their local tax-base. The EDF may thus become the cross-roads for the intersection of national, sectoral, and local authority policies with its own policies for the electricity service; it is a difficult situation for management. (Managements of other major public enterprises have similar situations to face.)

Nevertheless, it is crucial to recall that EDF is an enterprise, not an administration. This was the choice made in 1946; when the electricity companies were nationalised, there was the opportunity to have embodied them into a department, like the Posts and Tele-communications, rather than create a public corporation. The corporation having been preferred, it is necessary to accept the consequences of the choice, to recognise that EDF should be compensated for the performance of tasks conflicting with its aims as an enterprise and to understand that, though it may have a monopoly in the supply of electricity, it is exposed to competition from other energy forms.

From the point of view of EDF, transparency of accounts and of financial relations between itself and the State is the desired aim; this means, in particular, compensation from the State for the imposition on the enterprise of non-commercial functions. In principle, the notion of compensation implies an analysis undertaken by the State, aimed at determining whether using a public enterprise as an indirect means of achieving some object of public policy is a cheaper means than some alternative, frequently direct, means of public action; but the State is generally reluctant to make such analyses and compensation is often not given.

For EDF, the non-payment of compensation is damaging because it is in competition with four other public enterprises in the energy sector: Charbonnages de France, Gaz de France, Elf-Aquitaine, and the Compagnie française des Pétroles. Furthermore, the freedom conferred on EEC enterprises by the Treaty to locate anywhere within the Community constitutes a form of competition adverse to EDF's monopoly on the supply of electricity. It is thus essential that prices should reflect only the costs of supply, free of the burden of non-commercial activities.

To be a public enterprise may thus be the cause of many problems. The State can ease these problems by contracting with its enterprises – by the negotiation, that is to say, of *contrats de programme* or *contrats de plan* – thereby assuring the enterprises of its understanding and support. Unfortunately, a period of economic crisis and of counter-inflationary policies is not conducive to the negotiation of long-term contracts, particularly long-term in the case of EDF where the assurances of some stability in State policies have to allow for the interval of about nine years between the initial outlays on the study of a nuclear power project and the first receipts of revenue from the generation of power.

The concept of *contrats de programme* was first enunciated in France in the Nora Report in 1967 and was formally adopted by the French Government in 1969. In practice, however, the implementation of the concept has been slow and disjointed. Three contracts were negotiated initially – with EDF, the railways (SNCF) and the radio and television service (ORTF); this last contract was without effect because of the disbandment soon afterwards of ORTF. The original intention was for the contracts to be of five years' duration, coinciding with the national plan. They were to specify the strategic objectives for the enterprise in quantified terms, covering such matters as output or capacity, prices, quality of supply, and improvement of efficiency; they were to relieve the enterprises of a number of the a priori controls imposed by the government; and they were to assure the enterprises of the necessary external finance and other resources needed for the execution of the contract. The first contracts with EDF and SNCF encountered difficulties because of the economic recession of the seventies and the energy crisis. In the late seventies, further contracts were negotiated (but not with EDF) which were generally for periods shorter than five years and which sought to incorporate more flexibility as to the basic assumptions. However, the indications are that it is still proving difficult to eliminate over-optimism and to make the assumptions sufficiently flexible.

In conclusion, public enterprises are deeply conscious of the duality of their role. They have their particular mission; in the case of EDF to produce and deliver electricity to meet all the consumers' needs; and they have their mission of general economic interest, additional to their particular mission, which it is for the State to determine. The obligation to discharge these two missions simultaneously constitutes a distinguishing characteristic of such major public enterprises as EDF. It is the reason why EDF is described as 'a national service'. Originally, the term merely signified the difference between activities that were nationwide, as opposed to local; today, it is a political term, meaning service to the Nation in the fullest sense of the word.

NOTES

1. Principally by steel companies, and also by the nationalised railways and coal industry.
2. The CNR is a public enterprise in which the EDF holds 25 per cent of the shares. Its hydro-electric resources are operated by EDF.
3. The figures for employees in this section comprise staff at both headquarters and out-stations.
4. The Divisions mentioned in sections (1), (6), (7), (8), and (9) have a total complement of 10,000 employees.
5. Gaz de France (GDF) was also established by the Nationalisation Act of 8 April 1946 and was granted the monopoly − subject to certain exceptions − in respect to gas. It, too, is an *établissement public à caractère industriel et commercial*. General Administration, Personnel, and Distribution Divisions serve both enterprises jointly and though the billing and data processing sections of EDF and GDF Finance and Legal Services Divisions are under EDF management, the two enterprises are legally and effectively separate and distinct.

82 *Public Enterprise*

6. Until 1982, these *dotations* came from the 'Fond de Développement économique et social (FDES)', a special sub-head of the Finance Law. Since 1983, these *dotations* have been transformed into *participations*, derived from nationalised banks, on directions from the Ministry of the Economy and Finance.

SELECT BIBLIOGRAPHY

BOOKS

Bordier et Deglaire, *Electricité et Service Public*.
Ginocchio, *Législation de l'électricité*.
J. Virole, *Public Enterprise in the EEC*, Vol. IV, *France*, edited by W. Keyser and R. Windle (Sijthoff and Noordhoff, 1978)*.

ARTICLE

P. Questian, 'Financing the French nuclear programme', *Revue française de l'Energie*, 1980, p. 173.

DOCUMENTS PUBLISHED BY EDF

Electricité de France in France and in the world; *Updating of financial and economic data*; *Electricité de France, public corporation*.
Prospectus for several loans issued outside France.
Annual reports of EDF.
Studies of the Public Enterprises' European Centre (CEEP).

LAWS AND REGULATIONS

– loi du 8 avril 1946 sur la nationalisation de l'électricité et du gaz
– loi du 15 juin 1906 sur le régime de l'électricité
– loi du 16 octobre 1919 sur l'utilisation des richesses hydrauliques à des fins énergétiques.

* This book is the joint production of Maurice R. Garner and J. Virole.

5

ISTITUTO PER LA RICOSTRUZIONE INDUSTRIALE*

Dr. Veniero Ajmone Marsan

1. ORIGIN

When the onset of the world depression threatened disaster to Italy's three major banks, the government decided to set up a new agency – the Istituto per la Ricostruzione Industriale (IRI)[1] – with the double purpose of rehabilitating the distressed banks which came under its control and, at the same time, of disposing as early as possible of all the industrial assets which the new agency took over from the same banks. IRI at the start was in fact conceived as a temporary institution, on the assumption that private capital would be ready to step in and provide the equity base needed for the growth of the industrial enterprises which till then had relied on the backing of the deposit-taking banks.

The emergency phase in IRI's life was to last four years. In this period the new agency not only disengaged the three rescued banks from any controlling interest in industrial enterprises, but also took active part in preparing the banking reform of 1936 which imposed limits on the investment practices of commercial banks, in keeping with their fiduciary obligations. However important the contribution of IRI to the reorganisation of the Italian banking system (with its related benefits for the Central Bank and the Treasury) it was far exceeded by the role the new agency was able to play as an industrial holding.[2] Indeed, while engaging actively in the sale of its newly acquired assets (chiefly with regard to non-controlling shareholdings and minor companies)[3] IRI immediately started reorganizing its industrial interests.

By the end of 1936 it became obvious that there was no prospect of a complete disposal of IRI's assets: and since it had already shown

---

* All values appearing in the text have been converted into US dollars at the 1982 average exchange rate of 1,352 It. Lire to the $.

itself to be equipped with considerable managerial skills,[4] in 1937 IRI was converted into a permanent institution[5] entrusted with the management of the industrial enterprises which were to remain under state control.

2. GROWTH IN A CONTEXT OF STRUCTURAL CHANGE: 1937–82

IRI's development since 1937, when it became a permanent instrument of Government policy, covers more than four decades, during which momentous changes occurred in the political and economic context.

In the three years up to 1939, preceding the outbreak of the Second World War, asset sales were continued, mainly in the fields of light manufacturing (textiles, paper), electric power, agriculture, and real estate. At the same time important investments were made in capital-intensive sectors like shipping, heavy engineering and steel. In the latter the decision to build a new integrated coastal plant at Cornigliano (Genoa), marked a turning-point in the development of a modern steel industry in Italy.

Another feature of this early period was IRI's contribution to regional development. Italy's economic dualism is well known: compared to the North of the country, the South (with a population of almost 20 million, 38% of the Italian total) suffers from a weak productive structure, low overall productivity and a grave imbalance between the spontaneous flow of investment in modern activities and the growth of its labour force (almost twice as fast as warranted by its share in the national total).

IRI from the start was actively engaged in trying to meet the needs of the South. Among the first undertakings was the decision in 1939 to locate in the area a factory for the design and manufacture of military aircraft with the technical assistance of two northern IRI firms; the unit, employing 6,000 workers, was an important addition to the South's fledgling modern industrial sector.

The war inflicted heavy damage to IRI's productive structure, mostly in the shipping, steel, engineering, electricity and telephone sectors. However Italy's post-war recovery was relatively rapid and was followed by a decade (1953–62) marked by a very high rate of economic growth, both by international and by pre-war standards. For the IRI group this was a challenging period.

Reorganisation, conversion and internal growth of existing firms, entry into new sectors, acquisitions of private firms most often under the pressure of emergency situations, joint-ventures or partnerships with both Italian and foreign private companies, and – much less frequently – resale or closure of productive units, all contributed to the development of the group during those years.

Among IRI's achievements three deserve special mention:

(i)   the successful implementation of IRI's steel strategy, with the construction of two shore-based integrated plants, one of which was in the South (Taranto). The large capital requirements of such development were for the most part covered from market sources, including equity funds obtained through public share issues;

(ii) the contribution to the design and construction of a national system of toll-motorways;[6]

(iii) the impulse given to management education with the creation in 1959 of IFAP, a Management Development Centre in Rome, catering primarily to the group's needs. This initiative was prompted by the almost total lack at the time of business management schools, both within the universities and in the private sector.

After 1972 Italy experienced a growing instability of the social and economic context and the first emergence of inflationary trends which slowed down all progress in tackling the country's structural problems, those of the South in the first place. All this increased the difficulties of IRI's action together with the expectations of the Government for the group's contribution to the strategic ends of public policy.

Among the salient developments of this period of IRI's history one should include the diversification move which followed the nationalisation of the electricity industry.[7]

Important also was IRI's contribution to the building up of a national electronic industry, of strategic value for the country's industrial future. The group's multi-sectoral structure was in this case a crucial factor of IRI's prompt entrepreneurial response. The modernisation of telecommunications was consciously coordinated with manufacturing and research in related sectors and most of the new productive capacity was located in the South. Among the new ventures launched by IRI was also the setting up in 1969 of a computer systems and software house (ITALSIEL), which became the leader in its field in Italy, specialising in the design and implementation of large and complex EDP systems for both central and local public administrations.

Another feature of these years was the major role played by IRI in southern development. Two industrial projects, among the largest undertaken in Italy since the war, deserve mention in this context.

As Alfa Romeo saw the need for a smaller car to complete the range of models (traditionally middle- and large-sized) and proposed to build a new plant, IRI approved the project on condition that it be sited in Southern Italy. The Alfasud plant (after the name of the new model) was in itself a rather exceptional endeavour, considering that it was the first fully integrated (rather than just assembly) plant to be set up in Europe outside the traditional areas where the motorcar industry was born and developed since the beginning of the century.[8]

Moreover automobile manufacturing promised to induce a further expansion in the South of supplier firms capable of meeting the required standards of quality, cost and schedule observance. Ancillary activities did in fact develop[9] with an estimated employment of 13,000 by the end of 1974; such 'spread effects' were reinforced by FIAT's subsequent decision to locate in the South part of its motor assembly capacity.[10]

The other major investment undertaken in the 1960s was the doubling of the Taranto steel mill, raising its output capacity to over 10 million tons.

Measured at constant prices and converted into 1982 dollars, the group's investment in the South increased from a yearly average of $266 million in the four-year period 1959–62 to $752 million in 1963–66 (coinciding with the first stage expansion of the Taranto plant); it declined only slightly in the following four years ($711 million on average) but more than doubled again in 1971–74, when it reached a yearly average of $1658 million.

In the manufacturing sectors (the only ones where investment is relatively mobile)[11] the share of the South in IRI's total investment rose from 43% in 1959–62 to 75% in 1963–66; it was still over 51% in the next four years and increased again to 63% in 1971–74.

The growth of employment in the period examined followed closely that of investment. At the beginning of the 1960s the greater part of IRI's employees was, for historical reasons, in the North; only about 47,100, or 18.4% of a total of 269,000 were employed in the South (30,300 in manufacturing, equal to 19.1% of the corresponding group's total).

By the end of 1974 IRI's southern employment had reached 138,100 of which 104,500 was in manufacturing, equal to 29% and 34% respectively of the group's total workforce. Most of the expansion took place in the four-year period 1971–74, during which IRI contributed almost 38% of the new jobs created in southern manufacturing industry, while its share of the Italian manufacturing workforce was 6% at the end of 1970.[12]

After the first shock of the world oil crisis, the dominant objectives of IRI's action in the highly unstable world setting of the 1975–82 period have been: the rationalisation and conversion of its industrial structure; the promotion of innovation and of high technology sectors and the strengthening of the international position of the group. In pursuing these objectives, IRI faced its major problems in two directions: labour relations and finance.

A great deal has been done by way of joint ventures or technical and marketing agreements with both domestic and foreign companies. A few examples worth quoting are:

- the agreement between Alfa Romeo and Nissan Motor Co. to jointly produce a car in a new plant near Naples;
- the agreement between Italtel and GTE (USA) to join forces in developing a range of digital telephone exchanges;
- the joint ventures between Aeritalia, IRI's aerospace manufacturer and a number of foreign companies (Aérospatiale, Boeing, Embraer of Brazil, etc.)

Another sign of the group's ability to react to the adverse trend has been the increase in foreign sales by IRI's manufacturing companies. To a growing extent this was the result of the setting up, within the group, of firms specialising in the supply of complete plants with the associated engineering and manufacturing know-how (based on the varied in-group experience) as well as manpower training before start-up.

In civil engineering the grouping in 1970 of all of IRI's subsidiaries under a special sub-holding (Italstat), created a similar instrument capable of strengthening the group's export potential in the area of large construction projects.

Not surprisingly IRI's most difficult task in these years of crisis was that of carrying through the reorganisation and streamlining of the group's industrial structure. This required injecting capital and management in those ailing subsidiaries which appeared — once restructured and relieved of their surplus labour — to have a long term potential; but it also implied selling off those which — because of their field of activity or small size — could not serve the long term objectives of the group; finally there was the problem of closing down companies which clearly offered no hope of recovery.

Given the cut-back in the rate of growth and the constraints this imposed on employment, especially in the South of Italy, one should not underrate the relatively slow pace of progress achieved, until recently, in the restructuring process. In a few cases the entire programme of adaptation was carried through. In addition, between 1973 and 1982 four firms were sold, with a total employment of 5200. In the same context, however, the Government resorted to IRI for the rescue of a number of ailing enterprises. Indeed such rescues, which had tended to diminish in the 1960s, again acquired importance in the 1970s,[13] involving the takeover by IRI of 16,400 workers formerly employed by private firms in the shipbuilding, engineering and special steels industries.

3. FINANCIAL MANAGEMENT IN INFLATIONARY CONDITIONS

The counter-inflation policies pursued by the Government after the oil crisis undoubtedly aggravated in many ways its negative consequences for the IRI group. In the regulated service sectors the adjustment of prices to the continuing high level of inflation proved extremely difficult: thus IRI's telephone subsidiary SIP failed to obtain the tariff rises necessary to meet the increase in costs, even though Italy's telephone charges were already among the cheapest in Europe. As a result, SIP, which had regularly secured a fair return on capital (allowing a steady dividend distribution until 1978) saw its profitability increasingly eroded; in 1979 and again in 1980, as a consequence of a two-year tariff freeze, the company suffered a combined loss of over 730 million dollars.

However, by far the most severe and lasting impact of the restrictive policies pursued by the Government in the post-1974 years was on IRI's funding conditions. The requests which IRI made to the Government in 1969 and 1970 for an increase in its capital endowment in order to ensure, during the considerable gestation period of the planned investment, an adequate equity base to the group, appear with hindsight to reflect an underestimation of the risk capital needed for the purpose. For one thing endowment funding had secured throughout the 1960s a very minor proportion of the group's capital needs, so much so that between 1959 and 1969 IRI's endowment fund dropped from just over 10% to 8% of the total capital invested in the industrial section of the group (excluding the banking section). True enough the contribution of private shareholders (individual equity investors as well as partners in joint ventures) still provided at the time a much larger portion than the State's (24% in 1959 and 14% in 1969); however, it also tended to fall, and at a faster pace, so that the total equity base of IRI's industrial section was down to 22.3% in 1969 against 34% ten years earlier. This trend was due to continue in the subsequent low or negative profit years. By 1972 the private equity contribution had fallen to 9% of the industrial section's invested capital, practically the same proportion as that provided in the same year by IRI's endowment fund, causing total equity to shrink to 18%. This level remained unchanged in 1973–74, implying a very substantial recourse to borrowing, to cover the capital requirements of those heavy investment years. After the onset of the oil crisis, the gearing ratio of the group's industrial section accelerated its rising trend: on the one side the need for new funds was boosted by inflation which swelled investment expenditure, notwithstanding the fact that the volume of investment was down from the peak levels of 1971–74;[14] on the other side the proportion of capital needs covered by self-financing fell more than could be justified by the great increase in investment expenditure. In fact the decline reflected much more the adverse market trends in most of the group's sectors, the high costs of rationalisation programmes carried on under the constraint of political and union pressures which hampered the necessary adaptations, the delays in adjusting telephone charges to rising costs and, last but not least, the rapidly growing burden of debt service.

Chastened by experience of the early 1970s, IRI repeatedly stressed to the Government the need for an increase in endowment funding large enough to redress the debt/equity ratio of the group and to secure the financing of the investment programmes under way, which would still require the raising of a very considerable volume of funds on the domestic and foreign capital markets. However, the response of the State was nowhere near meeting such request: the awards to IRI's endowment fund after 1974 not only failed to strengthen the equity base of the group, but could not even prevent its further weakening[15] in a context in which virtually no reliance could be placed on a contribution from private shareholders[16] and even the sale of non-strategic companies was limited by the preconceived opposition of the unions to which the Government was not indifferent.

In the last eight years the ratio of equity to total capital invested in the industrial section of the group dropped by almost a third, from 18% to 13%, after having touched an all-time low of close to 8% in 1979. The part of risk capital contributed by private equity investors continued to fall more than proportionally, dropping from 9% in 1974 to 4% in 1982, i.e. by more than a half.[17] As a result throughout the period both IRI and its constituent companies had to resort to massive borrowing, paying the high interest rates which became part of the Government's counter-inflation policy.

By 1978 the net indebtedness[18] of the industrial section of the group reached $13.8 billion against $2.7 billion in 1969, a five-fold increase in nine years; by 1982 it had risen to $23.4 billion with a further increase of close to 70% in four years. Over the same intervals the average cost of borrowing was up from 6.9% to 12.6%, and 18%, with an overall increase of more than 11 percentage points.[19]

The combined effect of these rises was to increase the net interest charges of the group's industrial sections from some $190 million in 1969 to $1.8 billion in 1978 and $4.4 billion in 1982, corresponding to 8.5%, 15% and 18.2% of the section's total turnover in the years considered.

These figures must be kept in mind when judgement is passed on the financial record of the group in recent years. Compared to the pre-1974 years, when the profits of the service companies and the banks almost offset (and even exceeded, in certain years, such as 1969, 1970 and 1973) the losses of the manufacturing sectors (concentrated in shipbuilding and motor vehicles), the subsequent period saw a steep rise of the overall loss. In the service sector the profit of the telephone concessionary − as already noted − was squeezed and even turned into a heavy deficit in 1979 and 1980 because of the failure to adjust charges to rising costs; in the manufacturing sector losses increased rapidly owing to the mounting deficit of the steel companies (which accounted for over 70% of the group's total loss) but also to a general deterioration of the performance of the remaining companies, with few exceptions.[20]

As a result the overall modest profit of IRI's industrial section in 1973 ($7.4 million) was followed by a series of uninterrupted losses, rising to $668 million in 1978 and to a record $2.3 billion in 1981, only slightly reduced in 1982 ($2.1 billion). These results, however, cannot be considered meaningful, when making comparisons with private groups, in Italy or abroad, unless they are first corrected to take account of the impact exercised by constraints of the type exemplified in the preceding pages.

Over the years the employment constraint was the most frequent, especially for large-scale enterprises and plants located in depressed areas or in the South of Italy: in all these cases IRI's intervention was asked for to avoid the high social costs of closure and to carry through an inevitably lengthy process of adaptation. In other cases the policy objective was to start (or to ensure the survival of) activities which appeared of strategic value in the long term, as a base for technological innovation or for regional development, but entailed especially high costs which the existing incentive measures did not cover. In yet other cases the aim was to prevent an excessive penetration of multinational companies in particular sectors. Finally, in more recent years the heaviest constraint derived from the apparent concern of the Government (plagued by the problems of excessive spending) to minimise the allocation of endowment capital to IRI, trusting that IRI's credit-worthiness and that of the group's companies would secure the finance needed for the fulfilment of the investment programmes, as approved at each yearly review. In fact, an almost complete disregard seems to have prevailed for the problem of ensuring a minimum (if not an optimum) balance in the capital structure of the group.

In its yearly planning report to the Government, IRI includes an estimate of the extra costs entailed by specific political constraints; for 1981 they were calculated at $136 million; for 1982 at $145 million. This, however, does not include the burden deriving from the deficiency of risk capital which, so IRI argues, should be corrected if the group is to operate on an equal footing with its competitors on the capital market. On this score IRI companies compare very unfavourably with their European opposites which they must face within the tariff-free EEC market.[21] Considerable disparities emerge also from a comparison with the leading Italian companies in the private sector.[22] If the group's equity base had been proportionate to the average estimated for EEC companies, or even to the lower level prevailing in Italian industrial companies, the overall indebtedness of the IRI group would have been substantially lower. A calculation for 1980 (data are not yet available for more recent years) shows that, as a result, the group's financial charges would have been cut by an amount equal to between one-half and two-thirds of the group's losses in that year.

The additional recourse to borrowing which such cutback entailed for IRI and group companies had a financial cost of over $1.5 billion, corresponding to almost one half of the group's losses in the two years considered. It should be added that the earlier mentioned 'non-commercial' costs which IRI included in its programmes for the same two years, although acknowledged by the Government (and Parliament), were not actually covered by the Treasury until mid-1983.

One could hardly deny that in the situation described such management limitations as may have existed within the group were closely interrelated with the financial and other constraints which prevailed in these years.

The rationing of capital, in particular, clearly ceases to act as a stimulus to management efficiency when it reaches the point of absorbing virtually all of management's time and energies in seeking

solutions to day-to-day finance problems; this could not but seriously
hamper management in making timely decisions of long term strategic
value and inevitably weakened the overall bargaining position of
IRI companies vis-à-vis their providers of finance, suppliers, clients,
etc. In its latest investment programme, covering the 1983–85 period,
IRI has clearly stressed the impossibility of further delaying a solution
to its financial problems, pointing to the fact that although the
Government might postpone the provision of funds, it could not
reduce their amount; the real alternative in fact is either to use
them to make up for the capital losses (and social costs) which
would accompany any substantial cutback or delay of IRI's investment programme, or to support its implementation along the lines
which Government and Parliament have for the most part already
approved.

The crisis that has emerged involves in fact the very structure of
the relations between IRI and the political framework within which
it has to operate.

4. PRESENT SIZE AND DIVERSIFICATION

Within the Italian State-held system, which as already mentioned
comprises three holding agencies, IRI controls the largest and most
diversified array of activities. Compared to ENI, the second group
by size, it is twice as large in terms of consolidated assets and of value
added, but five times in terms of workforce (1982 figures), reflecting
the much greater share in the ENI group of capital-intensive activities
such as mining and petrochemical production. As to the third group,
controlled by EFIM, the disparities in terms of the same three indicators are of the order of 10:1.

As at the end of 1982 the book value of IRI's consolidated assets
was equal to $30.7 billion, over three-quarters of which corresponded
to the net value of plant; 70% of the latter was accounted for by the
telecommunications and steel sectors (45% and 25% respectively).
At the same date the group employed a total of just over 525,000
persons; about 83% were in the industrial sectors, 6% in the infrastructure and construction sectors and 11% in the banks. The largest
employer in the group was the steel sector with a labour force of
111,500 equal to 24% of the industrial total; it was followed by
engineering and telecommunications (19% and 17% respectively).

The value added produced in 1982 by the industrial sector equalled
$12.9 billion, 47.2% of which was accounted for by manufacturing,
43.8% by services and 9% by infrastructures and construction. The

largest single contribution came from telecommunications (29%) followed by steel (18%) and engineering (12%).

The share of the group in total Italian value added in 1982 was equal to 5.9% in manufacturing, 18.4% in transport and communications and 1.1% in other activities, giving a total in overall terms of 4.4% (excluding Public Administration from national value added). IRI's workforce at the end of 1982 was equal to 4.7% of total Italian dependent employment (excluding in this case agriculture, trade and construction in which the group is virtually absent); the proportion was higher (5.9%) in manufacturing and only 3.8% in services.

The group's exports of goods and services in 1982 amounted to $7.4 billion, representing about 9% of Italian exports; manufacturing exports, which contributed 78% of the group total, were concentrated in steel, heavy engineering, motor vehicles, aerospace, naval vessels and electronic products, which together accounted for 20% of the corresponding national export total.

Worth noting is the group's 33% share of the overall R&D expenditure by Italian industry in 1982; over 9500 technicians (full-time equivalent), half of which researchers, were engaged in the group's laboratories, mainly in the electronics, telecommunications and engineering sectors.

Between 1968 and 1982 IRI increased its percentage share of national value added by nine-tenths of a point and that of national industry and services employment (as above defined) by 1.3 points; in manufacturing alone the employment percentage was up by 2.6 points against three-tenths of a point in services. In the South, the progress was relatively much greater, reflecting the massive expansion of investment in the area which was commented upon earlier. In the whole of Italy the group's fixed investment in the 1971–78 period was equal to 11.5% of the national total (excluding residential construction), dropping to 7.9% in the subsequent four years; this is accounted for by the excess capacity prevailing in manufacturing (especially in the capital intensive steel sector), the slowing down of investment in the telephone network (caused by the tariff freeze of 1978–79) and the severe finance stringency suffered by the group.

In sectoral terms, IRI has an important stake in a number of key sectors. In 1982 the group's share in Italian iron and steel production was 100% for pig iron, 56% for crude steel, 70% for flat-rolled products and 36% for special steels.

In the same year the group accounted for virtually 100% of Italy's merchant and navy shipbuilding capacity. In engineering IRI companies contributed between one-half and two-thirds of electrical (including nuclear) equipment and between 30% and 40% of industrial machinery and aerospace products. In motor vehicles, Alfa Romeo's car output (number of units) was about 15% of the Italian total; the company's share of the home market was 6%–7%, rising to almost 20% for exports. Worth noting is also the group's production of diesel engines, especially in the medium and large range, both for automative use (13% of total Italian output) and for industrial and marine applications (30%).

In electronics, IRI accounts for almost half of Italy's manufacture of telecommunication equipment and about 30% of industrial equipment, radars and defence appliances; moreover, the whole of the Italian production of semiconductors is controlled by IRI. In the field of software IRI has a dominant position with Finsiel, ranking among the first ten European software houses.

In food processing the group has an 18% share of the Italian market for canned tomatoes and lower percentages for other preserves, vegetable fats, etc.; it accounts for 11% of deep-frozen and over 18% of ice-creams. In confectionery it has a leading position in baked products (35%–40%) and a fairly strong one in other lines (sugar products, crackers, chocolate, etc.). In modern retailing (food) the group operates a chain of seventy-seven supermarkets, of which fifteen are located in the South.

In the service area, IRI controls the entire urban telephone network and a good half of the domestic trunk network; at the end of 1982 subscribers totalled almost 15 million with close to 22 million telephones. IRI also operates Italy's transcontinental communications via submarine cables and via satellite.

Alitalia, among the ten largest world air-carriers operating international lines (and most of the domestic services), is controlled by IRI. In shipping, IRI companies account for one-third of the Italian dry cargo tonnage (almost two-thirds in the case of container vessels) which ensure regular international freight services as well as bulk transport of ores and coal.

The national radio and television broadcasting company RAI is under IRI control; since 1976, when radio and television services were liberalised in Italy, RAI has faced the competition of a large number of private companies, including six operating on a country-wide scale.

About 45% of the toll-motorway network is operated by an IRI company (Autostrade). In the construction sector the group has a modest share but includes two of the major Italian enterprises in the civil engineering field competing on the world market for large public works projects.

Finally the three banks under IRI control (Banca Commerciale Italiana, Credito Italiano and Banco di Roma) account for about 15% of total deposits of the Italian banking system; they have acquired a leading role in the finance of the country's foreign trade.[23]

Altogether IRI is easily the largest industrial group in Italy, a country in which large-scale enterprises can be counted on one's fingers and small and medium-size industry predominates much more than in the rest of the European Economic Community. For this reason alone IRI fills a key role in the delicate pattern of cooperative as well as competitive relations among large-scale groups, which is an essential feature of an advanced industrial system.

The large size of the group is matched at the company and plant levels. In 1982 forty companies accounted for 84% of the group's total sales of goods and services amounting to $24.8 billion; twenty-six were manufacturing companies, with turnovers ranging from a minimum of $140 million to a maximum of $3.4 billion accounting for over 83% of the group's manufacturing sales.

In the South, where IRI has concentrated over the years virtually all its new manufacturing units, 75% of the group's manufacturing workforce is employed in eighteen plants with more than 1000 workers (of which seven with over 4000 workers).[24]

International comparisons are always difficult, but it is safe to say that IRI, as a group, measures up to the top five or six European industrial companies by turnover,[25] though still nowhere near the biggest US corporations or Japanese *keiretsus*. It is highly diversified in product and market terms; in contrast it has, as yet, a limited presence in foreign countries, in the form of direct local production. Investment abroad (apart from the trivial cases in which it was imposed by the search for natural resources lacking in Italy, such as iron ore and coal) has been undertaken for the production of integrated circuits (in the Far East for the labour-intensive stages of production; in Europe and the US to gain access to local markets and advanced technological know-how), for local car assembly (to overcome tariff barriers, in South Africa and Greece) and for food processing (now limited to one company in Spain).

5. INSTITUTIONAL AND ORGANISATIONAL ARRANGEMENTS

The present section reviews the main aspects of the relations between IRI and the political authority as well as the internal organisation and management procedures of the group.

The problems and solutions devised in both these areas can only be understood against the historical background of the purposes leading up to the establishment of IRI as a permanent institution in 1937. From the brief description given in the first section it is clear that historical necessity brought about the decision by the Italian State to accept the role of an entrepreneur.

The fundamental issue was that in certain fields where the risks were too great for private enterprise or the capital requirements exceeded what the private sector was able to supply from sources other than deposit-taking banks, there was need for State economic initiative.

This, however, did not mean giving up the essentials of a market economy. On the contrary, State-held firms and private firms would continue to coexist in most sectors and compete under common rules of the game; and indeed the assumption by the State of directly productive functions was not conceived as an end in itself, but as an instrument which would eventually promote a larger amount of private enterprise investment than would otherwise come forth.

Another significant aspect to be stressed is that once the Italian State decided to take up its new role, this was entrusted to an ad hoc agency, accountable to the Government but separated from the bureaucratic framework and not subject to civil service procedures. In fact IRI was conceived as a holding concern and endowed with the degree of autonomy needed for the task of managing enterprises which maintained the status of joint-stock companies, regulated by private commercial law, requiring them to behave as a business. The reform of the industrial system thus went hand in hand with that of the State.

The gradual development of a formal framework

As an instrument of public policy, the new agency clearly had to serve the strategic ends of government, but at the same time preserve the conditions for enterprising management, which was the first requirement for the pursuing of those ends.

There have been circumstances in which the priorities of public policy were met by the group's initiative without any additional costs which current market prices could not cover. However, in many other cases public policy aims are at odds with market profitability at company level. In these situations the objectives of the public sphere turn into specific constraints in the sphere of enterprise decisions and it was obviously of crucial importance for IRI to establish rigorous criteria for meeting both its social and its commercial obligations.

In this respect IRI had to operate within a framework of imprecise statutory duties and constraints. The status of joint-stock companies undoubtedly implied that the profit criterion was the guiding rule for the management of subsidiaries. IRI's statute, however, even in its latest version approved in 1948[26] and still in force, stated simply that the Institute 'manages the holdings and other assets owned by it' and that 'the Council of Ministers is responsible for laying down the general guidelines to be followed by the Institute in the public interest'.

In this context the line of conduct initially followed by IRI was that of striving to keep the burden of low- or non-earning investments within the limits of its revenues from earning investments and profits on the sale of assets. This was virtually achieved in the pre-war years, without requiring any additional allocations of state capital, thanks also to the sizable proceeds from asset sales which IRI could effect in that period. After the Second World War the heavy engagement in recovery and conversion programmes was supported by fresh awards to IRI's endowment fund, thus allowing the Institute to carry on the rationalisation and development of such key sectors as steel, engineering and shipbuilding.

The reasoning behind the above-mentioned criterion was evolved, already in those early years, within IRI itself, by Professor Saraceno, then a senior staff member of the Institute.[27] The essence of Saraceno's position was that (a) the State could not refuse to take upon itself the burden of extra costs (or lower revenues), if any, caused to IRI by the pursuit of policy objectives and (b) the required compensation could be obtained through the State's contributions to IRI's capital by allowing the extra costs to absorb a part of, or all, the returns which the State would otherwise have derived from the endowment fund.

The year 1956 saw the emergence of a new formal structure which, with few changes, has governed up to the present IRI's relations with the political authority.[28] The new legislation provides that all State holdings be vested in 'Autonomous Management Agencies', such as IRI and other holding agencies established after IRI's model.[29] The direction and control of the system is entrusted to an Interministerial Committee and to a new Ministry of State Holdings which has the task of ensuring that the Government guidelines are pursued by the Autonomous Management Agencies. As to the latter, the law lays down that they must operate according to criteria of 'economic viability'.

This precept represents an important step in the formalisation of IRI's duties as an autonomous body within the framework of the

State holding system. Its purport obviously goes beyond the unques-
tionable profit criterion which is dictated for enterprises operating,
as all IRI's subsidiaries, under ordinary company law; what is at issue
is rather the problem of reconciling profit maximising activity with
the pursuit of the objectives of Government policy.

In this respect the creation of a sponsor Ministry and its inclusion
together with the technical or sectoral Ministries and the Treasury in
an economic planning Cabinet appropriately reflects the decision-
making process which, at the political level, leads to the formulation
of guidelines for the State-held system. As has been rightly stressed,[30]
Government policy in the various fields in which IRI operates (industry, telecommunications, transport, etc.) or which have direct
relevance for the group (Southern Italy, Research, Labour, etc.)
remains the responsibility of the non-sponsor Ministries which lay
down the policy goals and related strategies for the different areas
falling within their purview. The coordination of sectoral goals
and strategies is achieved within the Planning Cabinet in which the
Treasury ensures the necessary compatibility with budgetary policy.
In this context the Ministry of State Holdings received specific requests
relating to the possible contribution of State-held enterprises to the
policy objectives of the various non-sponsor Ministries. These requests
form the basis of the policy framework for the Ministry of State
Holdings, whose essential role at this stage is to ascertain whether and
on what terms and conditions the State-held system may respond to
Government policies without impairing the survival of enterprises
operating within the discipline of a market environment.

This in turn necessarily implies the cooperation of the Holding
agencies with the sponsor Ministry in order to: investigate all possible
opportunities for entrepreneurial initiative which may promote the
Government goals; make sure that the constraints due to social or
political priorities remain within limits which will allow efficient
management to gradually eliminate the ensuing extra costs or lower
revenues;[31] evaluate such costs and submit to Government the
problem of their funding as all other classes of public expenditure.
On this particular point the 1956 Law is silent; over a decade had to
pass until Law 675 of 1977 for the first time explicitly prescribed that
(non-commercial) burdens imposed on state-held enterprises, 'if not
otherwise compensated through existing State aids', must be specified
in the Holding agencies' programmes which are submitted yearly to
the relevant Interministerial Committee. The same law lays down that
the State capital awards to the Agencies' endowment funds are meant
to contribute to the financing of the investment programmes as well
as to 'cover non-commercial costs, if any'.

Although the formulation is still vague, Saraceno's longstanding approach appears to have been implicitly accepted by the law, which attributes to the endowment fund the dual role of risk capital and of a possible offset, through its non-remuneration, for the extra costs originating from the pursuit of public policy objectives.[32]

Since 1978 IRI has duly included in its yearly programme reports a description of the specific constraints which the group has accepted in response to political directives, with an estimate of the related costs. This type of assessment has been a regular feature of IRI's planning and control functions, carried on in close cooperation with the companies involved. The criteria adopted for the estimates[33] have been accepted (with minor modifications) by the Government. As to the form of compensation, Parliament has for the time being opted for a direct subsidy, which the Treasury will pay to IRI.[34]

Clearly the recourse to the endowment fund was practically ruled out in the present circumstances, given the already noted structural deficiency of the fund, which has in large measure contributed in recent years to the heavy losses of the group. To this should be added: the desirability of a closer governmental supervision over the criteria followed by IRI and the sponsor Ministry in determining non-commercial costs; the need to comply with a recent directive issued by the EEC Commission[35] requiring that Member States ensure 'transparency', i.e. adequate information as regards the provision of public funds to compensate public enterprises 'for the financial burdens assumed by them in pursuing other than commercial ends'.

IRI and the Government

The formal structure and systems of Government control over IRI are at present the following.

(i) At the summit are the two Interministerial Committees for Economic Planning (CIPE) and for Industrial Policy (CIPI).[36] The former has direct overview and guidance powers on all matters not delegated to the latter. Thus CIPE issues general guidelines in the framework of the national economic plan and verifies their observance on the basis of the annual Planning Report which the Ministry of State Holdings must submit to it. CIPE supervises in particular the field of services (for instance telecommunications), whereas CIPI carries out the same functions for the industrial sector proper. IRI's rolling multi-year programmes, however, are now submitted yearly to CIPI in their entirety. CIPE formulates the criteria for evaluating the extra costs of political origin which will be covered with the sums allocated by Parliament. CIPI expresses its opinion on the proposal which the Ministry of State Holdings makes concerning the awards to IRI's endowment fund;

(ii) The Ministry of State Holdings, as a member of both CIPE and CIPI, participates in the formulation of the general guidelines and thereafter supervises their implementation. To this end the Ministry has extensive day-to-day contact with IRI and has the right to prior information on important matters such as the acquisition or sale of controlling holdings, the creation of new companies, capital increases or write-offs of subsidiary companies, etc.

The Ministry's views are communicated to IRI but are not binding. IRI's Annual Report and Accounts are transmitted to the Ministry (as well as to the Treasury) for review and subsequent submission to Parliament together with the Ministry's yearly Planning Report and Estimate of expenditure.

The Ministry, moreover, is involved in the formative stage of IRI's medium-term planning, providing the political inputs and expressing its reactions to the Institute's proposals, valuations and requests. Here again the Minister formulates views and directives but cannot issue an injunction. IRI's compliance with the Ministry's guidelines must indeed be the result of an autonomous decision, having regard to the Institute's incumbent duty to safeguard the value of the capital (endowment fund) which it has been awarded by the State; moreover, it is IRI, not the Ministry, that has the responsibility of the overall funding of the group's programmes, which it has undertaken to carry out on the basis of the capital made available by the State and the resources that both IRI and its constituent companies must secure from the market.[37]

IRI's rolling multi-year programmes are submitted yearly to CIPI by the Ministry of State Holdings together with a detailed report on the implementation of the programmes already approved;

(iii) Parliament exercises its scrutiny and guidance on the basis of the formal information which flows from CIPI (investment programmes), the Ministry of State Holdings (IRI's Annual Report and Accounts) and the State Court of Accounts (reporting on the observance by IRI and the Government of the respective statutory and legal duties). Besides, Parliament holds hearings and carries out special investigations. IRI's Chairman and General Manager as well as the chief executives of the group's companies are regularly called upon to answer questions when the group's programmes and operations are scrutinized once a year. Ad hoc hearings are held whenever exceptional investment projects or other initiatives of national importance are being considered by IRI for inclusion in the group's programme. Parliament exercises its function through a Joint Standing Committee which is the counterpart of CIPI for the strategic direction and overview of national industrial policy and is composed of fifteen Senators and fifteen Representatives. The Government must obtain the opinion of this Committee on: IRI's medium-term programmes and the proposed awards to its endowment fund; the criteria for ascertaining and measuring the extra costs of political origin; the reports by the Ministry of State Holdings on the implementation of IRI's programmes; Government proposals for the appointment of IRI's Chairman and Vice-Chairman.

(iv) Finally, the allocations by law to IRI's endowment fund are made through the standing Budget Committees of the Senate and of the Chamber of Deputies, and a full House vote on the bill proposed by the Ministry of State Holdings.

Experience has abundantly shown that the present arrangements for political guidance are too lengthy to allow a proper functioning of the system. Especially the annual programme review procedures which are the principal vehicle for parliamentary scrutiny of IRI's strategies and achievements have proved to be a major obstacle to an effective decision-making process. The sequence of reviews and the number of Ministerial organs and parliamentary committees involved are such that considerable delays are inevitable in reaching the required formal decisions. Thus IRI's rolling medium-term investment programmes which were submitted yearly to the sponsor Ministry in the 1978–80 period, obtained the required opinion of the Joint Parliamentary Committee with time-lags of fourteen to nineteen months.[38]

The resulting uncertainties were seriously damaging for all participants: in particular IRI has had knowledge of the level of endowment funding which Government and Parliament were ready to provide only after its current year investments had been started; by the time the decision on IRI's initial requests for State capital were decided upon the group's needs had considerably grown, both because of unpredictable changes in outside circumstances (in a period of generally adverse short-term developments) and of the financial burden of the additional borrowing imposed on the group by the delay in State funding.

The same applies to the coverage of the extra costs to IRI of implementing political directives: the already mentioned allocations of funds for this purpose for 1981 and 1982 became operative only in May 1983, causing undue losses to the companies involved. The need for reform of the present review procedures of IRI's (and other holding agencies') programmes and achievements is now widely recognized and will be among the first tasks for the newly elected Parliament.[39]

Internal organisation and control systems

As a statutory agency, IRI is endowed with legal personality and its own capital awarded by the Treasury; it exercises stockholder's rights according to the provisions of ordinary company law; it raises funds on the market through all available forms of short- and long-term borrowing, which it uses, together with its own capital, for meeting the funding needs of the group's companies and maintaining its controlling (or equal partnership) stake in the same; its financial accounting and reporting conform to the standard principles followed by private companies; its staff is hired under private law and is regulated by the collective agreements applied in the banking sector.

In functional terms IRI is the central holding company of the group and its relations with its subsidiaries correspond to those of large private groups. So do the main areas of IRI's decision and control activity with respect to: the formulation of guidelines for the investment and production programmes of group companies; the provisions and allocation of the necessary sources of financing; the selection of the companies' top management and the adoption of efficient organisational structures and management systems.

IRI's administrative organs consist of a Board of Directors with a Chairman and a Vice-Chairman, an Executive Committee and a Board of Auditors.

The Chairman (full-time) and Vice-Chairman (part-time) are appointed by decree of the Head of State with the advice of the Cabinet and of the earlier mentioned Joint Parliamentary Committee, upon the recommendation of the Minister of State Holdings; their term of office is three years renewable no more than twice. The Board includes twelve Directors (part-time), nine of which are senior civil servants (two from the Treasury, and one from each of seven other Ministries, including the Ministry of State Holdings) and three are outside experts appointed by the Minister of State Holdings for a three-year term, renewable without limit.

The three 'expert' Directors, together with the Chairman and Vice-Chairman, form the Executive Committee, to which the Board of Directors delegates all decisions regarding the management of IRI and its relations with subsidiary companies, except for such matters as the purchase and sale of holdings and other assets, the issue of bonds, capital increases or write-offs, etc. In 1982 the Board held twelve meetings and the Executive Committee fifty-three.

IRI's statute provides that a General Manager be appointed by the Minister of State Holdings on the proposal of the Chairman after consultation with the Board. As a rule, General Managers have been drawn from the cadre of senior executives of the group.[40]

The Board of Auditors consists of five members appointed by the Minister of State Holdings; its functions are analogous to those of the corresponding private company auditing boards.

All meetings of the administrative organs of IRI are attended by a Magistrate of the State Court of Accounts (which is entrusted with the control of all agencies permanently financed by the State). The role of the Court is of special importance, as it must ensure that the capital awarded to IRI by the State is safeguarded, a condition which implies the constant observance, by Government and IRI alike, of the 'economic viability' criterion which the 1956 Law prescribes for the management of State holdings. In this context the Court is not concerned with the *merit* of managerial decisions, but with the correct application of the decision-making rules which are a precondition of 'economic viability'; this refers in particular to the requirement that any extra costs of political origin be accurately evaluated and fully compensated and that adequate financing will be forthcoming from the Treasury once IRI's programmes have been approved.

The Court's findings are included in a yearly report which is presented to Parliament. In recent years the Court has repeatedly called the attention of the political authorities to the deviations from the above-mentioned rules which have seriously affected IRI's financial results and prevented a meaningful assessment of managerial performance.

A fundamental feature of IRI's management system is the grouping of subsidiary companies operating in the same sector or in interrelated lines of activity (for instance: telecommunications and electronics) under a parent company which takes over from IRI the shareholdings in the relevant operating companies. At present there are eight sectoral subholdings of the type described; another two sectoral parents

(Alitalia and RAI) are 'mixed' holdings, combining both direct operating responsibilities and the control of a number of subsidiaries. These sectoral subholdings can be viewed, in part, as an extension of IRI, improving the guidance and control functions of the Institute and supplementing its financing capacity; but in part they are a vehicle of greater synergies for their subsidiaries in various areas (marketing abroad; research and development; joint-venture negotiations; EDP systems, etc.).

The management systems and practices within the group are not subject to any statutory or other outside regulations and correspond to current good practice in large private groups.

Appointments of board members and top level executives to be proposed to the shareholders' meetings of subsidiaries in which IRI has a direct stake (essentially sectoral subholdings and other parent companies) is based on general guidelines established by IRI's Board of Directors. Both executive and part-time members of boards are selected by IRI's Chairman and submitted to the Executive Committee whose role is to check that the candidates meet the qualifications specified in the guidelines.

Boards of subsidiaries include outside members consisting mainly of persons drawn from Italian public and business life, representatives of sizable minority shareholders, credit institutions, etc. appointed on a part-time basis. In addition the Heads of Departments at IRI's headquarters who are responsible for planning and liaison functions with subsidiary companies sit on the Board of Directors and sometimes on the Executive Committees of the first-level subsidiaries; for second-level subsidiaries similar arrangements are made with junior staff from IRI departments.

All other appointments within first- and second-tier subsidiaries are delegated to the top executives of the same; for major companies IRI's Executive Committee is informed of the appointments of full-time board members and of General Managers (who are normally also members of company boards). It should be stressed that, as in most other countries, the primary role of a board in Italy is in practice that of 'providing legitimacy and authority for management's actions'.[41] This justifies the inclusion in the Boards of non-executive appointees which often are *de facto* proposed to IRI by the sponsor Minister. Civil servants of the Ministry of State Holdings are normally members of the Board of Auditors of the major companies of the group; the Audit Boards of nearly all subsidiaries include IRI's comptroller or one of his senior staff, together with outside members drawn as a rule from the accounting profession.

The international organisation of the Institute is based at present (1983) on ten Departments[42] whose heads serve under the General Manager and are in charge of the Headquarters' general services and of the liaison with, and supervision of, the management of the subsidiaries. Total staff at IRI headquarters numbers 540, of which 140 are senior and junior managers.[43]

A Management Committee, consisting of the General Manager and the Heads of Departments, meets at irregular intervals to discuss problems of major importance proposed by any of its members.

A Group Policy and Coordination Committee, consisting of the General Manager, the Chairmen and Managing Directors of sectoral subholdings and other directly controlled subsidiaries, meets at least every three months to deal with problems and initiatives of common interest in areas of strategic relevance, such as human resource management, finance, exports, innovative developments, etc.

There is a continuous and close relationship between IRI and its major subsidiaries, which is maintained in a variety of ways. The two most important procedures consist of the annual review of multi-year programmes and the discussion and approval of the draft Report and Accounts of IRI's direct subsidiaries.

Investment programmes with a rolling multi-year horizon are now a standard practice in all subsidiaries.[44] IRI indeed initiated it already in the mid-fifties, in connection with the first published government projections and targets for the national economy.

The planning cycle starts in the spring with the formulation by IRI of general and specific guidelines and the fixing of basic external parameters to be used by all companies for their projections. The plans are submitted to IRI headquarters in October by sectoral subholdings and other parent companies which have the task to consolidate the operating companies' plans in a global sector perspective. The Planning Reports extend to 100–200 pages and discuss major policy matters, analysing investment proposals and projecting the profit or losses three years ahead. Funding requirements are estimated, indicating the expected contribution from IRI. There are separate chapters on employment, R&D and investment in Southern Italy.

Each plan is submitted to IRI's Executive Committee together with comments by the Planning Department and is discussed at a meeting attended by the top management of the relevant subholding or parent subsidiary.[45] By the end of the year these deliberations are completed. The overall funding requirements of the programmes are naturally of over-riding importance and represent a crucial issue for IRI and Government considerations. The consolidation of all programmes at IRI level closes the cycle with the submission of the group's multi-year programme at each year-end to the Executive Committee. Subsequently, when endorsed by the Board of Directors, the programme is submitted to the Ministry of State Holdings.

The draft Report and Accounts of the most important subsidiaries are discussed at two meetings of the Executive Committee: the first to debate a report by the Comptroller on the criteria which the company proposes to follow in drawing up its yearly accounts; the second to review the resulting financial statement with the comments of the Comptroller based on the trend over recent years and into the immediate future. These meetings are held in the spring and are attended by the chief executives of the company concerned. The Report and Accounts are subsequently submitted to meetings of shareholders for formal approval.

Important contacts are held between the Heads of Departments at Headquarters and their counterparts in the major subsidiaries (especially for coordinating, and assisting in, the raising of funds on the domestic and the international markets).

Negotiations with labour unions on wage agreements, redundancies etc. are handled by Intersind, in consultation with the company concerned. Intersind is an employers' association to which since 1957 IRI companies[46] belong (together with EFIM's subsidiaries) after their departure from the thereafter solely private employers' association (Confindustria).

This was the result of a parliamentary directive which was essentially motivated by Confindustria's increasingly 'political' attitude, leading to frequent conflict with Government. The directive stressed, however, that the disengagement from Confindustria did not imply any limitation of the autonomy of IRI companies in the negotiations with the unions, recognizing that this was essential for safeguarding the 'parity of conditions' with their private competitors which is required for the proper functioning of a market economy. Experience shows that, in actual fact, Intersind has duly defended its autonomy from 'outside' pressures during a long period of extremely difficult labour relations; no conclusive evidence has been produced that the agreements concluded by the Association were not negotiated to the best long-term advantage of the companies involved.

6. CONCLUDING REMARKS

A few conclusions from the preceding review of IRI's experience over almost half a century of Italian economic life may be drawn.

(a) The role played by IRI in a country struggling with the problems of capital accumulation for the achievement of fuller employment and greater regional balance has been significant. The recourse to the existing legal form of enterprise (the joint-stock company) pursuing profitability in a market environment has been an essential pre-condition for such a role. It permitted a cadre of dynamic managers to be enlisted to serve specific public ends, without hampering the operation and growth of private enterprise and the opening of the Italian economy to growing international competition.

(b) The role of public enterprise is in no way concluded; on the contrary the problems created by the worldwide crisis (the deepest since the 1930s when IRI was born) both for the adaptation of Italian industry and for the further progress of the South, leave no doubt that IRI's contribution will be required no less than in the past.

(c) IRI's position, after eight years of painful structural readjustment of the social and economic context in which the group operates, shows some encouraging signs:

   (i)   in labour relations, thanks both to a clearer realisation by the unions of the challenges the group has to face and to a greater effort on the part of management to secure a full understanding on the part of the workers of the options and constraints involved, so as to overcome differences before positions become entrenched;[47]

   (ii) in the opportunities which the wide industrial base of the group offers for exploiting technological innovation and new markets, with a growing recourse to joint ventures and partnership agreements with leading international companies for a pooling of know-how and markets;

   (iii) the gradual development of formal arrangements for isolating in a systematic manner from commercial costs the extra costs of public policy constraints and for providing the necessary compensation; even if further refinement of this framework will be called for, the prerequisites have been created for avoiding the confusion of responsibility which prevailed in earlier years, exposing group managers to negative assessments based on misleading financial results.

(d) On the other hand, IRI has to face the consequences of an extremely critical financial condition, which is mainly the result of two factors:

   (i)   First is the exceedingly heavy impact of the world depression.

This refers above all to the group's steel sector, which has accounted for an overwhelming proportion of IRI's losses in these years. The cut-back in capacity which is imposed on a European scale by a chronic world problem of over-production calls for an understanding and commitment by all the main parties involved; it undoubtedly requires political leadership and a readiness on the part of the State to provide the aid which has been granted considerably earlier in other European countries for a radical rationalisation of the Sector.

(ii) Second is the repeated failure of the government to ensure, together with the approval of investment programmes to which IRI became committed, adequate capital funding for carrying them out without disrupting the financing structure of the group. Not only has it been inherently difficult to reach agreement in advance on the endowment fund increases justified by the investments which were undertaken and by the risks associated with the inflationary environment and market prospects of the group, but the exceedingly lengthy reviewing procedures and the delays caused by subsequent changes in political priorities further aggravated the consequences of inadequate financing arrangements.[48]

In its latest programme report to Government IRI has clearly stated the urgent need to break the vicious circle of interest costs leading to deficits and further borrowing, a condition which imposes growing constraints on IRI's strategic planning, demoralises management, damages existing private shareholders and deters potential equity investors. The eventual coverage *ex post* of the losses by the State, if not accompanied by a commitment to consistent decision-making in the future, is hardly satisfactory to IRI and appears constitutionally incorrect, implying, as it does, that Government 'has effected an expenditure unauthorised by Parliament, relying on the credit which IRI is able to obtain on the market'.[49]

This is then, at the time of writing, the uncertain prospect confronting IRI and not the least of the many challenges for the newly appointed Italian Government.

NOTES

1. By Law n. 5 of January 23 1933.
2. Initially IRI included also an industrial finance section for the granting of medium-and long-term loans to Italian firms. With the banking reform of 1936 this section was dissolved and its role taken over by an investment bank (IMI) which the State had set up in 1931.
3. The banks and public utilities such as telephone, radio-broadcasting and electricity companies were excluded from disposal.
4. This was in no small measure due to the fact that, with the acquisition of a very diverse set of industrial firms, including profitable ones, IRI could muster a fairly large cadre of experienced managers. Add to this the appointment at the head of the Institute of men of outstanding professional competence and great integrity, such as A. Beneduce (Chairman from 1933 till his death in 1939) and D. Menichella (General Manager from 1933 to 1943).
5. By Law n. 905 of June 24 1937.
6. IRI was entrusted with the construction of almost two-thirds of the 3,200 km network which included, together with some profitable northern motorways, all the low traffic southern ones, which no private company would bid for. Note also that the concession of a network (rather than single turnpikes, which attracted private concessionaries) allowed IRI to apply the same toll rate to all its sections, so that the South could benefit from an implicit subsidy at the expense of the high revenue northern motorways, without impairing the profitability of the concessionary operation. (The concession to Autostrade provided that all income in excess of an 8% return on capital be passed on to the State.)
7. As the companies involved received considerable compensation funds for the surrender of their plants, IRI transformed SME, one of its former electricity subsidiaries, into a holding company for the taking on of new activities. SME's most substantial acquisitions were in the food industry. In part this was prompted by the desire to prevent a further extension (by way of takeovers) of the already strong presence of foreign multinational groups in the sector; however, a more important reason for choosing the food industry was the hope that its further development could be located, in good part, in the South.
8. A few years later a similar venture was undertaken in Spain (Valencia) by Ford (USA).
9. Both through expansion of existing plants and the setting up of new ones, mostly private (in certain cases in association with IRI's southern holding company SME). Secondary production lines located in the South include: batteries, glass products, tyres, plastic materials, paints, wires, wheels, ball bearings, etc.
10. Before this, the great expansion of Italy's private car manufacturers, sustained by two decades of high demand, was entirely concentrated in the North (and in foreign countries) where it could rely on the large inflow of labour, migrating from the South. FIAT's decision to move to the South was in part the result of union pressure (many of FIAT's workers, one should recall, are southerners).
11. That is, its location can be decided at the discretion of the investor; in other sectors, such as telephone and toll-motorways, investment is subject to technical constraints or government direction. Moreover, for airlines and shipping there is no meaningful way of defining the location of investment in aircraft or ships.
12. The gap between the last two percentages implicitly measures the deficiency of private enterprise investment in the South due both to general financial difficulties which held down overall investment by industry and to the fact that regional development policies were unable to create profit expectations for more than a modest number of new ventures in the South.

13. Notwithstanding the fact that in 1971 a new state finance company (GEPI) was set up with the specific aim of rescuing small firms in 'transitory difficulties'. GEPI has assisted over 200 companies employing at the end of 1982 some 31,000 workers.

14. Between 1971–74 and 1975–78 investment at constant prices fell by $2.7 billion, i.e. by 20%, but rose at current year prices by $3 billion, a 62% increase; in the subsequent four years a further decrease of investment in real terms by $1.9 billion was accompanied by a new expansion of expenditure of $4.4 billion, 57% more than in the 1975–78 period.

15. In the eight year period 1975–82, Treasury awards to IRI's endowment fund totalled $6.8 billion against an overall loss by the group's industrial section of $9.8 billion; in the same period IRI's industrial companies invested in plant the equivalent of $20 billion.

16. This reflected also the depressed state of the stock market during this period.

17. A sizable presence of private shareholders in the industrial section is now virtually limited to two of IRI's sub-groups, mainly STET and SME where outside equity holdings account for 22% and 41% of the respective total consolidated net worth. In 1974 the private component of equity in the same groups was equal to 59% and 70%; moreover, minority shareholders then held close to 56% of the total equity of the Finsider group, but owing to the heavy losses incurred during the worldwide steel crisis, the percentage is now 7%.

18. Measured in yearly averages.

19. The increase in the cost of borrowing reflected in no small part the fact that the existing system of state-subsidised credit to industry (for rationalisation programmes, R&D expenditure, investment in the South, etc.) was greatly hampered by lack of funds. The difficulty of borrowing on the domestic market forced the group to resort increasingly to the international capital market, where lower interest rates were in large part offset by exchange rate rises, especially in recent years. Between 1975 and 1982 total foreign indebtedness, mostly in US dollars, rose from less than $1 billion to $10.5 billion and from 12% to 40% of the group's total debts; close to nine-tenths of the total was borrowed on medium and long term.

20. Banks maintained their good profit performance throughout the period.

21. The most recent data available (1980) for European companies of comparable size give the following picture:

Sector	Equity as a % of invested capital	
	IRI companies	*European sample*
Steel	5	41
Shipbuilding	negative	49
Electrical engineering	18	68
Motor vehicles	43	52
Aircraft	31	41
Electronics	15	65
Food and confectionery	27	73

22. Data derived from balance sheets of a large sample of Italian private companies show that in 1969 their equity coverage of invested capital was on average twice and a half as large as that of IRI companies; since then the situation has deteriorated for both types of companies, but the disparity in relative terms had grown by 1981 to 4.4:1 (52.7%, against 12%), implying an 'equity gap' for IRI's industrial companies, of the order of $10 billion.

23. The presence of the banks within the group does not imply any privileged access to their resources by IRI or its operating companies. Thus the share of the total credit extended by the three banks which flows to IRI companies is entirely proportionate to the relative importance of the IRI group within the Italian productive system.

24. At the end of 1982 IRI accounted for over 52% of total southern manufacturing employment in plants with over 1000 workers.
25. Considering the top 100 European companies listed by the *Financial Times* (October 21 1982) for 1981, IRI's turnover at $21.5 billion appears comparable to that of Unilever and VEBA (third and fourth position) and more than two-fifths larger than that of Fiat (tenth on the list).
26. By Decree-Law n. 5107 of February 12 1948.
27. Professor Saraceno is at present General Economic Adviser to IRI.
28. The structure and system of outside control were defined by Law n. 1.589 of December 1956 and partly amended by Law n. 675 of August 1977 and Law n. 468 of August 1978.
29. At present ENI and EFIM.
30. See P. Saraceno, 'Il sistema delle partecipazioni statali', *Economia e Politica industriale* n. 29, 1981; pp. 50–51.
31. A permanent deficiency of revenue (as in the case of certain public services supplied at 'political prices'), can be compensated by direct subsidisation of the operating enterprise, public or private, in the framework of a concessionary regime. However, if the constraints imposed by political priorities are liable to become pervasive and unpredictable to the point of precluding an effective pursuit of profitability, the rational solution is outright nationalisation. This explains why in 1962 the electricity sector was not concentrated in IRI but nationalised; border cases, however, exist also within the group, such as RAI (responsible for television and radio broadcasting) and Tirrenia (providing regular link-up shipping services for Italian islands).
32. It is worth noting that in earlier years there was at least one significant instance in which the dual role of the endowment fund was correctly applied by the State: when the Taranto steel project was approved in the late 1950s, about 20% of its cost was covered by an IRI loan to Finsider at about one third of the going market rate. This was made possible by a prior increase of IRI's endowment fund conferred by the State, taking into account the extra costs associated with the southern location.
33. The estimates are necessarily the result of a subjective judgement by management, which is of course the rule for a host of similar evaluations required in the conduct of business. As aptly pointed out by Saraceno at a recent Senate hearing, 'the financial appraisal of a new investment or the determination of the depreciation allowance of a plant in operation are undoubtedly fraught with greater uncertainties than the estimate of the extra costs of a Government directive'.
34. Law n. 750 of December 18 1981 appropriated $335 million to compensate non-commercial costs for which IRI provided estimates in its investment programme for the three-year period 1981–83; the same law laid down that the criteria used for such estimates be approved by Government.
35. No. 80/723 of June 25 1980.
36. CIPE was established in the 1950s and consists of seventeen Ministers chaired by the Prime Minister, who normally delegates the function to the Minister for Economic Planning. CIPI was formed in 1977 and made responsible for the formulation and monitoring of policies in the manufacturing sector. It is limited to eight Ministers: Economic Planning, Treasury, Industry, State Holdings, Labour, Southern Italy, Regional Affairs and EEC policies.
37. Should there arise an insuperable conflict on a major issue the Ministry may propose the dissolution of the administrative organs of the Institute. On this whole argument, see Saraceno, *Il sistema* op. cit. pp. 50–51.
38. The review of the 1981 medium-term programme, owing to the premature interruption of the legislature, will probably be completed only two years after IRI transmitted the programme to the Ministry.

39. Elections were held on June 26 1983.
40. Over the last thirty-five years there have been six Chairmen and as many General Managers.
41. The definition is used by Professor R.F. Vancil (with reference to US practice) in an unpublished paper on management systems in the USA.
42. Planning and economic studies, Comptroller, Financial, Legal, International, Personnel and Labour problems (not negotiations), Public Relations, EDP systems, Chief Accountant, Administration.
43. There are some 1700 staff at the headquarters of the eight sectoral subholdings.
44. The time horizon of IRI's programmes is not uniform for all group sectors, as the length of the gestation period of the investment projects which will be carried out varies for different sectors; however financial projections are drawn up for a uniform, usually three-year, period for all sectoral plans.
45. A similar procedure will have been followed by the sectoral subsidiaries earlier with their own sub-subsidiaries, with IRI staff members present at the major meetings.
46. With the exclusion of the banks.
47. IRI has recently proposed to the unions new arrangements for a systematic exchange of information on the group's programmes in their formative stage, at the company as well as at the Institute level.
48. As noted earlier the delays applied also to the compensation for non-commercial costs.
49. P. Saraceno, *Il Sistema*, p. 60.

IRI GROUP MAIN ACTIVITIES (Excluding Banks)
(1982 figures)

Parent holding	Principal areas of activity	Main subsidiaries (number)	Employment at year end (thousands)	Annual Sales ($ bn.)	Planned investment 1983-1985 ($ bn.)	Net capital invested, at year end ($ bn.)	Financed with equity capital (per cent)	debt capital (per cent)	Return (interest and profit) on invested capital (per cent)
Finsider	Iron and steel; industrial plant engineering; cement	42	119.4	7.40	1.97	9.66	19	81	- 1.5
Finmeccanica	Motor vehicles; power plant; aerospace; diesel engines	33	79.8	3.23	.94	2.99	15	85	6.3
Fincantieri	Shipyards (building and repair)	13	29.4	1.53	.15	.69	20	80	- 5.0
Stet	Telecommunications; electronics	19	130.5	6.30	9.04	9.87	25	75	13.9
Sme	Food processing; confectionery; large-scale retailing	18	18.7	1.71	.20	.34	69	31	9.6
Finmare	Shipping (cargo line services and dry bulk)	11	11.2	1.42	.06	1.20	9	81	12.7
Alitalia	Air services	3	21.4	1.66	1.06	.83	28	72	2.8 (a)
Rai	Radio and Television	7	13.7	.76	.32	.05	100 (d)	-	.5 (b)
Finsiel	Software	6	2.1	.07 (c)	.02	.03	66	34	15.0
Italstat	Civil engineering; construction; toll-motorways and other infrastructures	67	28.0	1.70	2.16	2.97	20	80	13.6
Sofin	Miscellaneous	14	10.3	.46	.08	.25	26	74	7.0
Total (consolidated)		233	464.5	26.24	15.00	28.88	13	87	6.5

(a) 13.7% including capital gains on sale of aircraft.

(b) Return on equity.

(c) Excluding hardware supplied at cost of procurement.

(d) 25% on turnover.

6140 W. Germany

6

SALZGITTER AG

Ernst Pieper

1. PRELIMINARY REMARKS

The Salzgitter Group runs a wide range of industrial operations: iron and steel production and trade, shipbuilding, mechanical engineering, industrial plant construction, drilling for oil and gas and many industrial services.

With a turnover amounting to DM 11.7 billion in the business year 1981/82 and 55,000 employees, it ranks among the thirty major industrial concerns in the Federal Republic of Germany. At the helm of the Group is Salzgitter AG in Salzgitter, a holding company, whose capital shares are wholly held by the Federal Republic of Germany and are controlled by the Federal Minister of Finance in Bonn. Co-determination of the employees is based on the same understandings as in the private sector of industry. The concern has no specific statutory functions to fulfil.

However, there are some noteworthy special features in the relationship between proprietor and enterprise which are dealt with later on. In the fulfilment of its functions the enterprise has to consider directives which differ from those applicable to the private industrial sector.

Although an enterprise under government ownership, Salzgitter AG did not come into being by an act of nationalisation. Thus its origin is distinct from that of a number of other public enterprises.

2. ORIGIN OF THE INDUSTRIAL COMPLEX OF SALZGITTER

After World War I and the loss of the Lorraine ore mines, the German coal, iron and steel industries were faced with the necessity to look for new sources of ore supplies. The search for new supply potentials was supported by the Government by composition payments which were to be reinvested in deposit prospecting operations in Germany.

An outcome of this exploration work was the evidence of the existence of the largest ore deposits of the Continent, located in today's Salzgitter region, estimated from 1.5 to 2 billion tons of crude ore.

In 1936 a plan providing for the exploitation of the Salzgitter ores was submitted, which served as a basis for the foundation of the industrial complex of Salzgitter. The four-stage plan envisaged the erection of thirty-two blast furnaces as well as steel and rolling mills including all auxiliary plants. The planning was geared to a final capacity of 4 million tons of crude steel. The idea was to buy coal from the Ruhr mines to be transported over a junction canal linked with the Midland Canal in exchange for ore concentrate and steel products to be supplied to the iron and steel works and processing industries of that region.

In March 1938, construction of the first blast furnace was started; in October of the subsequent year the pig iron production began. During the war completion of the iron and steel works was given special impetus. By the end of the war, the enterprise was put under the property control of the British Military Government. By resolution of the Allies, dismantling of the industrial plants began in 1947, and were not brought to a stop until 1950.

3. DEVELOPMENT OF THE GROUP

The years thereafter were characterised by an intensive reconstruction of the iron and steel works. The enterprise employed 60,000 people, and profits were made. With a view to strengthening its economic efficiency several companies of the processing industry were added.

After around twenty years of existence − with interruptions − the enterprise had developed into a diversified coordinated industrial system and a remarkable steel processing industry. In the business year 1961/62 out of a labour force of 80,000, 42% were employed in the mining and energy sectors, 16% in the iron and steel production and one third in the processing industry. Since 1961 the concern has had the corporate name of Salzgitter AG.

In the 1960s the mining sector was losing importance, the steel sector sustained temporary shortfalls in profits, and some of the commitments proved to be considerable burdens. This was the reason why in 1967 a reorganisation of the group was initiated.

The group ceased activities with companies which proved to be too great an encumbrance. The steel commitment of the concern was considerably enlarged, followed by the merger of the former Ilseder iron and steel works in Peine and Salzgitter Hüttenwerk AG into today's Stahlwerke Peine-Salzgitter AG.

While emphasis in the Ilseder iron and steel works had traditionally been on the sectional steel sector, the Salzgitter iron and steel works produced mainly flat rolled steel, so that the two production ranges were complementary to one another.

The second sector of priority was shipbuilding, with the large shipyard of Howaldtswerke-Deutsche Werft AG, which was the result of the merger in 1968 of the two shipyards of Howaldtswerke in Hamburg and Kiel with Deutsche Werft AG.

Both commitments have proved to be decisions of great impact which caused the group to face enormous problems because of the coincidence of crisis developments in both lines today.

In the second half of the 1970s it became evident that the two main fields of the group, steel and shipbuilding, would not be going to grow but rather dwindle. Therefore, a strategy of consolidation and reorganisation had to be implemented, which took into account the worldwide changed economic setting.

This company strategy called for curtailment of capacities which were no longer profitable, modernisation and rationalisation of the remaining capacities with extensive capital investment programmes as well as the involvement in innovative growth fields. New know-how and the strengthening of research and development supplemented this strategy and enriched the performance programmes of subsidiaries in the sphere of sophisticated processing schemes.

4. PRESENT STRUCTURE OF THE GROUP

The fields of activity of most vital importance to the group today are sectors unrelated to consumption such as basic and producer-goods industries and the capital goods industry. In addition, trade and commerce and services play an ever-increasing part.

Breakdown by percent of the total turnover of the business year 1981/82 was as follows:

Steel production	23.9%
Steel trade	27.1%
Shipbuilding	8.6%
Foundries	2.2%
Rolling stock construction	2.4%
Machinery and steel construction	6.8%
Large-scale plant construction	10.7%
Energy	3.9%
Other trade and commerce	8.0%
Others	6.4%

Today the Holding is divided into four business lines: steel; ship-building; processing; and large-scale plant construction and energy.

4.1 *Business line: steel*

This line comprises the steel interests of the group, i.e. Stahlwerke Peine-Salzgitter AG (P + S) and its subsidiaries.

The steel sector is still highly crucial to the destiny of the concern. At present 58% of the total turnover is achieved in this sector; 36% of the group labour force is employed in this line. In the business year 1981/82 P + S had a share in the crude steel production of the Federal Republic of Germany, with an output amounting to 3.8 million tons, of nearly 10%.

Stahlwerke Peine-Salzgitter AG, like the iron and steel works in other countries of the traditional steel areas in Europe, is facing the challenge to accommodate to structural changes within the international steel industry.

Emphasis is laid by the European steel producers on reducing the existing excess capacities. P + S makes its contribution to this end. The last to be shut down was a complete blast furnace plant of the former Ilseder iron and steel works. In addition, considerable capital investment went into the reconstruction and modernisation of the works. Meanwhile, about 80% of the crude steel production is continuously cast at reasonable cost. As things stand today, further measures aimed at capacity adjustments will be inevitable.

The most important subsidiary of Stahlwerke Peine-Salzgitter AG is Salzgitter Stahl GmbH (STH) in Düsseldorf, which trades worldwide with steel and rolling mill products as well as steel pipes. Moreover, STH distributes a great number of products of other companies of the group and is intended to grow into the role of a trade organization.

4.2 *Business line: shipbuilding*

This line comprises the group's activities in the shipbuilding and ship-building related sectors: Howaldtswerke–Deutsche Werft AG (HDW) with shipyards in Hamburg and Kiel as well as their subsidiaries.

HDW is the largest shipbuilder in Europe, running the whole gamut of the branch, from merchant vessels of all types and marine vessels (ocean-going ships and submarines) to the offshore, machinery and mechanical engineering field, as well as a remarkable repair business. HDW's share in the total shipbuilding volume of the Federal Republic of Germany, including the marine vessels, accounts for about a quarter; in the repair and conversion business the market share is nearly 20%. The HDW shipyards employ just one-fifth of the total dockyard labour force in the Federal Republic of Germany.

As in the steel industry, the shipbuilding sector is suffering from worldwide excess capacity and from the subsidies in the competing countries which are in part markedly higher. Over and above this, there are considerable cost disadvantages in comparison with the shipbuilders in the Far East, some of which are still expanding. With a view to an adjustment to the changing market situation, HDW has for years pursued a company policy aimed at a reduction primarily of the merchant shipbuilding sector. This is to be offset by including production lines having little or no connection with shipbuilding, such as are dealt with by the HDW subsidiaries. Yet, for the purpose of securing the survival of HDW, an adjustment strategy had to be decided upon in the spring of 1983 providing for a reduction of the labour force by 4,000 people.

HAGENUK GmbH, with some 1,500 people on the payroll, is a manufacturer of radio communication systems for merchant ships and marine vehicles offering in its communication line a wide variety of telephone sets and extension sets.

HDW Elektronik GmbH with nearly 300 employees is a company specialising in the production of cable testing and control instruments as well as systems for ship automation.

4.3 *Business line: processing*

In the processing business line, employing 27% of the group labour force, 19% of the group turnover is achieved. The original dedication was to the processing of steel; the present-day shape of this line is widely diversified. The processing sector includes foundries, steel construction, mechanical engineering, wagon construction, building industry, heating, air-conditioning and ventilation, acoustics and noise abatement technology, and pollution control.

The range of products of these companies encompasses, for instance, motor blocks and gearbox cases made of cast iron, cylinder heads of aluminium, large-space wagons for the Intercity service of the German Federal Railways, sound-absorbing materials for passenger cars, deep-well pump gears, construction cranes, prefabricated garages, and many others. Here efforts are constantly directed towards product innovations with a view to filling market gaps. The last accomplishment was the introduction of an innovative low temperature heater.

Luitpoldhütte AG (LHA) in Amberg and Fronberg, and Kloth-Senking Metallgießerei GmbH in Hildesheim are the foundries of the concern. They employ respectively 1,700 and 800 people. There have been gradual enlargements of production ranges in these companies, as a sequel to changes in the demand structure. SMAG illustrates this in particular. Besides, strains in domestic markets have intensified the involvement of the companies in export sales, e.g., Linke-Hofmann-Busch GmbH.

More than 20% of the export sales of German industry consist of mechanical engineering products. Correspondingly the export intensity of this branch is higher than average, reaching at present nearly 60%.

The group's most important mechanical engineering companies are Salzgitter Maschinen und Anlagen AG (SMAG), Peiner Maschinen-und Schraubenwerke AG (PMS), Kocks GmbH, and Wolf Klimatechnik GmbH.

The requirements of the customers in the mechanical engineering sector are changing. There is a shift within the bundle of capital goods of equipment investments in favour of electrotechnical capital goods and to the detriment of specific mechanical engineering products. Thus the future of mechanical engineering lies in the interface of mechanics and electronics. Here are substantial innovation reserves open to being used, a task to which the mechanical engineering companies of the group are dedicated.

4.4 Business line: large-scale plant construction and energy

In the line of large-scale plant construction and energy there are about 12% on the payroll, mainly engineers, constructors, and technicians.

The German industrial large-scale plant construction sector has experienced a notable upsurge since the beginning of the 1970s. This field of activity is, in terms of its export share of 90%, an important export line of German industry. The Salzgitter Group is represented in this branch by Salzgitter Industriebau GmbH, the Dr C. Otto Group, Gg. Noell GmbH, and LGA Gastechnik GmbH.

Salzgitter Consult GmbH has specialised in development projects in Third World countries. The company gained a reputation in connection with the construction of one of the largest irrigation plants of the globe, the Tinajones Project situated in the north of Peru.

The Salzgitter Group's export turnover amounted in the business

year 1981/82 to DM3.2 billion, which corresponds to around 35%
of the group's total external sales. We are represented in thirty-eight
countries with offices, establishments, and associated companies.

In terms of turnover, the most important business partners are,
besides the EEC members, the USA, and the oil exporting countries,
the COMECON countries headed by the USSR and the GDR. A
natural location advantage of the Salzgitter Group is its proximity
to the COMECON countries.

Abroad the group has some 3000 employees, which is only 5% of
the total crew on the payroll. The most significant foreign interests
are the International Marine Services in Dubai active for the offshore
oil wells in the Arab Gulf, Feralloy in Chicago, a company of the steel
trading and steel processing line, as well as Otto India Ltd., essentially
engaged in the engineering and the construction of coking plants and
gas production plants in the Indian subcontinent.

5. STRUCTURE AND FUNCTIONS OF THE HOLDING COMPANY

Salzgitter AG is the holding company of the Salzgitter Group.
Salzgitter AG is, above all, concerned with adjusting the structure
of the group to the requirements of the market and with assuming
management functions and performing services on various levels:

- As a rule, the members of the Managing Board of Salzgitter AG
  take part as chairmen in the supervisory and advisory boards of
  the subsidiaries. In this way, the holding company exerts an
  influence on the appointment and recall of executive officers of
  the companies as well as on all subjects handled by the supervisory
  board, such as the investment policy of a company.
- By virtue of publishing intercompany directives and recommendations provision is made for uniform practices concerning
  specific regulations within the group of companies, including, for
  example, directions for accounting and reporting.
- A complex in-group control system with supervising functions in
  the fields of accounting, controlling, auditing, and several-years-
  ahead planning helps to discern and avoid misleading developments.
- Further, the divisions of Salzgitter AG assist the companies of the
  group directly with services, e.g., in the sphere of research and
  development, financing, and advice in tax and legal affairs.

In addition to these management functions, which are similar to those
of the majority of holding companies in industry, Salzgitter AG

assumes on behalf of the companies of the group specific management and control functions for the proprietor, which are partly statutory and therefore clearly defined in the 'Haushaltsgrundsätzegesetz' (Budget and Accounting Act) and in the Federal Budget Regulations.

This includes the following major provisions making it binding on Salzgitter AG to ensure that in any case where direct and indirect interests of the group exceed a 50% share:

- within the scope of the general audits the regularity of the management must also be examined;
- the auditors be instructed to set forth in their reports the development of the financial condition and the earnings base as well as the liquidity and profitability, loss-making operations pointing out reasons for a loss;
- the audit reports be submitted to the Federal Minister of Finance.

Pursuant to a formal obligation of Salzgitter AG, the auditors are bound within the scope of these regulations to make special reports concerning the remuneration of the managers and the members of the supervisory boards and to inform the Federal Minister of Finance accordingly.

Finally, the 'Bundesrechnungshof' (Federal Court of Auditors) may get direct information from the companies of the group, and to this effect may have access to the company, the books and the documents of the enterprise.

By virtue of these provisions, the control functions which Salzgitter AG is liable to perform go beyond the control possibilities provided for in the company law of the Federal Republic of Germany for joint-stock companies and/or the publicity commitments imposed on them.

According to the business rules of the Managing Board, the members are jointly responsible for the overall management. Therefore, the Managing Board of Salzgitter AG is a body organised on the collegial principle. The whole of the Managing Board is responsible for any and all of the fundamental questions as well as for affairs of substantial impact, including proceedings calling for authorisation to be given by the Supervisory Board or the Federal Minister of Finance.

Salzgitter AG is divided into nine divisions. Four divisions are responsible for the four business lines of the concern, thus looking after the companies of the group. The management function the Board Member has in the respective company of the group is generally covered by his being at the same time Chairman of the Supervisory Board of the respective company of the group. The Managing

Directors of the business lines are not directly responsible for the results, they rather exert, within the scope of their supervisory activity, an influence on the strategic management of the companies of the Salzgitter Group.

Five divisions are the so-called Central Departments responsible for cross-section tasks; they fulfil functions for the whole concern. These are the Central Departments of Chairman of the Managing Board, Finance, Research/Development and Economics, Labour Management, as well as Planning and Structure of the group.

The Central Department of the Chairman of the Managing Board covers the general business policy, coordination of the activity of the Managing Board, Public Relations, personnel matters of the executive officers of the group as well as the interface with the Supervisory Board and the Ministries. For this purpose, the General Secretariat and the 'Executive Officers' Personnel Division and also the Press and Information Division are under its control.

The Central Department of Finance accounts for the financial affairs of the group as well as for controlling and accounting, for central statistical inquiries and evaluations, for insurance matters, organisation, auditing, and for legal, tax, and real estate affairs. Seven divisions are assigned to this central Department.

The tasks of the Central Department of Research/Development and Economics include the coordination of research and development programmes within the concern, support of the subsidiaries in the development of new technologies, testing of the application of new technical processes and materials, central technical data and documentation, coordination of patent and licence affairs, and coordination of the administrative channels in the overall field of research and development. Evaluation of the global and single-branch developments and prospects with a view to the group interests, market analyses and matters concerning infrastructure are dealt with by the Economics Division. In addition to the divisions of Research/Development and Economics this Central Department covers the Postal Service and Telecommunications, whose function is to co-ordinate the use of communication systems of the subsidiaries.

The Central Department of Labour Management is headed by the Director of Labour Relations as provided for by the Coal and Steel Codetermination Supplemental Act. The Director of Labour Relations is responsible for personnel matters of the staff of Salzgitter AG with the exception of the executive managers and the fully authorised officers. Further responsibilities of the Director of Labour Relations refer to the coordination of the following spheres of functions in the group: retirement pension, scholarships, collective bargaining, work regulations, shop agreements, labour–management relations, personnel and education planning, housing, staff information, labour management, ergonomics, protective labour conditions, employee suggestion scheme, works sanitary conditions, and preventive medicine as well as social services of the company's social health insurance, and the catering system. The Personnel and Labour Management Divisions, which are in charge of these tasks, are under the control of the Director of Labour Relations.

In the Central Department of Planning and Structure principles and suggestions for setting up short-term, medium-term and long-term targets of the group are worked out, analyses prepared and partial plans coordinated. Furthermore, that Central Department includes the planning and control of investments as well as their coordination on a group level. The Central Department is involved in the implementation of structural measures such as organisation, production ranges, participations, sales and cost structures. The division of Planning and Industrial Management is within its competence.

The organisation of the Holding in its functional role featured by nine divisions is not reflected on the personnel side.

On this understanding, the Chairman of the Managing Board, in addition to his Central Department competence, is responsible for the business lines of steel and shipbuilding.

Each Board Member has control of two other business lines. The Board Member, who is responsible for the business line of large-scale plant construction and energy, is at the same time in charge of the coordination of sales and purchase and advertising in the whole group.

For the rest of the Central Departments one Board Member each is responsible, the Financial Directors and the Director of Labour Relations as Chairmen of the Supervisory Boards being in addition responsible for subsidiaries – the Financial Directors for Salzgitter Versicherungsdienst GmbH (Insurance Company), and Salzgitter Güterverwaltung GmbH (Land Administration), the Director of Labour Relations for Salzgitter Wohnungs-AG (Housing Company), and Salzgitter Wirtschaftsbetriebe GmbH (Catering Company).

Altogether the group is led by the Chairman of the Managing Board and six Members of the Managing Board.

The tasks of the Divisions of Salzgitter AG are derived from their provinces described in broad outline as follows:

- Consultation of the Managing Board of Salzgitter AG in its management functions.
- Performance of typical central group functions. For example, the Accounting Division prepares the consolidated balance sheet and issues the Annual Report. The Finance Division allocates funds to the subsidiaries suggesting at the same time investment possibilities; it undertakes similar functions for the subsidiaries as those performed by a bank. The Press and Information Division communicates with press, radio, and television and other institutions and groups which are of relevance to the Public Relations sector. The Advertising Department prepares the advertising formula for the group and provides for its presence at international trade fairs.
- Services for the subsidiaries. For instance, the Legal Department deals with legal matters for subsidiaries. Other divisions which render services are Research and Development, Postal and Telecommunications Service, and the Tax Division.
- Conduct of the Salzgitter AG company's own affairs, e.g. its own accounting or personnel organisation, property management, etc.

For services rendered by the Holding, lump-sum management fees are charged by a fixed code.

There is a total of around 570 people on the payroll of the holding company, of whom nearly 200 are employed in the Postal and Telecommunications Service, property management and in branch offices, so that around 370 employees are engaged in the actual management of the group. At present efforts are under way to streamline and reorganise the Holding.

6. ORGANS, CONTROL, CODETERMINATION

Salzgitter AG as an enterprise in public ownership, under the legal form of private law, is subject to the same control instruments and the same organs set forth in the company law as are provided for the private sector of industry.

Hence the company has articles of association defining essentially the object of the company, determining the amount of the capital stock (at present amounting to DM425 million), stipulating the responsibilities of the Managing Board, stating the nature and volume of the transactions subject to consent, and containing the regulations prevailing for the Supervisory Board and the General Meeting.

In contrast to the private industrial sector, the Federal Court of

Auditors is granted, in addition to the other bodies, wide-ranging control possibilities. According to the Basic Constitutional Law of the Federal Republic of Germany, the competence of the Federal Court of Auditors includes the audit of accounting, profitability and regularity of the budget and economic management of the Federal Government. This audit obligation, according to the Federal Budget Regulations and the Budget and Accounting Act, also refers to public activity for private law enterprises and therefore also to Salzgitter AG. The result of the audit is to be summarised in annual comments to be passed to the 'Bundestag', 'Bundesrat', and the Federal Government; and these are made accessible to the public as parliamentary publications. In the audit comments special mention is to be made of any objections of substance, and of measures recommended for the future.

Special stress is laid by the Federal Court of Auditors in its audits on acquisitions, foundations and mergers. By virtue of the Federal Budget Regulations, the acquisition of a direct federal participation, for instance, is dependent on the existence of a vital public interest, for which evidence has to be furnished that the purpose envisaged cannot be achieved in another more convenient and more economical way. This provision for the industrial participation policy of the Government is liable, in the case of a managerial-conducted participation policy, to come to a point where conflicts arise between public and entrepreneurial interests.

The comments of the Federal Court of Auditors constitute an auxiliary means for the parliamentary control of the industrial activity of the Federal Republic of Germany. These are referred to the Budget Committee, as a preparatory resolution body, to be considered in its sub-committee, the Auditing Committee, in the presence of Government representatives and members of the Federal Court of Auditors.

Thus it becomes apparent to what extent Salzgitter AG is not only subjected to additional public control but also to increasing publicity.

The General Meeting of Salzgitter AG, although, by virtue of the Companies Act, defined in the same way as private stock corporations, is not comparable with that of private shareholders. An interest majority — otherwise the rule — is not given to the proprietor, since the Federal Republic of Germany, represented by the Federal Minister of Finance, acts as an institution.

For Salzgitter AG the competent department in the Federal Ministry of Finance is the Industrial Federal Property Division. In certain cases it exercises consent and/or control functions, particularly in the event of changes in interests and personnel measures in the managements of vital companies.

Apart from this, the Federal Minister of Economic Affairs, too, has the power to exercise control over Salzgitter AG as far as the politico-economic and industrial interest of the Government is concerned.

In performing his control functions, the Minister of Economic Affairs makes use of the so-called *Spiegelreferat* (counterpart division), which corresponds to the relevant department in the Federal Ministry of Finance.

Therefore, Salzgitter AG is faced, on the proprietor's side, with two Ministries as controlling bodies. However, this interest control of the Government does not include any local auditing right as conceded to the Federal Court of Auditors by virtue of the Budget and Accounting Act, the Federal Budget Regulations and the articles of association of Salzgitter AG. Thus it is not authorised to carry out auditing on its own but has to rely on documentation submitted by third parties.

Another peculiarity in the interest control by the proprietor which deserves to be stressed is the fact that its function includes not only the actual control and supervision of Salzgitter AG but also the attendance of officers with supervisory mandates in all vital subsidiaries. This gives both Ministries the possibility of using direct influence on the preparation of decisions in the management policy.

The Supervisory Board of Salzgitter AG is composed in line with the provisions of the Coal and Steel Codetermination Supplemental Act of 1956. The most important regulation of this Act is the parity of the proprietor and employee-representatives in the Supervisory Board, i.e. ten representatives of the proprietor are faced with ten representatives of the group labour force and of the trade unions. The twenty-first member of the supervisory board is the so-called 'neutral man' whose vote turns the scale in stalemate situations. The 'neutral man' may not at the same time be chairman of the Supervisory Board.

The Federal Minister himself is, by virtue of the Federal Minister Law, not allowed to be a member of any Supervisory Board. In compliance with the Federal Budget Regulations, the Government is obliged to secure an adequate control over a Supervisory Board.

Appointments to Supervisory Boards are determined by the 'directives for the appointment of personalities to supervisory boards and other controlling bodies as well as to managing boards/managements of government-owned enterprises and other institutions as far as the Government is in control'. The intention is that, while the Government retains adequate control, an excessive representation by individual departments should be avoided and that, on the other hand, participation of conversant representatives of the industry should be secured.

In the present composition of the Supervisory Board of Salzgitter AG, this second point is particularly obvious: of the ten representatives on the proprietor side only two refer to the public sector, one being the Minister of Economics and Transport of Lower Saxony, the other a high official of the Federal Ministry of Economics. The other eight members hold top positions in the private sector of industry.

Consideration of regional interests — in the Supervisory Board of Salzgitter AG secured by the Minister of Economic Affairs of Lower Saxony — is also given in the other companies of the Salzgitter Group, and this not only in the event of a Federal land holding a financial interest in an enterprise. The Free State of Bavaria holds an interest with a blocking minority in Luitpoldhütte AG in Amberg/Bavaria and the land of Schleswig-Holstein holds also a blocking minority in Howaldtswerke-Deutsche Werft AG Hamburg and Kiel.

In the companies of the Salzgitter group occur all codetermination versions as provided for by the German law for industrial enterprises: The Coal and Steel Codetermination Act of 1951, the Employees' Representation Act of 1952, the Coal and Steel Codetermination Supplemental Act of 1956, and the Codetermination Act of 1976.

The Codetermination Act of 1976 is applied to joint-stock companies with as a rule more than 2000 people (employed). It is applicable in the Salzgitter Group to Linke-Hofmann-Busch GmbH, Salzgitter Maschinen und Anlagen AG, and to Howaldtswerke-Deutsche Werft AG Hamburg and Kiel.

Stahlwerke Peine-Salzgitter AG and Luitpoldhütte AG are subject to the Codetermination Act of the employees in the Supervisory Boards and the Managing Boards of the enterprises of the mining and the iron and steel producing industries, i.e., the Coal and Steel Codetermination Act, and Salzgitter AG is subject to the Coal and Steel Codetermination Supplemental Act of 1956.

Other companies fall within the province of the Employees' Representation Act of 1952 providing — with reservations — a one-third participation of the employees in the Supervisory Boards and by-passing the institution of a Director of Labour Relations.

The scope of experience the Salzgitter Group has gained with codetermination since 1951 is manifold, extending from unanimous vote to crucial vote.

7. FUNCTIONS AS A PUBLIC ENTERPRISE

At the time of its foundation in the 1930s and by the time of its reconstruction in the 1950s, the Salzgitter Group was vested with a public mission. The Salzgitter Group today has no longer to fulfil any clearly defined public assignment. However, one of its most vital functions is certainly still to make the jobs secure for a long-range time ahead in a region which, due to its situation near the border with the GDR and on the east edge of the European market, is lacking in strength in its economic structure.

About half of the 55,000 employees of the concern live and work in the structurally less fortunate area of South-east Lower Saxony; but also most of the other companies of the Salzgitter Group are located on the eastern edge of the European Community. Three-quarters of the group workplaces are in a fringe situation, stretching from the land of Schleswig-Holstein in the north of the Federal Republic of Germany with the Kieler shipyards to Bavaria in the south with the foundries in Upper Palatinate.

During the past ten years the Salzgitter Group invested more than DM4 billion in plants and constructions, most of these investments having been made in the fringe areas of Kiel, Peine, Salzgitter, Hildesheim, Goslar, and Amberg. A total of more than 80% of the group's capital expenditure went into these regions.

Hence the investment activities and projects of the concern are largely in line with the aims of the Government and the *Länder* as defined in the joint edition *Improvement of the Regional Economic Structure*. They are a substantial contribution to their achievement.

A similar effect in terms of increasing the economic strength of the region stems from the large-scale plant export of the concern. For instance, various companies from the region were involved as sub-contractors in the construction of the air terminal Scheremetjewo II in Moscow. The majority of these enterprises would hardly be in a position to canvas export orders of the kind on their own.

In the long term, these targets of regional policy can only be attained if in addition to workplaces on-the-job training facilities are offered correspondingly. The Federal Government expects of public enterprises an example-setting function with a view to providing on-the-job training facilities. Vocational training policy has always been considered by the concern to be of paramount importance to a company committed to overall social interests.

On the understanding that a depopulation of the fringe area along the frontier with the GDR and a migration from structurally less fortunate regions of, above all, young people can be met only with an ongoing training policy, the training scheme of the Salzgitter Group – which is generally recognised to be excellent – is designed so as to offer more apprenticeships than are needed to cover the group's own requirements. For the last decade the excess of training places has been about 20%.

Hence the training scheme of the concern is a contribution to the longer-term labour policy and, with its inherent strengthening of the regional labour force potential in terms of quantity and quality, creates vital prerequisites for pursuing a promising regional economic policy within the framework of trade promotion programmes sponsored by the Government, the *Länder* and the municipalities.

This, however, is not the original management assignment for the concern. The typical criteria of the enterprise economy also prevail in the Salzgitter Group. No enterprise which is subject to the rules of a market economy system can in the long run conceivably pursue aims unrelated to company objectives without jeopardising its existence.

The Salzgitter Group will increase its commitment in future – even more than in the past – to the field of development and application of environmental technologies. The group of companies already possesses high-grade know-how in this ever-growing market. In this way, the concern will contribute to curbing the persistent great environmental impact commonly considered to be a socio-political problem in the Federal Republic of Germany.

Based on the experience of the group, it can be stated that in a well-functioning market system the principle is true, also for a public enterprise, that the proprietors, the employees, and the customers will achieve the best results if the company strives for its maximum long-term profit while competing with other firms. It is this attitude alone – based on a business management approach – that ensures that costs will be lowest, products cheapest, productivity highest and, as a result, jobs most secure.

BIBLIOGRAPHY

Hans Birnbaum, *Stahljahre. Unternehmer in unruhiger Zeit* (Düsseldorf – Wien, 1980).
Klaus Broichhausen und Klaus Wiborg, *Kaufherren und Konzerne im deutschen Norden. Hanseaten und Hannoveraner zwischen Wolfsburg und Waterkant* (Stuttgart, 1974).

Geschäftsberichte der Salzgitter AG, diverse Jahrgänge.

Kontrolle öffentlicher Unternehmen, 2. Vol., Schriftenreihe der Gesellschaft für öffentliche Wirtschaft und Gemeinwirtschaft, Heft 17 (Baden-Baden, 1980).

Ernst Pieper, 'Erfahrungen in der Führung öffentlicher Verwaltung und öffentlicher Unternehmen', in: *Zeitschrift für öffentliche und gemeinwirtschaftliche Unternehmen* (1978).

Matthias Riedel, *Vorgeschichte, Entstehung und Demontage der Reichswerke im Salzgittergebiet* (Düsseldorf, 1967).

6140
6150
US
author

131 — 163

THE PORT AUTHORITY OF NEW YORK AND NEW JERSEY*

TABLE OF CONTENTS

* Permission to reproduce this article given by Louis J. Gambaccini, Assistant Executive Director and Director of Administration, The Port Authority of New York and New Jersey.
© Port Authority of New York and New Jersey (1983).

7

THE PORT AUTHORITY OF NEW YORK
AND NEW JERSEY

EVENTS LEADING TO THE CREATION OF THE PORT AUTHORITY

Nearly five thousand feet above sea level, in a tiny New York State lake called Tear-of-the-Clouds, rises one of the most important rivers in the United States. Flowing almost straight south for three hundred miles, the Hudson River empties into the Atlantic Ocean, where its excellent natural harbor served to determine the site of New York City. Serving the states of New York and New Jersey, and providing the largest port in the United States, the 'river in the middle' has also created its share of jurisdictional crises — for within its water lies the boundary line between the two states.

One of the earliest crises occurred in 1824 when a monopoly granted by the State of New York for navigation in the New York harbor was successfully challenged in the courts. So significant was the outcome, even in those days, that by 1825 the number of steamboats plying in and out of New York harbor increased from 6 to 43. In 1834, following another dispute, a treaty between New York and New Jersey finally established the center of the Hudson River as the boundary between the two states. New York retained jurisdiction over the waters, while New Jersey received title to all land beneath the water on its side of the boundary line, with exclusive jurisdiction over wharves, docks, and improvements upon her shores. The treaty, then, made an important distinction between sovereignty and jurisdiction, as will be seen again later on.

In the fifteen or so years that followed, the New York side of the port experienced rapid population and commercial growth, while the New Jersey portion remained much as it was. The growth of railroading after 1850 changed the economic picture for New Jersey. The railroads developed large terminals on the river's west boundary (New Jersey side) with extensive carfloating, lighterage, and ferry service to New York.

With increased realization of the importance of port facilities to the area, in 1911 each state appointed a three-man commission to investigate the problem of developing the port. The two commissions, however, concentrated primarily on problems having to do with their own state's port facilities, and the large problem of planning a unified and coordinated port was obscured.

A successor board to the New Jersey commission later enlarged the problem by charging that existing railroad rates, which were the same from inland to all parts of the port area, discriminated against New Jersey. The board contended that New Jersey was entitled to lower shipping rates because of a more efficient operation which did not entail the additional cost, delay, breakage, and so on, associated with lightering goods across the river. In May, 1916, charges to this effect were filed with the Interstate Commerce Commission. The ICC denied a rate adjustment on the grounds 'that historically, geographically, and commercially, New York and the industrial district in the northern part of the State of New Jersey constituted a single community'. The decision went on to say that only cooperation and initiative, and not division and competition, would bring about the improvements and benefits sought by the complainants.

In New York meanwhile, members of the Chamber of Commerce, with interests on both sides of the Hudson, worked hard to reconcile the various interests. New Jersey's newly elected governor, Walter Edge, joined in, stating 'I want to see industrial New York and industrial New Jersey cooperating ... I would like to see a joint commission appointed representing the two states ... with one thought that this responsibility is to develop the port of New York.'

In 1917, bills which would achieve that effect were introduced in both state legislatures, and two commissions were created to act jointly in recommending policies for the development of the common harbor. Breaking with all tradition, the commissioners organized themselves into a single body which they called the New York, New Jersey Port and Harbor Development Commission. A year later, in its preliminary report, the commission recommended a comprehensive development scheme for the entire port area, and another year later the committee recommended that a permanent agency be created to accomplish this job.

THE BI-STATE COMPACT*

The same principle observed in the treaty of 1834, that of distinguishing between sovereignty and jurisdiction, provided the framework for establishing a public corporation exercising jurisdiction by compact under the sovereignty of each state. The recommendation for a bi-state compact which first emerged in late 1918, underwent a series of revisions over a two year period. In the course of these revisions, the concepts emerged of establishing an agency which would not have any regulatory powers, but which would be empowered to develop proposals that could then be approved by the elected representatives of the two States, following which the agency would transform these proposals into specific programs for action.

Earlier drafts of the compact provided for appointment of commissioners by the two governors, but New York City partisans insisted on the City's right to fill two of New York's three positions. Each proposed compromise was rejected by one side or the other until 1921, when both States enacted legislation providing for the creation of The Port of New York Authority, to be governed by 3 commissioners (later increased to 6) from each state, appointed by the governors of New York and New Jersey with the consent of the respective state senates. An important stipulation by the two States was that the new Authority must be completely self-supporting; it would not have the power to tax, neither would it have the right to pledge the credit of either State without specific approval by both state legislatures. This provision forced the agency to undertake projects which, taken in toto, had to be self-supporting.

Under the terms of the Compact, the Port Authority was charged with two vital tasks, developing terminal and transportation facilities in the port of New York, and promoting trade and commerce within what was called the 'Port District', an area roughly described as falling within a radius of 25 miles of the Statue of Liberty. However, the Compact also provided in Article VI that 'the Port Authority shall have such additional powers and duties as may hereafter be delegated to or imposed upon it from time to time by the action of the legislature of either state concurred in by the legislature of the other.' This provision has made possible projects which could not have been foreseen by the compact's authors in 1921. In addition the Authority is encouraged in Article XII to 'make recommendations to the legislatures of the two states ... based upon study and analysis ... for the better conduct

---

* A copy of the Bi-State Compact creating the Port of New York Authority is shown in Appendix I.

of the commerce passing in and through the Port of New York, the increase and improvement of transportation and terminal facilities therein; and the more economical and expeditious handling of such commerce.'

This was an invitation to creative, entrepreneurial thinking which the Port Authority has always been quick to grasp — especially in recent years. The World Trade Center and Teleport* projects exemplify this creativity, which is one of the prime strengths of the Authority.

Since 1921, the Port Authority has built or acquired, and today operates, four interstate bridges, two interstate tunnels, three airports, two heliports, seven marine terminals, two bus terminals, a truck terminal, a World Trade Center and is developing three industrial parks. In 1962, the Port Authority acquired a rail rapid transit system between New York City and several communities in nearby New Jersey, which it operates through a subsidiary, the Port Authority Trans-Hudson Corporation. In 1970, the Authority opened The World Trade Center, a major addition to the port's facilities for servicing international trade. This project ranks with J. F. Kennedy Airport as one of the Authority's most ambitious and successful projects and houses the Authority's headquarters within its 10 million square feet of office space.

BOARD OF COMMISSIONERS

A suggestion that the Commissioners be paid annual salaries was rejected by members of the New York, New Jersey Port and Harbor Development Commission, who insisted that the Port Authority's Commissioners serve without compensation. It was strongly felt that a commitment to public service should be both motivation and reward for the Port Authority Commissioners. When the Compact was formally adopted in 1921, it provided for five-year terms of office (later changed to six-year terms) to expire in a staggered pattern, and no compensation for the Commissioners. In the past, Commissioners have generally been drawn from successful executives in the financial business and legal communities; this ensured a highly competent board which was somewhat conservative in its outlook. In recent years, commissioners have had more diversified backgrounds, including a number of people with public service experience.

---

* A facility to provide space for an electronic data processing center in conjunction with a ground station for satellite communication being constructed in the 1980s by the Port Authority's World Trade Department.

The original six-person Board of Commissioners was charged by the Compact with directing the activities of the Port Authority, and with legal responsibility for all actions taken by the organization. The Compact specifically authorized the Commissioners to elect a Chairman and Vice-Chairman from among their ranks, and to make all such appointments necessary to conduct the business of the Authority.

The Chairman, according to the Compact, was directed to preside over meetings of the Board, sign official documents, and exercise general supervision over business and affairs of the Port Authority. In fact, the Chairman also serves as spokesperson of the Port Authority, in conferences with the governors and other public executives, and represents the Port Authority at major civic events, and has legal responsibility for all actions taken by the organization. The Vice-Chairman, who was directed to perform the duties of Chairman in the latter's absence, has traditionally been from the other state, and often acts as spokesperson and liaison with officials from his or her home state. Both the Chairman and Vice-Chairman were designated in the Compact as ex-officio members of all Committees of the Board.

ORGANIZATION OF THE BOARD

The need for Committees of the Board was evident from the very start. Today, the Executive Director is the operating head of the organization. However, in the early days of the Authority, there was no need for a full time executive officer, and the Commissioners themselves were responsible for administration, as well as policy making. In order to carry out all of their responsibilities, the Commissioners found it necessary to divide the work into manageable pieces, and each Commissioner took personal responsibility for particular segments of the work of the organization.

When the position of General Manager (forerunner of Executive Director) was created, the Commissioners were able to take a less active role in administration, but they continued to rely on the Committee structure for policy review. This process intensified as a result of acquisition by the Port Authority of the Holland Tunnel. This first public facility to span the Hudson River had been built by two individual State Commissions, one each from New York and New Jersey, each with its own offices, officers and policies. The Port Authority proposed to the two State legislatures in 1930 that it acquire the Holland Tunnel and absorb the two state tunnel commissions, so as to be able to provide comprehensive planning and coordinated service for crossing the Hudson. In both States, bills which designated the

Port Authority as the agency to purchase and operate the tunnel were enacted into law. This legislation abolished the two tunnel commissions and amended the compact to provide for a Board of twelve Commissioners (6 appointed by the Governor of each state) with six-year overlapping terms. The continuance of the policy of having staggered terms of reasonably long duration is significant because it provides continuity in a constantly changing environment.

The legislation directed the Board to meet promptly to organize to carry out its new responsibility. Approximately a dozen committees of the Board were created soon after.

Functions of the new committees were closely related to both the programs and the activities with which the Port Authority had been concerned throughout the 1920s. There were separate committees established for personnel, publicity, finance, purchasing, and insurance. Other committees had the responsibility for bridge construction, tunnel construction, marine terminals, and freight terminals. There were also separate committees for municipal activities (responsible for arrangements between the Port Authority and the municipalities in which it exercised jurisdiction), operations (to keep abreast of facility operations) and port protection (charged with responsibility for Port Authority appearances before regulatory agencies). There was even a program and work committee, whose assignment it was to recommend 'such programs as will enable the Port Authority to perform its duties effectively, in due relation to their order of importance.'

The committee structure evolved slowly. Responsibility for all terminals – marine, rail, freight, and other – was consolidated in one committee, another was made responsible for all Port Authority construction projects, regardless of type.

A decade later, however, the Port Authority was operating a number of facilities, and experience gained during the years of growth pointed up the need for reorganizing the workload of the Board of Commissioners. Some committees had but little activity, while others were carrying much more of a burden than was anticipated, and the multiplicity of the committee structure caused divided responsibility on almost any subject.

In 1943, the Board reorganized into four standing committees (Port Planning, Finance, Construction, and Operations), each of which corresponded roughly with the then major departments of the Port Authority. For nearly forty years thereafter, the committee organization of the Board remained unchanged until 1981, when the Audit Committee was created. Briefly, committee responsibilities are as follows:

- The Committee on Port Planning keeps informed of the duties
  of the Port Authority and the needs of the Port District, and
  authorizes or recommends to the full Board actions concerning
  terminal and transportation facilities. The Committee also authorizes agency appearances before courts, boards and commissions,
  to protect the interest of commerce in the port district.
- The Committee on Finance considers all questions relating to the
  organization's financial affairs, including selection of depositories
  for Port Authority funds, investment of Port Authority funds,
  issuance and retirement of Port Authority bonds, acquisition of
  assurance policies, and insurance of sound and prudent fiscal
  policies.
- The Committee on Construction has general supervision over all
  construction and demolition contracts, and the acquisition of real
  property.
- The Committee on Operations is responsible for developing and
  reviewing policies governing the operations of the Port Authority,
  and has general supervision over the operation and maintenance
  of all facilities, including personnel transactions, procurement,
  and operating standards.
- The Audit Committee has general supervision over the books and
  accounts of the Port Authority and the auditing of the books and
  accounts by internal auditors (the Audit Department) and independent public accountants hired by the Authority.

Note, however, that the Port Authority has changed drastically
from its pre-World War II operations; by 1965 investment in facilities
soared to more than $1.5 billion from less than $250 million in 1943.
At the end of 1981 investment in facilities was $4.4 billion, an aston-
ishing and gratifying record of growth (see Appendix II). To keep pace
with its increased public responsibility, in 1952 the Port Authority's
staff underwent a major reorganization (see below, pages 143–5).
The Board, however, did not find it necessary to change the assign-
ments and responsibilities of its committees.

Not only has the basic structure of the Board remained the same
since 1943, but its size and character did not change in any significant
way between 1930 and 1962, at which time the Hudson and Manhattan
Railroad was acquired.

The Port Authority's acquisition of the Hudson and Manhattan
Railroad is a special case and represents an innovation in U.S. public
enterprise. Prior to the acquisition of the Hudson and Manhattan
Railroad, the Commissioners of the Port Authority arranged to have

a careful study made of a series of alternative ways in which this new enterprise could be most efficiently and effectively managed. It was finally decided by the Commissioners that the best method would be to establish a wholly-owned subsidiary corporation, to be known as the Port Authority Trans-Hudson Corporation (PATH). The Board of Directors of the Corporation would be the Commissioners of the Port Authority, and the Executive Director of the Port Authority would be the President of the Corporation. Accordingly, the legislation that was passed by the two States authorized the commissioners to establish this subsidiary corporation and enabled them to set up the necessary legal, financial, and operating arrangements to carry out this concept.

There were many reasons for setting up the management of the railroad in this way. For example, the railroad fell under the jurisdiction of a federal regulatory agency, the Interstate Commerce Commission, and its employees were covered by the Railway Labor Act, a federally regulated pension program. Neither of these governed the Port Authority or regular Port Authority employees, and some policies which did apply to Port Authority employees did not necessarily cover railroad personnel, many of whom were represented by national railroad labor unions. Through the device of a subsidiary corporation, the corporate identity of the railroad was retained, its personnel and labor relations remained distinct and unique, regulatory acts were confined to the subsidiary, and operationally the railroad was able to function as a facility within the appropriate line department (Rail Transportation Department).

POLICY FORMULATION

Naturally, the Board of Commissioners establishes all important Port Authority policies. There are two primary means by which the Board is able to do so effectively.

First, as discussed earlier, there is the committee structure of the Board, each committee, like the full Board, meets once every month, and each commissioner serves on one or two committees. The small size and informal committee structure encourages thorough discussion of staff recommendations. Once a committee recommendation is developed, it is presented to the full Board for final approval. An added benefit accrues from being able to assign commissioners to those committees in which they are especially interested, or for which they are particularly qualified.

Second, and closely related to the first, is the means by which items are brought to the attention of commissioners. In the Port Authority, a set procedure has been established for developing agenda items. Agenda items are special reports, prepared according to an established format by originating departments, for the information of the Board of Commissioners or a committee of the Board, as a basis for taking action.

Agenda items are prepared by staff and subject to several reviews before submission to the Executive Director for presentation to the Board or one of its committees. The Director of Finance, for example, reviews all proposed revenue projects, and the Chief Engineer reviews all items involving contracts for construction. At an agenda review meeting, all items are analyzed and discussed by the Executive Director and appropriate staff members, following which the items are prepared for advance distribution to Commissioners prior to their Committee meeting. This gives Committee members an opportunity to request further information if they feel the need for additional data and is an important point of contact and interaction between the Executive Director and Commissioners. At the monthly meeting of the full Board, the calendar is composed almost entirely of items which have been previously reviewed by the appropriate committees of the Board. Agenda items approved by the Board of Commissioners* are not final until they pass scrutiny of the governors of both states. Under Article XVI of the Compact 'each State reserves the right hereafter to provide by law for the exercise of a veto power by the governor thereof over any action of any commissioner appointed therefrom.' This power was given to the governors and in recent years they have exercised the veto power on several occasions to block some project or action they opposed or to compel some action by halting Port Authority progress on new projects or day to day business. Just as important as formal reports and memoranda which the Executive Director uses extensively to keep the Commissioners informed, is discussion at informal meetings and conversations between the Commissioners and the Executive Director. These informal contacts provide an invaluable opportunity to exchange ideas and keep each other up to date, and provide an excellent means for maintaining a successful working relationship.

---

* Under Article XVI of the Compact agenda items must be approved by a majority of the Board, at least three members from each state must be present at a meeting, and at least four votes must be cast for an item, two from each State. No item can pass with merely a tie vote.

FINANCIAL STRUCTURE OF THE PORT AUTHORITY

The Compact directs the Port Authority to be financially self-sustaining; and, as such, it must obtain the funds necessary for the construction or acquisition of facilities upon the basis of its own credit, its reserve funds and its future revenues. The agency has neither the power to pledge the credit of either state or any municipality nor to levy taxes or assessments.

The Port Authority has no stockholders or equity holders; cash derived from operations and other cash received must be disbursed for specific purposes in accordance with provisions of various statutes and agreements with holders of its bonds and others. The costs of providing facilities and services to the general public on a continuing basis are recovered primarily in the form of fares, fees, tolls, rents and other user charges.

From its creation through December 31, 1981, the Port Authority had issued over $4.9 billion in obligations, of which over $2.0 billion was outstanding on December 31, 1981.

In 1982, faced with record interest rates in the bond market, the Port Authority for the first time began issuing tax exempt notes with a maximum interest rate of 10 percent maturing no later than a maximum of 270 days from date of issue. This type of debt instrument supplemented the long term bonds and one year notes traditionally used by the Port Authority to borrow capital funds. The interest rate would be significantly less than that paid on long term bonds or one year notes.

Statutes which govern the Port Authority established the principle of pooling revenues from facilities with established earning power to aid in the development of new projects and to offset those facilities which, though necessary for public service, prove not to be self-sustaining. The statutes also provide for the utilization of available net revenues to maintain the General Reserve Fund at the prescribed amount of at least 10 percent of the total par value of the Port Authority's outstanding bonded debt, in accordance with Port Authority bond resolutions, secured by a pledge of such Fund. After payment of debt service on Consolidated Bonds and Notes, and payment into the General Reserve Fund of such amounts as may be necessary to maintain that Fund at its statutory amount, all net revenues upon which such Bonds and Notes have a first lien are paid into the Consolidated Bond Reserve Fund.

As of 1982, the General Reserve Fund and the Consolidated Bond Reserve were pledged in support of the Port Authority's outstanding bonds and notes other than New York State Guaranteed Commuter Car Bonds and the Port Authority's bank loans.

Bonds for an additional facility cannot be issued with a pledge of the General Reserve Fund unless the Port Authority commissioners certify the investors that the issuance of the bonds, or that such a pledge, will not materially impair the Port Authority's sound credit standing, the investment status of its bonds, or its ability to fulfill its commitments and undertakings.

It is the Port Authority's long-established policy to retire debt as rapidly as sound financial management permits and to maintain, at year-end, in its reserve funds, including reserve funds trust, a combined amount equal to at least the amount of the next two years' mandatory bonded debt service. Acceleration of debt retirement before mandatory dates may be accomplished by use of the General Reserve Fund only to the extent that available reserve funds exceed the ensuing two years' mandatory bonded debt service.

A statutory covenant with holders of affected Port Authority obligations, which was enacted in 1962 by the legislatures of New York and New Jersey, permits deficit financing of passenger railroad facilities in addition to the basic PATH system only within specified financial limits. The covenant was adopted as part of the statutes authorizing the Port Authority acquisition of the interstate Hudson and Manhattan Railroad. In 1973, the legislatures of New York and New Jersey enacted legislation to preclude application of this covenant provision to Port Authority obligations issued after May 10, 1973.

ORGANIZATION STRUCTURE OF PORT AUTHORITY STAFF 1921–1946

When the Port Authority was created in 1921, the organization was chiefly a planning body, a small assemblage of planners, engineers, statisticians, accountants, and lawyers. It was not until 1926 that the organization appointed its first chief operating executive, a position then referred to as General Manager.

In 1926, there were four 'process' (or 'functional') departments in the Port Authority, one each for engineering, administrative, legal and developmental activities. With several facilities becoming operational within the next decade, the operations function was broken out of the development unit and became a separate organizational unit. In the subsequent decade, the organization changed little: separate departments for the real estate, personnel, medical, purchasing and audit/control functions were created from the old administrative unit, which was disbanded. Port Development, Operations, and Engineering remained the major departments.

During this period, the Engineering Department was charged with design responsibilities and construction supervision for all new facilities; Port Development was staffed with planners, statisticians, economists and traffic analysts and was responsible for both port promotion and facility planning; and the Operations Department directed both the operation and maintenance of all tunnels, bridges, and terminals. This was the way the Port Authority functioned for some twenty years, during which period it acquired or developed some dozen terminal, marine terminal, tunnel, and bridge facilities.

ORGANIZATION STRUCTURE OF PORT AUTHORITY STAFF – 1947

In the late 1940s, however, the Port Authority became the agency responsible for operating the major airports in the New York metropolitan area. With the coming of the air age it became increasingly difficult for the historic staff organization structure to accommodate the needs of the agency. Several attempts were made to avoid a major reorganization through piecemeal changes in responsibilities and relationships. For example, in 1947, an airport development office was created in the Port Development Department, reflecting realization by Port Authority management of the technical specialization required to develop modern air facilities. (Reflecting the importance of this function, the unit was raised to departmental status in 1949.) Also in 1947, the Operations Department was expanded considerably, and organized on a 'product' (or 'purpose') basis. Within the department, separate divisions were established for tunnels and bridges, terminals, and airports, as well as for maintenance. The Operations Department also housed several offices, such as safety and traffic engineering, which provided specialized auxiliary services to the various facilities.

The restructuring of the Operations Department in 1947 met with only limited success. The organization structure best suited to operating a small number of like facilities simply proved inadequate once a wider variety of new responsibilities was added.

For one thing, the problems involved in resolving competing demands among the various process departments for a wide variety of facilities placed an undue burden on the Office of the Executive Director. Frequently, for example, the Office of the Executive Director had to step in and resolve problems which the process structure did not permit to be resolved at a lower level. In addition the organization structure tended to produce narrow functional specialists rather than broad-gauged executives, in an organization which placed great emphasis on training and development and promotion from within.

Because these conditions existed, the Executive Director, in 1952, asked several members of the staff to participate in a Task Force established to 'determine if the methods and procedures of policy determination of the Board of Commissioners, the management methods and controls of the Executive Director's Office, and the basic form of organization of the Port Authority staff could be improved.'

ORGANIZATION STRUCTURE OF PORT AUTHORITY STAFF – 1952

As a result of this study, made with the assistance of an outside management consulting firm, a decision was made to reorganize so as to centralize responsibility below the Executive Director for each group of like facilities. The new organization placed all of the major line functions – development, negotiation, operation, and maintenance – for airports in a new Aviation Department; for marine terminals in a new Marine Terminals Department; for bus and truck terminals in a Terminals Department, and for tunnels and bridges in a new Tunnels and Bridges Department. For the first time, the Executive Director could look to one person – the Director of Aviation – for overall success of the Port Authority's airports, including planning, operations, maintenance, and financial and level of service results. Likewise, the directors of other line departments could also be held accountable for similar overall responsibilities in their respective fields.

With the line department organized on a purpose basis, the remainder of the Port Authority retained a 'process' type organization. Separate staff departments for personnel, engineering, financial, purchasing, real estate, and other similar responsibilities were created, or retained, to service the new line departments as well as the Executive Director.

Within this new organizational framework, the Operations Department was substantially changed. It was re-named Operations Services Department. It would no longer be in direct command of individual facilities but rather was to provide a number of staff support functions. The old divisions of that department became the nuclei of the new line departments, and appropriate transfers were made of their personnel and funds to those new departments. The Operations Services Department was then reorganized in such a way as to provide a variety of functions, some of which were concerned with providing central service, some of which were of an advisory nature and others of which involved standard setting, inspection evaluation and control.

In short, the reorganization resulted in the establishment of line departments with the necessary authority to manage their facility operations and programs, subject to reliance on central staff departments for technical services, and some limited controls delegated by the Executive Director. This relationship will be explored later.

The fundamental strength of this arrangement is that it enables conflicts to be dealt with far more effectively than before. In the first place, the number of conflicts which only the Executive Director can resolve are reduced i.e., most of the conflicts between people concerned with planning, operations, and revenue development are resolved at the line department director level. Under the old set-up these were all coming up to the Chief Executive.

Secondly, with net revenue responsibility clearly delegated to a level below the Executive Director fewer appeals are actually made to that level from the central staff units than was the case previously.

Finally, under the new arrangement, when an issue arises between a central staff unit and a line department, its resolution is aided by the high specificity of goals within which the issue is dealt with, e.g., what's the best way to organize and staff to achieve an optimum level of service at and revenues from tunnels and bridges facilities, etc.

Another healthy facet of this structure is the effect it has on the people of both line and staff groups – each learns much about the differences in perspective and value systems of the other so that potential conflicts can be anticipated and often avoided. The issues that remain for resolution at the highest levels are the real tough ones to decide.

In addition to more efficient and more effective management of conflict, the new structure encourages the development of broad-gauged executives in the line departments concerned with all of the functions involved in running public facilities in an efficient business-like way.

The success of this approach is evident from the fact that no need for major reorganization has arisen since 1952. A real test of this organization structure was the ease with which three completely new line departments (World Trade, Rail Transportation and Economic Development) were subsequently created, staffed, and incorporated into the organization framework.

ORGANIZATION STRUCTURE CHANGES 1953–1982

On July 1, 1972, the name of the organization was changed from the 'Port of New York Authority' to 'Port Authority of New York and New Jersey.' This amendment to the compact was made by the legislatures of the two states to reflect properly the importance of New Jersey to the bistate port district. The action was taken following a resolution of the Board of Commissioners inspired by a request from the then Governor of New Jersey.

In the years 1953–1982, but especially in the past ten years, the organizational structure foundation first laid down in 1952 has continued to prove quite resilient and able to adapt to changes in the mission of the organization. Additions/changes to the basic organization structure include the following events:

● Creation of the Industrial Development Department in 1978 to effectuate economic development projects and facilities including resource recovery facilities. This department is charged with developing several industrial parks with the goal of attracting and holding job-creating industries in the Port District. The department's mandate was broadened in 1982 to include the investigation of projects to revitalize those areas of the waterfront which have fallen into disuse and decay and for this reason the name of the department was changed in 1982 to Economic Development Department.

● Combination of the Tunnels & Bridges and Terminals Departments into a single department in 1979 to strengthen development of Trans-Hudson bus, auto and truck transportation as an integrated system. This department combined the functions of operating the Port Authority's tunnels and bridges connecting New York and New Jersey and the operation of the Port Authority Bus Terminal in midtown New York City – the world's busiest bus facility.

● Creation of an Audit Department in 1980 to put increased emphasis on the internal auditing function and reinforce the independence of the audit function from all other Port Authority activities.

● Combination of the Marine Terminal Department with portions of the World Trade and Planning and Development Departments into a new Port Department in 1979 charged to realize maximum economic benefit to the region from operation of all of the port's facilities and related services.

- Abolition of two departments: The Operations Service Department was abolished in 1974 and the central services it provided (as described on p. 145) were transferred to other staff departments that also provide central services to line units. The Real Estate Department was abolished in 1974 and its function of leasing and marketing consumer services space at the facilities transferred to the various line departments which operate these facilities.

- Establishment of special units of less than department size and status to address important problems facing the region and the Port Authority's ability to deal with them:

Office of Infrastructure Renewal (1979) addresses the problem of the deterioration of bridges, highways, sewers and mass transportation in the region by working with government officials to develop financing, participating in regional and national coalitions and sponsoring campaigns to inform the public about the problem.

Office of Strategic Planning (1979) sets corporate goals in consonance with the changing needs and problems of the region.

Office of Energy (1979) conducts research on energy supply and demand in the region, effects of technical developments affecting alternate energy sources, surveys local, state and Federal actions regarding energy policy, reviews energy charges paid by the Port Authority, etc., develops facilities for the export of coal and the importation of crude oil.

PHILOSOPHY OF ORGANIZATION

At the time of the Port Authority's reorganization in 1952, the Executive Director made some telling comments on the Port Authority's philosophy of organization. He wrote:

> The form of organization determines the manner in which responsibility for a job and authority to do a job is delegated from the chief executive to a specific individual and the manner in which the individual is held accountable for accomplishment of his assigned job. The form of organization is not an end unto itself, it is the means by which the work and efforts of individuals are directed to an end result. The effectiveness of a staff ... depends, therefore, not only upon the competence and ability of the individual but also upon the manner in which individual efforts are coordinated through the form of staff organization.

To that end, the Port Authority adheres to certain basic premises with respect to its organization structure. For one thing it is not bound by doctrinaire approaches to problem solving. Some activities may be centralized, for example, while others are decentralized. In every situation, such factors as public service, economy, and personnel are taken into account before one alternative is chosen over another. This flexible attitude sometimes creates conflict, but conflict, per se, is not unwelcome. To the contrary, conflict is considered beneficial when it represents different approaches to the same problem, and it ultimately results in the best solution to a problem. Conflict arising from personality differences, preoccupation with personal or jurisdictional status, confused responsibilities or the like is undesirable and every attempt is made to avoid it.

Many of the organizational principles observed in the Port Authority are adapted from those used in other successful enterprises both public and private. Some of the more important ones include:

1. Defining objectives for both the organization as a whole, and each of its subdivisions. This includes examining what must be done, the reasons for doing it, and setting this down in writing so that it can be understood and questioned.
2. Grouping related tasks together in a logical fashion, to achieve economy and proficiency, avoid duplication and where desirable centralize responsibility.
3. Pinpointing accountability for performance. This simply refers to establishing criteria against which both unit and individual performance is evaluated. It complements the Authority's policy of employing competent personnel and giving them the tools with which to do their job.
4. Striking a sensible balance between having too many layers of supervision, and too many people reporting to a supervisor. This concept is intended to achieve manageable workloads while not creating excessive and delaying chains of command.
5. Creating clear lines of command, while encouraging free informal channels of communication. This refers to making each person aware of his or her job relationships and responsibilities, so as to know who can be called upon for direction, for delegation, or for advice.
6. Emphasizing that organization has to do with people, depends on human effort, and must satisfy human needs. This is an extension of the philosophy that the most important single factor in the success of an enterprise is its personnel. This belief is formally

carried forth in the organization's personnel policies and, infor-
mally, in supervisory relationship with subordinates. Thus the Port
Authority believes that the organization structure should be
designed not only to achieve the most effective planning and
execution of Port Authority functions but should also contribute
to high morale, personal development and work satisfaction for
the employees.

DELEGATION IN THE PORT AUTHORITY

Another fundamental principle in the Port Authority is delegation
of authority. Over the years, the Board of Commissioners has developed a close and effective working relationship with the Executive
Director, and the Board has delegated to that position considerable
freedom in decision making, while retaining ultimate control.

Since its earliest years, for example, the Board of Commissioners
has adhered to a policy of delegating to the Executive Director responsibility for carrying out its policies. (In practice, these are frequently
policies which have been developed by staff and recommended to the
Board of Commissioners. However, all policies established by the
Board are transmitted to the administrative staff by the Executive
Director, and all staff recommendations are made through him or
her.)

Approximately 30 people report directly to the Executive Director,
a span of control which, at first glance, may seem unduly large. A
key factor which enables the Executive Director to manage effectively
so great a number of immediate subordinates is delegation. This
delegation is accomplished in two ways.

First, the Executive Director relies on a small and highly competent
staff within his office. The members of this cadre know exactly what is
expected of them and how they can best relieve the Executive Director
of unnecessary detail, for example one staff member clears, processes
and coordinates all items which are to be presented to the Board of
Commissioners or one of its committees. Another staff member is
responsible for primary liaison with the legislature and executive
branches of the governments of the States of New York and New
Jersey.

Three staff members, in particular, deserve special mention because of their close relationship to the Executive Director. The three
Assistant Executive Directors have each been delegated substantial
authority by the Executive Director. Documents sent to the 'front
office' for approval are frequently acted upon by one of them, and

each is delegated, from time to time, responsibility for staying close to particular program developments. One Assistant Executive Director is also the Director of Administration; another is also General Counsel and, as the organization chart indicates, in those other roles they have a considerable staff reporting to them. In this manner, much of the Executive Director's workload is screened before reaching him, so that he can concentrate on the important jobs of assessing the Port Authority's directions and goals and maintaining relationships with the commissioners, other top governmental officials, the press, and the public. Each of the three Assistant Executive Directors has particular expertise in a vital area – Law, Finance, and Administration.

LINE AND STAFF

Second, the Executive Director makes important delegations to department directors. Generally speaking, line department directors are delegated responsibility for the success of all facilities under their supervision. This includes overall responsibility for plans, operations, maintenance, tenant relations, security, and policies on public service matters.

In executing this responsibility, however, line departments are obligated to utilize specialized services performed by central staff departments whenever appropriate. Also, the line departments are in some cases subject to limited staff department controls.

INTERDEPARTMENTAL RELATIONSHIPS

Complementing these delegations to line and staff departments is the responsibility of department directors to make proper use of available staff services. Departments must not only seek staff services, but they must then act in such a way as not to dismiss what the staff specialist has recommended without good reason. It is taken for granted that a line department will adopt the recommendations of a staff department if they are sound, and will reject them only for compelling reasons. When there is a disagreement, either the line or staff department director may take the problem to the Executive Director for resolution.

For example, a staff department director may recommend to the Director of the Port Department that a certain level of maintenance be utilized for a particular type of cargo terminal building. The Port Director may disagree with the recommendation on such counts as the following:

(1) the rental available for such buildings would not support such a high maintenance cost;
(2) prospective customers are agreeable to a lower level of building maintenance; and
(3) the useful life of the building with the lower level of maintenance would be sufficient to make it self-supporting.

The staff department director may then argue that the building would last longer with the higher level of maintenance and that such maintenance is required to meet the standard of a first-class marine terminal. Both directors may then together bring the matter to the Executive Director for decision. Regardless of the outcome in such a conflict, the line department director understands the importance of the role played by the staff department, and must consider the staff position before taking a final course of action.

MANAGEMENT CONTROLS

Because of the extensive interaction between departments, the Port Authority has developed several means of measuring how well a department carries out its assigned tasks.

Net revenue responsibility is the principal device used to hold line departments accountable for financial return on investment. This measures the department's overall success in forecasting requirements, conducting operations, and staying within financial plans.

Line departments are also held accountable for furnishing high levels of safety, service, and convenience to the patrons of its facilities. Public service criteria, therefore, represent important indices of patron satisfaction. These include written and verbal statements from patrons and tenants, periodic public opinion surveys, the character of relationships with municipalities and state agencies, press coverage and editorial comment, and damage suits and tort claims. Since there is some potential conflict between public service and net revenue responsibility, the line departments have the difficult task of balancing the two considerations.

Various types of standards are also applied in individual departments, particularly in the fields of maintenance, cleaning, typing, economic analysis, and personnel. Other standards are continuously being developed, not only for programs that lend themselves to quantitative measurement, but also for those that involve considerable use of judgment.

Another measure of performance stems from use of the 'responsible department' concept. When more than one department shares involvement in a problem or project, the Executive Director designates one department accountable, with provision made for transferring this designation at a later time.

USE OF OUTSIDE SERVICES

Until very recently, the Port Authority has not relied heavily on outside contractors to provide services such as security, maintenance, engineering design, field surveying and so on. However, with the increased service demands being made by, and on, the line departments, the criteria that apply to the use of such services are being carefully reviewed. This is not simply a problem of economy, but rather, involves policy questions regarding public service responsibilities, and the extent to which the organization can expect an outside contractor to give proper attention to those responsibilities. Reliance on outside services also entails audit and control measures which are less necessary with self-operation. Like the question of centralizing or decentralizing staff services, the problem of using outside services can profoundly affect both the appearance of the organization chart and the economics of the organization.

In general the guidelines for employing outside services are as follows:

1. It can be demonstrated that the outside firm has a special expertise that is not available in a staff unit or when it can be demonstrated that the outside firm can give equal or better service at substantially lower cost than the Port Authority staff unit; and
2. By so doing, other Port Authority activities are not adversely affected; and
3. There is no compelling reason of Port Authority policy or public service which would dictate use of Port Authority staff.

CONCLUSION – AN OVERVIEW OF THE PORT AUTHORITY OF NEW YORK AND NEW JERSEY

In summary, the Port Authority is a corporate instrumentality of the States of New York and New Jersey created by compact between the two states in 1921 with the consent of the Congress of the United States. It is authorized and directed to plan, develop and operate terminals and other facilities of transportation and commerce, and to advance projects in the general fields of transportation, economic development, and world trade that contribute to promoting and protecting the commerce and economy of the Port District, defined in the Compact, which comprises an area of about 1,500 square miles in both States, centering about New York Harbor.

The Port Authority is empowered to undertake only those projects authorized by the two States.

The Governor of each State appoints six of the twelve members of the governing Board of Commissioners, subject to confirmation by the respective state senates. Each governor has from time to time exercised the statutory power to veto the actions of the commissioners from his state.

The commissioners serve six-year overlapping terms as public officials without compensation. They establish Port Authority policy, appoint an Executive Director to implement it, and also appoint a General Counsel to act as legal advisor to the Board and to the Executive Director.

The Executive Director is responsible for the management of the daily operations of the agency's facilities through line and staff departments comprising 7,800 career personnel. The Executive Director also guides proposals to the point of presentation to the Board of Commissioners, including the planning and developing of recommendations to the two states and the federal government to increase and expedite Port District commerce.

As a public corporation combining sound business and governmental principles and practices, the Port Authority endeavors to provide high quality public service and employs and develops personnel to that end.

Detailed policies and procedures are promulgated and communicated to all employees to guide the operation of each department. To assure compliance with the Port Authority's standards, and to protect the assets of the Port Authority, a system of internal controls has been developed. This system is reviewed by a staff of internal auditors which conducts examinations of the Port Authority operations and reports on management's performance to the Executive Director and to the Audit Committee of the Board.

A budget incorporating guidelines for expenditures is adopted annually after stringent examination of all proposed expenditures. It is designed to enable the Port Authority to continue in the most economical manner the construction and operation of its facilities to the maximum public benefit. It should be made clear however that the Port Authority budget is a financial planning tool outlining the estimated expenditures for programs already authorized, or to

be considered by the Board of Commissioners. It is not an author-
izations allocation, and approval of the budget does not in itself
authorize projects. Each project must be separately considered and
approved by the Board.

Upon approval, the financial plan becomes a means of achieving
systematic control of program expenditures to insure they are made
in accordance with the policies and financial decisions of the Board,
and the requirements of the By-Laws of the Port Authority. Continuous planning is undertaken to prepare for future developments.

The Port Authority entered the 7th decade of its existence prosper-
ous and confident, with dynamic, creative top management alert to
new opportunities, improved ways of operating its facilities and
serving the public and imbued with the desire to remain at the 'cutting
edge' of modern corporate management.

APPENDIX I

Excerpts from

COMPACT

BETWEEN THE

States of New York and New Jersey

1921

For the Creation of the 'Port of New York District'
and the Establishment of the 'Port of New York
Authority' for the Comprehensive Development
of the Port of New York

Entered into Pursuant to Chapter 154, Laws of New York, 1921; Chapter 151,
Laws of New Jersey, 1921

WHEREAS, In the year eighteen hundred and thirty-four the states of New York and New Jersey did enter into an agreement fixing and determining the rights and obligations of the two states in and about the waters between the two states, especially in and about the bay of New York and the Hudson river; and

WHEREAS, Since that time the commerce of the port of New York has greatly developed and increased and the territory in and around the port has become commercially one center or district; and

WHEREAS, It is confidently believed that a better co-ordination of the terminal, transportation and other facilities of commerce in, about and through the port of New York, will result in great economies, benefiting the nation, as well as the states of New York and New Jersey; and

WHEREAS, The future development of such terminal, transportation and other facilities of commerce will require the expenditure of large sums of money and the cordial co-operation of the states of New York and New Jersey in the encouragement of the investment of capital, and in the formulation and execution of the necessary physical plans; and

WHEREAS, Such result can best be accomplished through the co-operation of the two states by and through a joint or common agency.

Now, therefore, The said states of New Jersey and New York do supplement and amend the existing agreement of eighteen hundred and thirty-four in the following respects:

ARTICLE I.

They agree to and pledge, each to the other, faithful co-operation in the future planning and development of the port of New York, holding in high trust for the benefit of the nation the special blessings and natural advantages thereof.

ARTICLE II.

To that end the two states do agree that there shall be created and they do hereby create a district to be known as the 'Port of New York District' (for brevity hereinafter referred to as 'The District') which shall embrace the territory bounded and described as follows: ...

ARTICLE III.

There is hereby created 'The Port of New York Authority' (for brevity hereinafter referred to as the 'Port Authority'), which shall be a body corporate and politic, having the powers and jurisdiction hereinafter enumerated, and such other and additional powers as shall be conferred upon it by the legislature of either state concurred in by the legislature of the other, or by act or acts of congress, as hereinafter provided.

ARTICLE IV.[1]

The port authority shall consist of twelve commissioners, six resident voters from the state of New York, at least four of whom shall be resident voters of the city of New York, and six resident voters from the state of New Jersey, at least four of whom shall be resident voters within the New Jersey portion of the district, the New York members to be chosen by the state of New York and the New Jersey members by the state of New Jersey in the manner and

[1] As amended by C. 419, Laws of N. Y. 1930, approved April 12, 1930 and C. 244, Laws of N. J. 1930, effective April 21, 1930. This article originally read:
'The port authority shall consist of six commissioners – three resident voters from the state of New York, two of whom shall be resident voters of the city of New York, and three resident voters from the state of New Jersey, two of whom shall be resident voters within the New Jersey portion of the district, the New York members to be chosen by the state of New York and the New Jersey members by the state of New Jersey in the manner and for the terms fixed and determined from time to time by the legislature of each state respectively, except as herein provided.
'Each commissioner may be removed or suspended from office as provided by the law of the state for which he shall be appointed.'

for the terms fixed and determined from time to time by the legislature of each state respectively, except as herein provided.

Each commissioner may be removed or suspended from office as provided by the law of the state from which he shall be appointed.[2]

ARTICLE V.

The commissioners shall, for the purpose of doing business, constitute a board and may adopt suitable by-laws for its management.

ARTICLE VI.

The port authority shall constitute a body, both corporate and politic, with full power and authority to purchase, construct, lease and/or operate any terminal or transportation facility within said district; and to make charges for the use thereof; and for any of such purposes to own, hold, lease and/or operate real or personal property, to borrow money and secure the same by bonds or by mortgages upon any property held or to be held by it. No property now or hereafter vested in or held by either state, or by any county, city, borough, village, township or other municipality, shall be taken by the port authority, within the authority or consent of such state, county, city, borough, village, township or other municipality, nor shall anything herein impair or invalidate in any way any bonded indebtedness of such state, county, city, borough, village, township or other municipality, nor impair the provisions of law regulating the payment into sinking funds of revenues derived from municipal property, or dedicating the revenues derived from any municipal property to a specific purpose.

The powers granted in this article shall not be exercised by the port authority until the legislatures of both states shall have approved of a comprehensive plan for the development of the port as hereinafter provided.

ARTICLE VII.

The port authority shall have such additional powers and duties as may hereafter be delegated to or imposed upon it from time to time by the action of the legislature of either state concurred in by the legislature of the other. Unless and until otherwise provided, it shall make an annual report to the legislature of both states, setting forth in detail the operations and transactions conducted by it pursuant to this agreement and any legislation thereunder. The port authority shall not pledge the credit of either state except by and with the authority of the legislature thereof.

ARTICLE VIII.

Unless and until otherwise provided, all laws now or hereafter vesting jurisdiction or control in the public service commission, or the public utilities commission, or like body, within each state respectively, shall apply to railroads and to any transportation, terminal or other facility owned, operated,

[2]R. S. N. J. 32:1–5.

PE–F*

leased or constructed by the port authority, with the same force and effect as if such railroad, or transportation, terminal or other facility were owned, leased, operated or constructed by a private corporation.

ARTICLE IX.

Nothing contained in this agreement shall impair the powers of any municipality to develop or improve port and terminal facilities.

ARTICLE X.

The legislatures of the two states, prior to the signing of this agreement, or thereafter as soon as may be practicable, will adopt a plan or plans for the comprehensive development of the port of New York.

ARTICLE XI.

The port authority shall from time to time make plans for the development of said district, supplementary to or ammendatory of any plan theretofore adopted, and when such plans are duly approved by the legislatures of the two states, they shall be binding upon both states with the same force and effect as if incorporated in this agreement.

ARTICLE XII.

The port authority may from time to time make recommendations to the legislatures of the two states or to the congress of the United States, based upon study and analysis, for the better conduct of the commerce passing in and through the port of New York, the increase and improvement of transportation and terminal facilities therein, and the more economical and expeditious handling of such commerce.

ARTICLE XIII.

The port authority may petition any interstate commerce commission (or like body), public service commission, public utilities commission (or like body), or any other federal, municipal, state or local authority, administrative, judicial or legislative, having jurisdiction in the premises, after the adoption of the comprehensive plan as provided for in article X for the adoption and execution of any physical improvement, change in method, rate of transportation, system of handling freight, warehousing, docking, lightering or transfer of freight, which, in the opinion of the port authority, may be designed to improve or better the handling of commerce in and through said district, or improve terminal and transportation facilities therein. It may intervene in any proceeding affecting the commerce of the port.

ARTICLE XIV.

The port authority shall elect from its number a chairman, vice-chairman, and may appoint such officers and employees as it may require for the performance of its duties, and shall fix and determine their qualifications and duties.

ARTICLE XV.

Unless and until the revenues from operations conducted by the port authority are adequate to meet all expenditures, the legislatures of the two states shall appropriate, in equal amounts, annually, for the salaries, office and other administrative expenses, such sum or sums as shall be recommended by the port authority and approved by the governors of the two states, but each state obligates itself hereunder only to the extent of one hundred thousand dollars in any one year.

ARTICLE XVI.[3]

Unless and until otherwise determined by the action of the legislatures of the two states, no action of the port authority shall be binding unless taken at a meeting at which at least three of the members from each state are present, and unless a majority of the members from each state present at such meetings, but in any event at least three of the members from each state, shall vote in favor thereof. Each state reserves the right hereafter to provide by law for the exercise of a veto power by the governor thereof over any action of any commissioner appointed therefrom.[4]

ARTICLE XVII

Unless and until otherwise determined by the action of the legislatures of the two states, the port authority shall not incur any obligations for salaries, office or other administrative expenses, within the provisions of article XV, prior to the making of appropriations adequate to meet the same.

ARTICLE XVIII.

The port authority is hereby authorized to make suitable rules and regulations not inconsistent with the constitution of the United States or of either state, and subject to the exercise of the power of congress, for the improvement of the conduct of navigation and commerce, which, when concurred in or authorized by the legislatures of both states, shall be binding and effective upon all persons and corporations affected thereby.

ARTICLE XIX.

The two states shall provide penalties for violations of any order, rule or regulation of the port authority, and for the manner of enforcing the same.

---

[3] As amended by C.419, Laws of N.Y. 1930, approved April 12, 1930 and C.244. Laws of N. J. 1930, effective April 21, 1930. This Article originally read:
  'Unless and until otherwise determined by the action of the legislatures of the two states, no action of the port authority shall be binding unless taken at a meeting at which at least two members from each state are present and unless four votes are cast therefor, two from each state. Each state reserves the right hereafter to provide by law for the exercise of a veto power by the governor thereof over any action of any commissioner appointed therefrom.'
[4] R. S. N. J. 32:1–17.

ARTICLE XX.

The territorial or boundary lines established by the agreement of eighteen hundred and thirty-four, or the jurisdiction of the two states established thereby, shall not be changed except as herein specifically modified.

ARTICLE XXI.

Either state may by its legislature withdraw from this agreement in the event that a plan for the comprehensive development of the port shall not have been adopted by both states on or prior to July first, nineteen hundred and twenty-three; and when such withdrawal shall have been communicated to the governor of the other state by the state so withdrawing, this agreement shall be thereby abrogated.

APPENDIX II

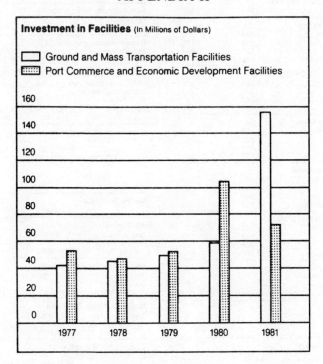

Cost of facilities is composed of the following:

	December 31,	
	1981	**1980**
	(In Thousands)	
Completed Construction:		
Air Terminals	$1,386,376	$1,338,237
World Trade Center	1,025,737	1,022,206
Tunnels & Bridges	599,569	588,323
Marine Terminals	554,568	544,543
Rail Facilities	264,830	260,070
Bus Terminal	139,510	138,120
	3,970,590	3,891,499
Construction in Progress	188,026	169,756
	$4,158,616	$4,061,255

THE PORT AUTHORITY OF NY & NJ
Facility Traffic 1980 - 1981

Tunnels and Bridges

(Eastbound Traffic in Thousands)	1981	1980
All Crossings		
Automobiles	80,699	77,372
Buses	1,635	1,702
Trucks	8,925	8,884
Total Vehicles	91,259	87,958
George Washington Bridge		
Automobiles	38,463	37,312
Buses	246	253
Trucks	3,747	3,831
Total Vehicles	42,456	41,396
Lincoln Tunnel		
Automobiles	15,050	14,470
Buses	1,222	1,259
Trucks	1,883	1,862
Total Vehicles	18,155	17,591
Holland Tunnel		
Automobiles	10,167	9,359
Buses	48	87
Trucks	1,667	1,618
Total Vehicles	11,882	11,064
Staten Island Bridges		
Automobiles	17,019	16,231
Buses	119	103
Trucks	1,628	1,573
Total Vehicles	18,766	17,907
Cumulative PA Investment in Tunnels and Bridges		
(In Thousands)	$646,400	$635,800

Air Terminals

	1981	1980
Totals at the Three Major Airports		
Plane Movements	793,500	821,900
Passenger Traffic	54,081,000	53,487,000
Cargo—Tons	1,346,800	1,312,000
Revenue Mail—Tons	221,700	228,300
Kennedy International Airport		
Plane Movements	286,000	307,500
Passenger Traffic		
Total	25,753,000	26,796,000
Domestic	12,422,000	13,767,000
Overseas	13,331,000	13,029,000
Cargo—Tons	1,191,500	1,169,800
LaGuardia Airport		
Plane Movements	308,200	317,600
Passenger Traffic	18,146,000	17,468,000
Cargo—Tons	36,800	35,300
Newark International Airport		
Plane Movements	199,300	196,800
Passenger Traffic	10,182,000	9,223,000
Cargo—Tons	118,500	107,200
Cumulative PA Investment in Air Terminals		
(In Thousands)	$ 1,473,900	$1,434,800

Terminals

	1981	1980
All Bus Facilities		
Passengers	72,100,000	74,200,000
Bus Movements	3,084,000	3,183,000
Port Authority Bus Terminal		
Passengers	55,000,000	56,500,000
Bus Movements	1,901,000	1,950,000
George Washington Bridge Bus Station		
Passengers	7,800,000	8,000,000
Bus Movements	318,000	327,000
PATH Journal Square Transportation Center Bus Station		
Passengers	9,300,000	9,700,000
Bus Movements	865,000	906,000
Cumulative PA Investment in Bus Facilities		
(In Thousands)	$203,500	$186,800

Marine Terminals

	1981	1980
All Terminals		
Ship Arrivals	3,053	3,234
General Cargo (Long Tons)	13,056,029	12,181,897
New Jersey Marine Terminals		
Ship Arrivals	2,188	2,326
General Cargo (Long Tons)	12,264,762	10,920,815
New York Marine Terminals		
Ship Arrivals	865	908
General Cargo (Long Tons)	791,267	1,261,082
Cumulative PA Investment in Marine Terminals		
(In Thousands)	$571,600	$559,800

PATH

	1981	1980
Total Passengers	47,923,000	35,865,000
Passenger Weekday Average	169,800	163,600
Cumulative PA Investment in PATH		
(In Thousands)	$284,800	$279,000

	1981	1980
Total Port Authority Cumulative Invested in Facilities, Including the Above		
(In Thousands)	$4,375,500	$4,148,300

Operating Results 1980–1981

Gross operating revenues by operating segment exclude interdepartmental revenues primarily relating to the World Trade Center of $20,040,000 in 1981, and $15,141,000 in 1980. In the table below, gross operating income (loss) consists of gross operating revenues less operating and maintenance expenses and depreciation. General administrative and development expenses, financial income, interest on debt and interdepartmental revenues and expenses are not considered in calculating gross operating income (loss). Allocated general administrative and development expenses for the Ground and Mass Transportation group are $34,523,000 in 1981 and $28,394,000 in 1980, and for the Port Commerce and Economic Development group are $34,255,000 in 1981 and $28,228,000 in 1980.

	Ground and Mass Transportation				Port Commerce and Economic Development				Combined	
	Tunnels & Bridges	Bus Terminal and Bus Program	Rail	Total	Air Terminals	Marine Terminals*	World Trade Center	Total	1981	1980
	(in Thousands)									
1981										
Gross Operating Revenues	$148,026	$17,902	$16,449	$182,377	$333,656	$52,400	$130,680	$516,736	$699,113	
Gross Operating Income (Loss)	75,584	(10,226)	(49,000)	16,358	90,827	13,098	48,884	152,809	$169,167	
1980										
Gross Operating Revenues	142,825	17,309	12,397	172,531	313,927	51,151	110,038	475,116		$647,647
Gross Operating Income (Loss)	76,988	(2,606)	(37,452)	36,930	87,194	10,771	31,202	129,167		$166,097
General Administrative and Development Expenses									(68,778)	(56,622)
Income from Operations									100,389	109,475
Financial Income									102,489	86,516
Interest Expense									(103,630)	(101,371)
Cumulative Effect on Prior Years of Changing to a Different Security Valuation Method (Note A-4)									–	9,503
Net Income									$99,248	$104,123

8

CORPORACIÓN VENEZOLANA DE GUAYANA

Enrique Viloria

1. THE INCEPTION OF CVG

Corporación Venezolana de Guayana (CVG) (or Venezuelan Corporation of Guyana) is one of the important agencies in the public sector of Venezuela, concerned with regional development and as a holding complex. It has also been the base for the emergence of public enterprises in the field of basic industry in the rich and yet unexploited region of Guyana, which represents about 50% of the Venezuelan territory.

The zone is characterised by its climatic diversity and a varied geographic landscape. It is rich in minerals, hydric and forest resources. Mention may be made, in particular, of the 2,000 million tons of iron resource of high concentration (52%), and the proven resources of about 200 million tons of bauxite. Besides, there exist gold and diamond reserves, and several non-metallic resources like clay, sand, gravel, quartz, silica sand, limestone, dolomite, white clay, granite and marble. The Guyana region has rivers with a great hydroelectric potential: for instance, the Caroní has a potential of 18,000 megawatts. With the Orinoco and the Caura besides, the region is of inestimable importance as a source of energy. In addition, the resources of wood are quite extensive.

The region was practically uninhabited until 1950, except for such places as Cindad Bolivar and San Felix. Activities that would promote the economic utilisation of the resources of the region began to be developed about 1948, culminating eventually in the establishment of CVG. The earliest studies of the Caroní River were initiated in the Venezuelan Development Corporation (Corporación Venezolana de Formento) (CVF), with a view to its hydro-electric exploitation. The Ministry of Development (Formento) was established in 1953, as also the Commission for Studies of Electrification of the Caroní, which was made responsible for the continuation of studies initiated by CVF. The 'Office of Special Studies of the Presidency of the Republic' was established as a converging point for all the studies initiated in respect of the establishment of a national iron and steel industry.

The construction of the central hydro-electric station Managua I was commenced in 1956, as also the construction of the Orinoco steel plant. In 1958 the Venezuelan Institution of Iron and Steel (Instituto Venezolano del Hierro y el Acero) was created as an autonomous public entity responsible for supplementing the technical studies initiated in this industry, for supervising the construction of the Matanzas steel plant and for commercial exploitation of the steel products manufactured in Venezuela.

In 1958 the Commission for Studies on the Electrification of the Caroní was transferred to the Venezuelan Development Corporation, with the rank of a department. A Presidential Commissioner of the Republic of Guyana (Comisionado de la Presidencia de la Republica de Guayana) was set up and entrusted, together with the Central Office of Co-ordination and Planning (Oficina Central de Coordinacion y Planificacion) (CORDIPLAN), with the task of making recommendations leading to the establishment of a permanent agency devoted to assist, programme and promote the development of the Guyana region. The strategy consisted in the creation of a nodal point for economic development utilising the resources of the region, structuring a vast complex of heavy industries; for developing a programme of hydro-electric exploitation; and for developing a new city as an urban nucleus complementary to industrial development. In order to execute this programme a decentralised public agency was created under the name of Corporación Venezolana de Guayana.

2. THE OBJECTIVES OF CVG

CVG was created by Decree-Law No. 3430 of 1960 as the organ responsible for formulating and executing a programme for the development of the Guyana region. It is an autonomous institute, partaking of the Venezuelan laws relating to decentralised entities. It has certain characteristics of a national entity: direct attribution to the Presidency of the Republic through the Ministry of the Secretariat of the Presidency, governing boards appointed and removable by the President, headquarters in Caracas and jurisdiction confined (though extendable) to the region of the resources it was intended to exploit.

The Decree assigned to CVG an array of objectives characterised by diversity and complexity. As per Article 7 'CVG will have the following objectives:

(1) to study the resources of Guyana, within as well as outside of the development zone, whenever this becomes necessary;
(2) to study, develop and organise the progress of the hydro-electric potential of the Caroní River;
(3) to programme the integral development of the region in accordance with the policies and within the context of the Plan of the Nation;
(4) to promote the industrial development of the region within the public sector as well as in the private sector;
(5) to coordinate the activities of the various official organs in the region in the economic and social fields;
(6) to contribute to the organisation, programming, development and functioning of public services necessary for the development of the zone;
(7) to undertake, as per the decision of the National Executive, any other task which could relate to operations outside the zone, when there is a close relationship with those undertaken within the zone.'

It may be seen that CVG's functions range broadly over studies of problems and potentialities of the region, implementation of projects, co-ordination of activities carried out by official agencies in the economic and social fields, and contribution to the organisation and functioning of public services necessary for the development of the region.

The primary objectives of CVG were extended so as to cover certain others derived from the policy of administrative regionalisation adopted by the State in 1969. Within this policy CVG was converted into a key element of the system, by being charged with one of the administrative regions (namely, Guyana) and not merely the small zone of resources, with respect to which it would assume the totality of functions (co-ordination, planning, etc.) assigned to the different regional organs foreseen under the regulations.

The Corporation has also been handling, with some success depending on the case, many other areas of functions indispensable for the 'integral development of the region'. These areas are not limited to the city of Guyana, but extend to the various zones of the region. For example, one can cite the activities accomplished in the field of urbanisation which involve Urban Planning, execution of urbanisation activities, housing programmes, equipment, etc., the carrying out of matters of formal education, from the elementary up to the higher levels, training of human resources, promotion of scientific and cultural development, programmes of medical assistance that involve both the construction of installations and the presentation of services, community development programmes, programmes for the protection and rise of natural resources, etc.

All this shows the enormous complexity that marks the development programme of the region and consequently the responsibilities of CVG. And this is how the formal objectives of CVG have been translated into a concrete form of diverse activities.

3. THE ACTIVITIES OF THE VENEZUELAN CORPORATION OF GUYANA

It would be useful to distinguish CVG's activities by the criterion of focus: (i) urban; (ii) regional; and (iii) industrial.

(a) *The urban activities*

One of the fundamental objectives of the programme of Guyana was the creation of an urban centre that would provide the locus for complementing the programme of resource exploitation which would generate and develop an important nucleus of industrial activity. With this in mind, the creation of a new city, Ciudad Guayana, was considered essential, on the banks of the Caroní River.

The decision regarding the birth of a new city was adopted by the National Executive, on the basis of studies and proposals of the Public Works Ministry's Directorate of Urbanism, undertaken with the intent of promoting investment programmes at the instance of the State in the zone, and as an appropriate habitational alternative to the proposal for the construction of a special community (camp site) for the workers and employees of the steel industry. Such was the core of Decree No. 228 of March 1960, that defined a polygon within which the real estate required for the urban development would be subject to expropriation. The decision to build a new city centred around the attainment of a conglomerate of activities that would guarantee its stability and permanence as a first rate urban centre in the region and make imperative and proper synchronization between the urbanisation process (city development) and the development of the industrial programmes that the public and the private sectors would generate in the area.

To attain this objective two main functions were assigned to CVG:

the co-ordination of the activities of different official organs and the contribution, organization, programming, development and performance of the public services needed in the context of a population growth (in the city).

Nevertheless, it may be noted that the 'urban' activities by CVG have, as time passed, undergone a change. Today, because of changes in policy, inadequacies of the city and failures attached to other official organs, CVG has had to relinquish its co-ordinating role in being directly concerned with the fulfilment of the vast programme of building and infrastructure, which might jeopardise, in the long run, the fulfilment of its other obligations of a regional or industrial nature.

(b) *Regional development activities*

The concept of what must be understood by regional development is confusing. It may refer to programmes of administrative or economic decentralization, or to the co-ordination of activities among the several elements of the public sector and of the latter with the private sector. It can be said to the credit of CVG that it has been able to provide a clear conceptualization in respect of its regional endeavours.

Hence, the CVG has clarified the difference between actions of regional development in a strict sense, and the development actions in the least developed areas within the region.

(i) *Activities of regional development*

These refer to those programmes oriented to the gradual, rational and orderly achievement of the initiatives rendered possible by the resources offered by the region, its comparative advantages and costs, and its complementarity perspectives. In this sense the role of CVG has been to deepen the knowledge we have of the very vast Guyana region, and to propose, having in mind the existing resources, the action programmes deemed rational within the regional context.

In concrete terms, these have allowed the discovery of the 'regional vocation of Guyana'. We may emphasise that the activity of studying the resources and the possibilities has been the main engine in Guyana's development. It has allowed the launching of a group of industrial programmes which have enabled the economic utilization of the rich resources in water, mining, forestry, etc. As evidence of the purposiveness of the resource-study we may point out the energy possibilities of the Caroní River, taken up by one of CVG's affiliates, CVG-Caroní Electrification (EDELCA), and bauxite prospecting in

'Los Pijiguaos', which is in the process of exploitation by yet another company affiliated to CVG, 'Bauxita Venezolana' (BAUXIVEN).

(ii) *The development actions in the most backward regions*

Due to successive extensions of the territorial range of activity, as a result of a number of decrees issued in the context of the government's policy of administrative regionalization, CVG has put into effect certain programmes, though of a modest and limited nature, which aimed to assist the least developed regions within the Guyana region. These have a fundamental agricultural and infrastructural character. This has been the case with the programme known as 'Orinoco Delta', in which major investments have been made to recover terrain for agricultural use. Similar have been the development programmes in the Grand Sabana region.

(c) *The industrial and entrepreneurial activities*

Within the context of regional development CVG has had to concern itself with the administration and control of a number of investment participations in industrial enterprises. This has helped in concretising the fruits of studies on the resources of the Guyana region, its comparative advantages and complementarities into industrial projects of a viable nature. These programmes in water, electricity, mineral, forest and iron, by their magnitude, importance, complexity and long periods of gestation, have called for systematic co-ordinative action in the conception, execution, supervision and evaluation of the projects and programmes, with due regard to market conditions, national and international, economies of scale, technical interrelationships between the products made for the different industries whose activities are complementary and indispensable for other production activities, etc. Complementary actions have also been required for ensuring the timely availability of indispensable elements of infrastructure, urban and industrial, as well as the training of human resources which has been necessary at all levels. CVG has legal competence in promoting the formation of the enterprises which have been necessary for fomenting the development of the zone. CVG has directly participated in the capital of the enterprises promoted, and in constituting a conglomerate of enterprises which facilitate the complementary utilisation of the resources of the region. In illustrating this we may look at the production of iron alloys of silicon in charge of FESILVEN, the production of cement in Cementos

Guyana, the production of valves, elbows and other devices for the petroleum industry in the Metalmeg, etc.

In coherence with the basic attributes in respect of state enterprises for the development of Guyana, the organic statute placed a double obligation on CVG. For one thing, it had to constitute, in conjunction with the patrimony of the former Institute of Venezuela for Iron and Steel, one or several enterprises for the development of the iron and steel industry; and for another, it had similarly constituted, given the patrimony forthcoming from the electrification of Caroní, several enterprises which allowed full utilization of the hydroelectric potential of the Caroní River.

Further, Decree 580, which reserves to the State the exploitation of the iron industry, lays down that CVG, in the exercise of its right to promote State enterprises, and to construct the installations along with the equipment and other goods of the ex-concessionary enterprises, can set up one or various enterprises for the management of nationalised industries. In this way, CVG created the CVG-Ferrominera Orinoco (iron).

In accordance with the juridical norms of Venezuela, CVG has, within the entrepreneurial context of the State, a large number of functions and responsibilities. It has therefore been promoting and developing enterprises which serve as an instrument for the execution of the integral development policy of the Guyana region.

The enterprises promoted and directed by CVG are noted for their high degree of complementarity; and by exploiting the hydraulic, energy and mineral resources located in the region, CVG has developed an industrial programme which pursues a rational and integrated exploitation of the resources. In this way it has made an important contribution to the development of the national economy. Further, the economic effects of the CVG enterprises in terms of exports, savings in hard currency and generation of income have been conspicuous.

In recent years there has been a shift of CVG's share in the role of financial participation in industrial enterprises located in the Guyana region. The Venezuelan Investment Fund (El Fondo de Inversiones de Venezuela) (FIV) – a state enterprise – has participated significantly in the enterprises promoted by CVG – e.g., Sidor, Venalum, Alcasa, Interalumina and Fesilven. CVG has ceased to be the only (public sector) shareholder of these enterprises; correspondingly there has been a reduction in its management and control powers over them. CVG's shareholding proportions in

CVG's SHAREHOLDING

ENTERPRISE	SOCIAL CAPITAL	CVG's HOLDING	% OF CVG's HOLDING
(1)	(2)	(3)	(4)
Ferrominera Orinoco, C. A. (FERROMINERA)	750.000.000,oo	750.000.000,oo	100
Siderúrgica del Orinoco, C. A. (SIDOR)	12.350.000.000,oo	5.300.000.000,oo	42,91
Electrificación del Caroní (EDELCA)	7.225.000.000,oo	3.626.000,oo	50,19
Minerales Ordaz, C. A. (MINORCA)	22.500.000,oo	11.475.000,oo	51,00
Bauxita Venezolana, C. A. (BAUXIVEN)	200.000.000,oo	199.990.000,oo	99,995
Interamericana de Alúmina, C. A. (INTERALUMINA)	2.500.000.000,oo	127.500.000,oo	5,1
Industria Venezolana de Aluminio (VENALUM)	1.000.000.000,oo	187.550.000,oo	18,755
Aluminio del Caroní, S. A. (ALCASA)	565.000.000,oo	82.500.000,oo	14,60
Fior de Venezuela, S. A. (FIOR)	100.000.000,oo	33.333.333,oo	33,33
Cementos Guayana, C. A.	40.000.000,oo	10.00n.000,oo	25,00
Metalmeg, S. A.	12.500.000,oo	6.000.000,oo	48,00
Sociedad Financiera Atlántica, C. A.	44.498.000,oo	1.500.000,oo	3,37
Fábrica Nacional de Tractores y Motores, S. A. (FANATRACTO)	50.000.000,oo	22.500.000,oo	45,00
Venezolana de Ferrosilicio, C. A. (FESILVEN)	21.500.000,oo	3.308.000,oo	15,386
C. A. Pulpa Guayana	1.000.000,oo	400.000,oo	40,00
Puerto de Hierro, S. A.	450.000,oo	225.000,oo	50
Promotora de Desarrollo Urbano Region Guayana, C. A.	50.000.000,oo	20.000.000,oo	40
C.V.G. Internacional, C. A.	1.000.000,oo		
Comercializadora Rofi, S. A.	100.000,oo		
	24.933.548.000,oo	10.382.281.333,oo	42

the different enterprises are shown above. Only in two of the big enterprises (Ferrominera and Bauxiven) is CVG's ownership almost complete. In aggregate it comes to 42% only.

4. CVG'S ORGANISATIONAL STRUCTURE

In order to have a view of the organisational nature of CVG, we shall refer to the following aspects: top management, planning, financing, personnel and control.

(a) *Top management*

CVG is managed by a board composed of six members, one of whom is the President and the remaining five are principal directors, all of whom are designated by the President of the Republic, who will additionally designate five substitute directors. The President of the board represents the Corporation and is designated as Presidential Commissioner in the Development of Guyana. Temporary absences of the President of the board will be covered by the director (any of the directors) designated by him in consultation with the President of the Republic.

However it is to be noted that in accordance with the stipulations of the Law on Representation of the Workers of Autonomous Institutions, Enterprises and Economic Development Agencies of the State, an additional director has been added to the CVG board to represent the workers. This representation is exercised by the most representative Federation or Union in the respective economic sector, which, in the case of CVG is Fetrametal.

The board will have a Secretary, who could be that official of the Corporation who holds the post of Secretary of the President, or else the official designated by the board. The Secretary of the board will be responsible for everything concerning notice of meetings, agenda, drafts, minutes, books, files, documents and any other matter related to the meetings of the board.

Board members, exceptions considered, do not perform their functions full time. Their contacts with the organisation are kept by means of their attendance at the meetings of the board. The board's decisions need support from no less than three of its members, one of which must be the Presidential Commissioner for the Development of Guyana.

Evidently and logically, the duties of the board are related to the fundamental aspects of the Corporation's management, and by way of example we can underline the following: to authorise and approve studies, programmes, establishment of subsidiary enterprises or participation as shareholder in enterprises; approval of the investment and expenditure budget, and, of course, control of the enterprise's management and of the management of affiliated enterprises.

The highest authority of CVG is its President, who is responsible for the daily management of the Corporation, to which end he is endowed with ample assistance, of which the following stand out: legal representation of CVG; appointment and removal of managerial personnel, presentation of reports and accounts to the President of the Republic and, in general, all such functions geared towards a normal accountability and development of the activities of the Corporation.

The conduct of the programmes of CVG is in charge of the managers, who report to the President directly.

In matters of internal organization, as may be seen in the following organization chart, CVG has the traditional staff or support units (personnel, finance, public relations, legal counsel and planning), together with the organisational units which execute the programmes connected with the achievement of the Corporation's objectives (urban, agricultural, and industrial development).

As regards the relations of CVG with its subsidiary enterprises and affiliates, the fundamental mechanism of approval and transmission of directives rests with the assemblies of shareholders. In these meetings the plans of investment and budgets of expenditure are approved; the administrative and financial management aspects are also approved; and the directors are designates who represent CVG on the subsidiaries' boards.

The day-to-day organisational relationships of CVG with its subsidiaries revolve around the directors, who generally are managers in CVG or persons closely related to the organisation. Further the relations and direct and frequent contacts between the presidents of the enterprises with the President of CVG play an important part as a permanent channel of information and consultation.

(b) *Planning*

CVG has a unique status in that, as an organisation responsible for the development and execution of important programmes of investment in the Guyana region, it at once constitutes an important piece in the processes of national and regional planning in Venezuela. The planning system is directed by the Oficina Central de Coordinacion

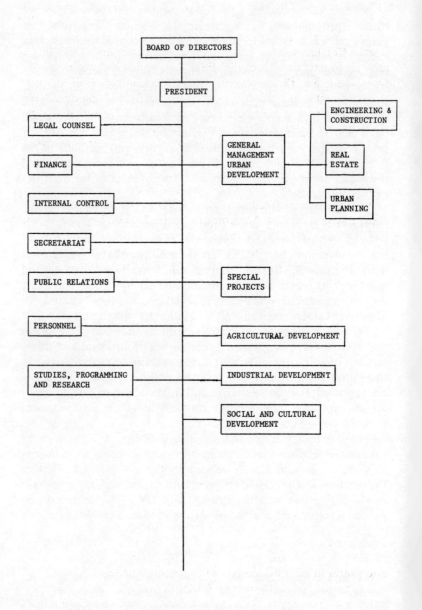

BOARD OF DIRECTORS

PRESIDENT

LEGAL COUNSEL

FINANCE

INTERNAL CONTROL

SECRETARIAT

PUBLIC RELATIONS

PERSONNEL

STUDIES, PROGRAMMING AND RESEARCH

GENERAL MANAGEMENT URBAN DEVELOPMENT

ENGINEERING & CONSTRUCTION

REAL ESTATE

URBAN PLANNING

SPECIAL PROJECTS

AGRICULTURAL DEVELOPMENT

INDUSTRIAL DEVELOPMENT

SOCIAL AND CULTURAL DEVELOPMENT

y Planificacion (CORDIPLAN) and is based on analysis, projections and formulations of general goals, complemented by consultation with the public sectors (for the compatibility of the Plan) and the private sectors (for harmonised activity). Under this system, CVG has a relevant role to play, from the standpoint of its contribution to the formulation and the consistency of the Plan in respect of the programmes that bear a relation to its own objectives. A good example of this relates to its assistance in the industrial sector, in which the electricity, iron and steel and aluminium projects undertaken by the CVG group of enterprises represent a good part of the industrial investment of the country. The same may be said as regards its programmes of investment in infrastructure (e.g., roads, education and hospitals) in which CVG's involvement has been substantial.

The organisational relationship of CVG with regional planning is even more pronounced. According to Decree 1331 on Regionalisation and Participation of the Community in Regional Development, a Regional Office of Coordination and Planning has been set up as an ancillary to CORDIPLAN in each of the nine administrative regions set up under the Decree. In the case of the Guyana region, CVG has assumed the functions of the Regional Office of Coordination and Planning. In this sense the principal responsibility of CVG consists in the elaboration of the projects of regional plans and in the evaluation of the execution of those plans with a view to proposing any necessary revisions.

(c) *Finances*

Here we have to distinguish between the aspects related to the capitalisation (patrimony) of CVG and those related to the financing of its programmes. In accordance with the organisation statute, CVG's capitalisation is made up as follows: in the first place, the amounts fixed by the Law of the General Budget of Public Revenues and Expenditures – these are determined by the National Executive; in the second, assets of any type which emerge in the course of its activities in areas assigned for the creation and expansion of Ciudad Guayana and whose sales have constituted an important source of its revenues; and in the third, assets, rights, obligations, participations and shares in its subsidiaries and mixed enterprises.

From another point of view CVG, in order to finance the programmes whose execution is entrusted to it, can, apart from relying on its own resources (grants from the Executive and revenues obtained directly), contract credits with national as well as international

financial institutions. In respect of such contracts CVG has to
comply with the requirements and procedures set out in the Organisational Law of Public Credit. Further it has to highlight the loss
in its financial position caused by any changes in the policy of
financing the programmes executed by its enterprises. In the past
the normal practice was for the Executive to determine in consultation
with CVG, the nature and magnitude of CVG's contributions to
the subsidiaries and mixed enterprises. In this way the National
Executive transferred to CVG, via the budget, a Group of Funds
with the object of providing capital (by adding to their social capital
with subscription to new shares) or authorising credits to them.
However, with the creation of the Investment Fund of Venezuela
(FIV) the situation has changed substantially, since the Fund has
become the financial organ for industrial investment in the public
sector in Guyana. By subscribing to the shares of the CVG enterprises,
the Fund has come to be the major shareholder in many cases,
curtailing CVG's administrative and control powers over the subsidiaries.

(d) *Personnel*

The Organic Statute of CVG stipulates that its personnel should be
subject to the provisions of the Law of Administrative Career and
its regulations. However, it is necessary to distinguish the technical
workers and administrative workers on monthly pay roll from the
daily paid workers, to whom the provisions of the Labour Law apply.
For this reason the latter are not considered as public functionaries.
They have the right to unionise themselves and negotiate collective
agreements for the improvement of their general conditions, under
the provisions of the Labour Law.

The personnel in the service of the enterprises in the CVG group
are not considered as public functionaries; and the general rules
of the Labour Law apply to them in all cases, even when they all
reach collective agreements regularly establishing labour relations
and the general conditions of work in respect of each enterprise.

(e) *Control*

CVG by virtue of its being an institution of public (autonomous)
character, is subject to several modalities of control: e.g., control
exercised by the Ministry of the Secretary of the Presidency, and
control by the Controller General of the Republic and by Parliament.

The control exercised by the Ministry of the Secretary of the Presidency, which is also the Ministry to which CVG is attached, has the object of guaranteeing coherence and proper execution of state policies. It is not direct hierarchical control. This control is fundamentally translated into direction and guidelines to the Corporation, as also into controls over its actions calling for the approval of the Ministry (e.g., procurement of goods or contracting of works beyond a certain amount).

The control exercised by the Controller General of the Republic on CVG corresponds to the so-called control of the superior financial entities. In accordance with the Venezuelan constitution, the Controller General of the Republic is an auxiliary organ of the Congress charged with the exercise of fiscal control over public administration. In this sense, Article 234 of the Constitution establishes that the function of the Controller's Office is to exercise 'control, vigilance and inspection of the receipts, expenditures and national property, as also the operations related thereto'. For accomplishing this control, the Controlaria General of the Republic opened an office (Delegated Controlaria) at the headquarters of the Corporation with the object of exercising efficient managerial control on the activities carried out by CVG.

The control which Congress exercises on CVG is manifested fundamentally through the requirement that each enterprise should submit periodic information on the physical and financial execution of their respective budgets. In this way, Parliament is informed of the achievements of CVG and its constituent enterprises and can formulate appropriate observations on the management.

Further, Congress can also order that investigations be initiated on specific problems of concern relating to CVG and its enterprises. In this case, the directors and employees of the enterprises are obliged to appear before the legislative bodies or their committees and must submit the information and documents required by Congress.

Finally, Congress exercises control over the creation of subsidiary enterprises on the part of CVG; they cannot be constituted without the corresponding authorisation of the Finance Commission.

5. CVG AND FIV

There is no doubt that by clear legal mandate, CVG has been assigned a broad group of functions, rights and responsibilities for the execution of the integral development policy of the Guyana region. This has several implications.

(a) The abundant natural resources of the Guyana region have been developed at a much faster pace than the regions located elsewhere in the country.

(b) Economic policies and opportunities of investments have dictated that many of the industrial projects should be realised in a relatively short period of time.

(c) The size, pace and diversity of industrial development has put great pressure on the available human and financial resources.

(d) The financial requirements of the investment projects of the firms of the CVG Group were not equalled by the direct financial capacity of CVG. To this must be added the fact that the high initial investments involved long periods of amortisation, deferred profitability and high financing costs; and the generation of cash flows was affected.

A significant number of its firms have been under-financed or have a capital structure that does not assure an adequate net return on invested capital.

In brief, the main bottleneck suffered by the industrial projects undertaken by the CVG firms consisted of the insufficient direct financial capacity of the Corporation. The National Executive, however, with the objective of solving, in part, the financial difficulties of the projects, has been using, with increasing frequency, financial mechanisms that have tended to weaken CVG's position as the principal instrument for the development of the sectors under its legal responsibility. A good example of this situation is provided by the loans given by the 'Venezuelan Investment Fund' (FIV) to some of the firms in the CVG Group.

The initial purpose of FIV was to channel a substantial part of the oil income obtained by Venezuela from successive increases in oil prices, into the financing of the expansion and diversification of the economic structure of the country. FIV had to place funds in secure and profitable foreign investments. Thus FIV was created as a typical financial institution with authority to invest in foreign assets and to finance some projects related to the expansion and consolidation of the basic Venezuelan industry.

Due to the inadequacies in the financial capacity of CVG and considering the financial policy guidelines of the Government, FIV, using its resources, has been participating to a substantial degree in the financing of the industrial projects of the CVG firms, through subscriptions of shares, common and preferred. This gradually meant that FIV became the main shareholder of the majority of the firms that were once controlled by CVG. Thus, SIDOR, ALCASAVENAUM, INTERALUMINA are today controlled by FIV. In the same way, industrial projects of other firms like BAUXIVEN depend to a large degree on FIV for their financing.

With the intention of clarifying the relative positions of FIV and CVG (one a financial institution and the other an institution for business administration and control) the two institutions signed an agreement on 8 February 1979, containing a detailed description of their respective functions and responsibilities in relation to the direction, administration and control of the CVG firms. The agreement established that FIV, with its financial interests in the CVG firms, would always designate a representative to the meetings of the firm. In the same way FIV would nominate the external auditor of the firms. CVG, as a business administrator of the firms, would nominate the directors of the firms, including the directors corresponding to the FIV shares. The agreement also established that the investment programme and the annual investment budgets of each one of the firms in which CVG and FIV were shareholders, would be approved by both 'Assemblies'.

Finally, as a consequence of the transitory character of the ownership of shares of the CVG firms by FIV under the financial arrangements, the Agreement established the procedure by which CVG could take over the shares owned by FIV in a short time.

Experience has shown that, in spite of the Agreement, FIV, due to its financial capacity, has been assuming a very important influence in the administration and control of the CVG firms. In this way the original role of the FIV as a financial institution has been progressively changing into that of direct and increasing participation in the direction and control in the firms it finances. This situation becomes more relevant when account is taken of the fact that many of the CVG firms are under-financed and that the financing capacity of CVG continues to be insufficient. In this way the dependence of CVG and its firms on the decisions of FIV has been accentuated, and this affects, directly or indirectly, the business capacity of CVG and contradicts the original financial purpose of FIV.

From this situation it is possible to infer some consequences that affect the functioning of the projects of the CVG firms.

(a) There is a negative impact on the decision-making process, especially if account is taken of the sensitivity in terms of costs of the projects to decisions not taken at the right time.

(b) There is a duplication in efforts and scarce human resources, given that both CVG and FIV are involved in creating the structures to administer and control the CVG firms.

(c) There is a distortion in the purpose and functions for which FIV was originally created. This brings it into deep involvement in the management of the CVG firms, without a significant improvement in their management or an efficient substitution for the role legally assigned to CVG. If this distortion were to continue, FIV would become a super-holding company with direct involvement in the management of a large number of state-owned firms.

Finally, in so far as CVG is concerned the consequence is evident: it is affected in its main purpose, viz., the administration, direction and control of the firms that are the instruments of the Guyana programme.

9

NATIONAL FERTILIZER CORPORATION OF PAKISTAN LIMITED

Riyaz H. Bokhari

More than 71% of Pakistan's population lives in rural areas and a majority of all persons in employment (ten years and above) depend for their livelihood on agriculture. The Government of Pakistan has been making concerted efforts over the years to improve agricultural productivity through the use of fertilisers.

1. THE BEGINNINGS AND GROWTH OF NFC

Pakistan has eight fertiliser manufacturing facilities at present. Three of these are in the private sector and the remaining five form the National Fertilizer Corporation group, which accounts for nearly 52% of the total nitrogenous and 100% of phosphatic fertiliser manufacturing capacity in the country. Of the five, two are large and three are small. (Besides these, the group has a small plant for the manufacture of a micronutrient (zinc sulphate) also.) There is also a marketing subsidiary, viz., National Fertilizer Marketing Limited (NFML), which looks after dispatches from the factories, construction and operation of large warehouses in the consumption areas and distribution and sale of the fertilisers through an extensive network of dealers all over the country.

The manufacturing units are (i) the Pak-American Fertilizers Limited (PAFL) at Daudkhel, set up in 1958 to manufacture ammonium sulphate (present capacity: 90,000 tons per annum); (ii) the Lyallpur Chemicals and Fertilizers Limited (LC&FL), the two plants of which were set up in 1957 and 1967 to manufacture single super phosphate (present capacity of both plants: 90,000 tons per annum) – a small plant to manufacture zinc sulphate (600 tons per annum) was added in 1980; (ii) the Pakarab Fertilizers Limited (PFL) set up at Multan as the Natural Gas Fertilizer Factory (NGFF) in 1962 and modernised and expanded in 1978/79 to manufacture calcium ammonium nitrate (450,000 tons per annum) and nitrophosphate (304,500 tons per annum) besides 59,400 tons per annum of urea; (iv) the modern ammonia/urea plant of the Paksaudi Fertilizers Limited (PSFL), commissioned at Mirpur Mathelo in 1980 for manufacturing 557,000 tons of urea per annum, and (v) the Pakchina Fertilizers Limited (PCFL), completed in 1982 at Haripur with a capacity of 96,000 tons of urea annually.

The holding company, National Fertilizer Corporation of Pakistan Limited (NFC), was set up in 1973. The operating plants of PAFL, LC&FL and NGFF as well as the project for modernisation and expansion of the facilities at Multan were owned by the West Pakistan Industrial Development Corporation (PIDC) till their transfer to NFC in 1973/74. Since many of the characteristics of organisational structure, and practices and procedures followed by the public sector fertiliser industrial units have been inherited from PIDC, it would be useful to note certain facets of PIDC itself (described in Annex 1), especially those relating to its board of directors, its direct involvement in project promotion, its top management structure, and government stipulations concerning accounting and financial control; and of the Board of Industrial Management which came in the wake of large scale nationalisations in 1972.

The initial years of PIDC were marked by a spirit of trail blazing, flexibility in operations, quick and independent decision-making and emphasis on results achieved rather than on mere adherence to rigid rules. Over the years, however, with expansion in operations and responsibilities, there was a trend towards over-centralisation, strict observance of rules, constraints on flexibility, overstaffing, multiplicity of audits and greater involvement/interference of government functionaries in PIDC's decision-making process. The 'negative' role and the 'vetoing power' which could be exercised by the financial director of the Corporation under his charter of financial control and by virtue of the requirement that his dissenting views must be reported to the Government came in for increasing criticism and was put forward as an excuse for the lack of progress or initiative in achieving major objectives or in arriving at quick decisions. It was even held that the experience of PIDC proved that the public sector organisation was not adequate to run and manage a large number of enterprises. Quite a few of the units in the public sector were involved in losses, and the view was generally accepted that, while the public sector had the responsibility for assuming a pioneering role in setting up units in difficult locations and problematic sub-sectors, it could not be regarded as a regular and successful entrepreneur in the industrial sector.

Another point of historical significance needs mention here in view of its relevance for the origins of NFC. In December 1971 political power in the country passed to a party which subscribed to the philosophy of transferring the major categories of industrial activity to 'the control and command of the people'. In pursuance of this objective, the management of thirty-two large units operating under ten basic industrial categories in the private sector was taken over by the Central Government under the Economic Reforms Order of January 1972. These were later nationalised and transferred to the public sector on the basis of a compensation formula. There were two operating fertiliser plants in the private sector at that time but these were not nationalised, perhaps because these had foreign participation. However, a third small unit which was yet in a project-implementation stage in the private sector was taken over by the Government.

In order to manage these nationalised units a Board of Industrial Management (BIM) was established under the Development of Industries (Federal Control) Act, 1972. A Production Division was also created in the Government. The object was to ensure that these units were managed efficiently and in accordance with sound business principles. The Minister for Production was the Chairman of the Board and the members, including the finance member, were appointed by the Government to look after groups of units. Subsequently, a Vice-Chairman was also appointed. The Board had a full-fledged secretariat headed by its Secretary and in addition to the objectives mentioned earlier, it was expected to co-ordinate the activities of the individual public enterprises and to evaluate their performance; it was to undertake 'watchdog' functions over the nationalised industries on behalf of the Ministry of Production. The BIM was entrusted, among other duties, with the responsibilities of:

(i)   approving annual operating budgets of operating units;
(ii) arranging short and medium term credit facilities to meet the requirements of operating units;
(iii) making recommendations to the Ministry on matters of common concern to all units, for example, staff bonuses, working hours, working conditions and dividend policy;
(iv) assisting the units/corporations with their labour problems;
(v)   exercising control over contracts and purchases of major equipment by operating units; and

(vi) preparing periodical reports and conducting annual performance reviews of operating units/corporations.

It was soon realised that a large measure of decentralisation was necessary to enable BIM to carry out its managerial and planning functions. In 1973, by an amendment to the original order, the public sector industrial units operated by PIDC together with the thirty-two units that had been nationalised under the Economic Reforms Order of 1972, were reorganised and distributed on an industry-basis among ten public corporations incorporated under the Company's Act. NFC is one of these corporations. All the PIDC fertiliser plants and projects were transferred to it, along with the private sector project which had been nationalised in 1972.

NFC, whose offices are located in Lahore, is to spearhead the development of the fertiliser industry in the public sector. According to its mandate, it is responsible for the efficient operation, at optimum levels of capacity utilisation, of existing fertiliser plants, the establishment of additional fertiliser production facilities and the development of a distribution and marketing infrastructure for fertilisers. It is wholly owned by the Government with an authorised share capital of Rs. 1000 million and paid up capital of Rs. 700 million. Since 1974, the Corporation has launched three new companies viz., the Paksaudi Fertilizers Ltd. (PSFL), the Pakchina Fertilizers Ltd. (PCFL) and the National Fertilizer Marketing Ltd. (NFML). The projects for the modernisation of the old Multan plants and for setting up new facilities of PSFL and PCFL have been successfully completed. Three large warehouses for storing fertilisers in consumption areas during the off-seasons and thus reducing pressure on the country's transport system during the peak demand periods have been constructed and work is in hand at two more locations. A project estimated to cost US$49 million for the rehabilitation of old plants and facilities is being initiated with financial support (US$38.5 million) from the World Bank. This project includes the setting up of a Technical Training Centre also. A scheme for starting a Fertilizer Industry Research and Development Centre has also been drawn up and submitted to the Government for approval. Feasibility studies are in hand for additional large and small fertiliser plants.

From 1973 to 1982 the NFC Group's output of fertilisers went up from 211,500 tons to 1,302,600 tons. (With combined sales revenue of about Rs. 2.4 billion during 1981/82 the Group ranks as the third largest industrial enterprise in Pakistan.) Capacity utilisation improved to 71% in 1980/81 and to 83% in 1981/82; and the market share of NFC products went up from about 14% in 1973/74 to 44% in 1981/82.

2. THE GROUP AND THE CAPITALISATION STRUCTURE

Let us note some facts of interest as regards the capital structures of NFL and the subsidiaries.

The extent of NFC's shareholding in the subsidiaries was as follows in June 1982:

NFC's shareholdings

	Subsidiary (1)	NFC's share in capital (%) (2)
(i)	Pakarab Fertilizers Ltd (PFL)	52
(ii)	Paksaudi Fertilizers Ltd (PSFL)	100
(iii)	Pakchina Fertilizers Ltd (PCFL)	100
(iv)	Pakistan Fertilizer Co. Ltd (PFCL)	100
(v)	Pak-American Fertilizers Ltd (PAFL)	100
(vi)	Lyallpur Chemicals and Fertilizers Ltd (LC&FL)	75
(vii)	National Fertilizer Marketing Ltd (NFML)	50

The structure of capitalisation of these companies and of NFC is indicated below. Two points of interest may be mentioned: the loan–equity ratios are quite diverse; and loans from non-government sources have been quite important.

NFC inherited an investment of Rs. 160 million in the operating units transferred to it from PIDC during 1973/74. The book value of NFC's investment figure rose to Rs. 1823 million on 30 June 1982. Apart from channelling Rs. 700 million as the Government's equity in its subsidiaries, Rs. 746 million was raised by NFC as cash development loan from the Government and another Rs. 907 million was raised through the issue of debentures to a consortium of banks. Of the total funds raised by NFC, Rs. 1221 million were invested as share capital in the subsidiaries and the balance was passed on as loans. It is not difficult to see that under such an arrangement where a substantial part of a holding company's investment in the equity share capital of its subsidiaries is financed out of borrowed funds, considerable strain is put on the liquidity position of the parent company when

Capitalisation of NFC Group (Rs. Million)

(1)	30th June, 1978								30th June, 1982							
	PFL (2)	PSFL (3)	PCFL (4)	PAFL (5)	LC&FL (6)	PFC (7)	NFML (8)	NFC (9)	PFL (10)	PSFL (11)	PCFL (12)	PAFL (13)	LC&FL (14)	PFC (15)	NFML (16)	NFC (17)
Equity Capital	646	275	51	90	4	10	0.5	286	646	600	188	90	7	11	0.5	700
Loans from NFC/Government	320	-	-	0.7	12	6	-	535	238	117	87	-	4	13	44	746
Loans from others	692	797	-	0.7	-	18	-	492	582	695	381	-	-	17	-	354
Reserves	-	-	-	5	5	-	-	117	480	-	-	5	6	-	-	118
Unappropriated Profit/(loss)	1	-	-	0.1	(16)	-	1	(132)	103	203	7	2	3	-	8	85

the redemption of loans and interest payments start falling due, particularly if the projects have not by that time gone into profitable production and are thus not in a position to pay dividends and meet the commitments. In fact NFC has been facing this situation, what with the long gestation periods of its projects and unavoidable slippages in their completion. The interest payments could have been 'capitalised', but for a number of reasons it was considered advisable to charge these to the annual profit and loss account of the Corporation. The figure of accumulated losses of NFC, mainly on this account, rose to Rs. 132 million on 30 June 1978. However, with the commissioning of the new plants in subsequent years, NFC has started receiving dividend incomes. Adjustments have also been carried out consequent upon the conversion of a part of the Government's development loan into equity shareholding and the consequential refund (by adjustment) of interest previously paid. As a result, the accumulated loss was wiped out completely by June 1982 and the Corporation will now be in a position to pay a return on government equity out of its dividend income from the subsidiaries. The details of how the accumulated loss situation of 1977/78 has been dealt with are shown below.

ACCUMULATED LOSS/PROFIT POSITION OF NFC (Rs. million)

Year	Net Income/(loss)[1]	Interest paid on development loans utilised as equity in subsidiaries	Accumulated (loss)/profit at end of year
(1)	(2)	(3)	(4)
1977/78	(7)	48	(132)[2]
1978/79	(4)	28	(98)[3]
1979/80	15	28	(111)
1980/81	41[4]	52	(122)
1981/82	278	70	85

1. Dividend and Managing agency commission received less office and establishment expenses of NFC.
2. Accumulated losses at end of
   1974/75   Rs.   5 million
   1975/76   Rs. 56 million (including loss of Rs. 33 million on sale of NGFF assets to PFL)
   1976/77   Rs. 77 million
3. After adjustment of refund of interest (Rs. 66 million) previously paid to Government on loans which were converted into equity.
4. Dividend due from subsidiaries for 1980/81 accounted for in 1981/82 on receipt.

3. THE HOLDING COMPANY ROLE OF NFC

NFC, as the main instrument of the Government in the fertiliser field, has the responsibility for implementing national policy and for achieving the goals set for it. At the same time, it is concerned with protecting the interests of the Government as a shareholder of the subsidiaries. It has, therefore, to balance its operations between these two major responsibilities. It must ensure that its subsidiaries are operating efficiently and profitably and at the same time undertake activities or risks which may be necessary in order to accelerate the development of the industry but which the private sector may not want to undertake. It identifies the industry's needs, e.g. availability of warehouses, rehabilitation of old plants and projects and schemes: it monitors closely the performance of the subsidiaries with reference to budgeted targets and designed consumption ratios, and approves those projects which generally have an impact on the overall efficiency and profitability, the direction of the growth of the industry or the subsidiary. It has also to keep in view the Government policies and specific directives issued to it from time to time. NFC's role towards its subsidiaries has been mainly that of a holding company and principal shareholder, acting as financial supervisor, monitor of performance, guide in respect of government policies, channel of communication with various government authorities and agencies, agent for bulk procurement of a limited number of items and a central body for facilitating recruitment and career development of middle and senior management level executives. In the case of two subsidiaries, namely PAFL and LC&FL, it has agreements for acting as their managing agent.

NFC is accountable to the Government for the performance of the public sector of the fertiliser industry and is, therefore, ultimately responsible not only for its own operations but for the operations of its subsidiaries as well. The Corporation has perceived itself as a holding company and as a mechanism for channelling sound investment in fertiliser and related projects. It is responsible for the initiation, evaluation, planning and execution of new projects. Learning from the experience of PIDC, NFC does not, as a matter of policy, get involved in the direct management of projects and expects the subsidiaries to operate as autonomously as possible. For this purpose even the task of implementation of new projects is handled by setting up new independent subsidiaries rather than as projects of the parent body. NFC adopts a relatively passive role by controlling and guiding the operating subsidiaries through their respective boards of directors.

This is facilitated by the fact that the Chairman and the chief executive of NFC is concurrently the chairman of each of these boards also. This is quite an effective arrangement and the fact that NFC has full responsibility for monitoring and co-ordinating the activities of on-going projects and subsidiaries is never lost sight of.

Although the key officers of the subsidiary companies are technically NFC employees, they are encouraged to feel accountable to their respective boards of directors. These companies view NFC primarily as a major stock holder and rely upon it for overall guidance and direction through the Chairman of NFC.

NFC's policy of autonomous operation by subsidiaries has many points to commend itself. While the entire Group has to be seen as a single system, great care is exercised to avoid centralisation in the management and operations of the group. The subsidiaries are separate legal entities and the units are geographically dispersed. There are differences in technology: in the case of all but two units the size of operations and investment are substantial; and these units are capable of managing themselves. NFC's approach of not centralising helps in training executives and managers for shouldering responsibilities at a later stage at higher levels of policy formulation and supervision. It also enables NFC to pinpoint responsibility for the performance of specific projects. One of the reasons for adopting this approach has, of course, been the shortage of experienced and qualified managers who could be spared for appointment in staff positions at the Corporation head office itself.

It is to be appreciated that in the nature of NFC's structure the need for close co-ordination and efficient communication is very critical. With the dual objectives of keeping the lines of communications open as well as to develop future senior managers within the Corporation, monthly review meetings are held with the subsidiaries. These are presided over by the Chairman who is assisted by his staff officers. The top management of the subsidiaries along with the second, and at times even the third, tiers of management are encouraged to participate in a free and frank discussion of their affairs. Problems which hinder the achievement of targets − physical and/or financial − are identified and analysed objectively. Attempts are made to find optimum solutions and to devise such lines of attacking the problems as are indicated by consensus as likely to have the maximum chance of success at the earliest and with the least cost. The executives concerned are encouraged to make presentations about their respective areas of responsibilities. Ways and means are discussed to improve co-ordination of operations among the sister companies, and in particular with the marketing subsidiary. In order to facilitate full coverage of a maximum number of problems faced by a subsidiary, NFC's staff officers hold preliminary and informal meetings with the subsidiary's officers and departments concerned. Problems which require discussions at length and/or at higher levels are brought before the review meeting the following day. Formal minutes of these meetings are recorded and 'follow up' action is discussed in subsequent meetings. Apart from ensuring co-ordination and providing a quick means of feedback and control over significant aspects of operations or project implementation, these procedures help the executives of subsidiaries to overcome their shyness and to learn from their seniors on matters pertaining to the human factor and decision-making.

By this approach, it has been possible to monitor, control and guide the subsidiaries in an economical manner and with the minimum deployment of resources, particularly of highly experienced technical personnel. The head office strength is watched very closely and is not allowed to expand on marginal pretexts. The purpose is not only to keep the expenditure down but to obviate the operation of Parkinson's Law and over-centralisation with consequent bottlenecks and inefficiencies. Under the set-up, the spheres of responsibility are clearly defined at various levels so that accountability can be enforced quickly.

In the matter of supervision of the subsidiaries the main role of NFC is to set targets in respect of each of the projects/companies, in consultation with the management concerned. NFC then monitors the progress in respect of the achievement of the targets, on a regular basis. The areas of weakness are identified speedily and remedies that are required to overcome the deficiency are immediately brought into play. The essential nature of this monitoring and information system is that maximum authority is delegated to the units concerned and it is for them to find ways and means to regulate their performance in order to achieve the targets in terms of physical achievement as well as timely completion within the allotted resources. A standardised reporting system has been introduced for reporting the physical and financial activities of the units.

It has not been felt necessary to continue in the NFC Group the 'watchdog' functions of PIDC days, which allowed the right of 'direct access to the Government' and virtual 'veto power' to one of the directors. It is clearly understood that the responsibility for the decisions and their consequences rests squarely with the chief executive of the Corporation/unit concerned.

A brief account of the comprehensive budgetary and financial control system in operation in the NFC Group would illustrate the nature of internal relationships within the Group. The object of the system is to secure optimum utilisation of the resources. Detailed guidelines have been developed and laid down for the preparation of budgets for production and sales in the operating plants and their linkages with the budgets for purchases of raw materials, packing materials (bags, liners), spare parts etc., plans for maintenance, budgets for expenses and financial requirements, proposals for personnel hiring, etc. Proposals for capital investment for replacement of worn-out assets, addition of new equipment to improve efficiency of operations and to achieve reductions in operating expenses, and welfare measures for staff are also drawn up as part of this exercise.

Budget committees have been formed in each company to set out the budget assumptions and guidelines for determining production and sale plans, to review the budgets for each cost centre and department, to compile and integrate the budget for the company and to present it to the company's managing director before finalisation and submission of a 'skeleton' budget to NFC at least four months in advance of the start of the year.

The draft (or skeleton) budgets are reviewed in detail in NFC to check up production targets in the light of long and short term plans for improvement of rated capacity utilisation, sales prospects, inventory levels, etc. The expenditure budgets are reviewed in the light of prescribed consumption ratios and standard inputs. Variance analyses are carried out to segregate the impact of changes in prices, volumes and usages of inputs in the proposed budget as compared to the actuals for the preceding periods.

Based on the above reviews detailed discussions are held with the managing directors of the subsidiaries concerned. In all these meetings the chief executive of the marketing company is also present so that the targets for production, sales/dispatches and inventory levels are kept internally consistent. It is also ensured that the budgets conform to the overall plans and strategy of NFC, as a group. Targets of achievement in various areas are finalised during these discussions and, if necessary, the companies concerned revise their detailed budget components (cash flow, budgeted profit and loss statement, sale value and volume, production volume, plant utilisation, inventory levels, cost of sales, materials consumption ratios, production overheads, general administrative expenses, financial charges, stores levels, capital budget etc.) and submit these to NFC before the start of the year. These budgets are also presented to the respective boards of directors for discussion and approval.

A system of reviewing budget performance of the subsidiaries at quarterly intervals is in operation. The actual expenses/income/out-flows are compared with (proportionate) budgeted provisions for the period. Deviations from the budget are isolated for detailed discussion and remedial action is chalked out for improving performance (inputs and expenses) and for making up deficiencies in meeting the targets. These reviews and discussions form the basis of financial control and performance evaluation of the companies.

The Management Information System (MIS) in the NFC group consists of balance sheets, operating results, statements of sources and application of funds and product cost analysis. An integrated system of accounting has been introduced whereby financial and cost accounts are maintained in one set of books. An elaborate cost system has been introduced to compute costs according to carefully estab-lished cost centres. Unit costs of utilities and the production depart-ment are worked out on a monthly basis and compared with the planned costs. The identity of variable and fixed cost is maintained right up to the stage of the end-products.

The accounting system has been organised in such a manner as would facilitate the preparation of management reports on a month-ly basis. Income statements and balance sheets supported with the necessary schedules are prepared by 15th of every month following the month of accounts.

As part of an overall MIS, NFC companies prepare the following monthly and quarterly statements: monthly: (1) operating results, (2) cost of goods sold, (3) production report, (4) sale report, (5) personnel position, (6) income statement, (7) cash flow and (8) balance sheet; and quarterly: (1) inventory statement, (2) finished goods stock report, (3) status of loans, (4) balance sheet, (5) cash and deposits, (6) ac-counts receivable ageing summary, (7) tax and duties and (8) product prices.

The following ratios are worked out by the companies as part of the preparation of periodical financial statements: finished stock turn-over, labour turnover, productivity of employees, capacity utilisation, inventory levels in terms of annual production, and production hours loss due to plant shut-down. Monthly operation returns are also used for trend analysis by comparing actual performance with the budget targets.

The senior officers in NFC's head office function as 'staff officers' to the chief executive of the Corporation. They provide assistance to him in the respective areas assigned to them and do not exercise direct authority over the chief executives (or other officers) of the subsidiaries.

The experience so far has not brought out any major points of friction between NFC and the subsidiaries. There are sometimes differences of opinion about such matters as the need for enforcing certain minimum standards and conditions prior to the promotion of executives, extent of concessions to be allowed to labour and the collective bargaining agents at the time of periodical negotiations, revisions in the established consumption ratios, steps necessary to improve productivity of labour, the creation of additional positions in the approved organisation chart, and proposals for additional capital expenditure on particular items preferred by the companies but not necessarily in line with the long-term plans of the Group; but it has so far been possible to resolve these issues amicably by frank discussions through a comprehensive analysis of the pros and cons of the proposals and a mature appreciation of the various constraints in which public sector enterprises operate.

4. THE BOARDS OF DIRECTORS

The board of NFC has a full-time chairman and four other members – all drawn from the public sector: two of them from the Government (Additional Secretaries of Ministry of Production and Ministry of Food and Agriculture) and the other two from public enterprises (managing director of Bankers Equity Ltd. and chairman of Federal Chemical and Ceramics Ltd).

The boards of the subsidiaries are broadly similar in constitution. The chairman in every case is the chairman of NFC. Annexe 2 gives details. Two points may be mentioned. One is that, except for the chairman of NFC or the managing director or general manager of a subsidiary, there is no full-time or functional director on the boards. Second, there are no directors from outside the public sector. The four representatives from Abu Dhabi on the Pakarab Fertilizers board themselves come on behalf of Abu Dhabi National Oil Co. Ltd., whose principal shareholding is governmental.

NFC deals directly with the Ministry of Production but not with the other Ministries, except through the Ministry of Production. This has grown in size over the years. It has today one secretary, two additional secretaries, five joint secretaries, a large number of deputy secretaries and section officers and a full-fledged Expert Advisory Cell.

5. THE INTERNAL STRUCTURE OF ORGANISATION

The structure of internal organisation of NFC is shown in Annexe 3. The chairman, who reports through the board of directors to the Minister of Production, is assisted by four general managers for Technical and Planning; Finance; Commercial; and Personnel and Administration. The broad functions and responsibilities of these departments are summarised below.

Planning Department

(i)   Preparation of feasibility studies for new projects/schemes, discussions with concerned government agencies;
(ii) monitoring physical progress of the on-going projects; and
(iii) developing a suitable Management Information System and computerisation programme for NFC subsidiaries covering procurement, civil works, and erection activities for projects under implementation.

Technical Department

(i)   Technical assistance and guidance to the operating units so as to maintain a standard level of consumption efficiencies;
(ii) monitoring production programmes of the operating units and identifying reasons for any shortfalls for remedial action;
(iii) co-ordinating maintenance programmes in the units and introducing preventive maintenance techniques as well as maintaining significant data on the breakdown of critical equipments for future reference;
(iv) assistance in planning and selection of the process/design criteria for new plants; and
(v)   forward manpower planning for the group's requirement for engineers and technicians and selection of suitable training programmes both inside and outside the country.

Finance Department

(i)   Formulation of annual development programme for the on-going projects/schemes and monitoring of fixed capital investment; determining credit requirements of the projects and raising funds from the Government's annual development programme as well as from financial institutions through debenture issue; also negotiating loans with foreign lending agencies;

(ii) introduction of finance and cost control through budgets in the operating units; chalking out internal audit programmes for NFC units; arranging cost verification and notification of ex-factory prices of fertilisers produced in the group and obtaining ad hoc and final release of payments for the units;

(iii) preparation of accounts and periodical reports for the Corporation and consolidating financial results on a Group basis; maintaining liaison with the various cells and units of the Ministry of Production on financial matters; and

(iv) looking after corporate affairs, taxation and audit of the Corporation and rendering technical advisory services in this regard to the subsidiary companies; dealing with government auditors and performance evaluation teams; and organising administrative functions in the branch office at Islamabad.

Commercial Department

(i)   Matters relating to import of raw material, especially rock phosphate and sulphur for the companies in the Group;

(ii) co-ordination of purchase/import of packing material, cloth or polypropylene bags and liners;

(iii) co-ordination of verification of fertiliser dispatches to various provinces and obtaining confirmation from the agencies concerned; and

(iv) organising clearance and dispatch of the imported materials through the Karachi Office.

Personnel and Administration Department

(i)   co-ordination of recruitment policies with the Government and arranging for recruitment of executive employees on a centralised cadre basis;

(ii) maintaining personnel records;

(iii) conducting and co-ordinating negotiations with the collective bargaining agents and rendering advice on labour management to the subsidiaries; and

(iv) organising office and general services including transportation and security in the head office at Lahore.

NFC is responsible for the recruitment of all persons in executive grades and also the staff required to run the NFC head office. All recruitment is on the basis of merit and primarily against public advertisements. As compared to a total staff strength of 3164 persons (173 executives/managers and 2991 non-executives) on 30 June 1974, NFC group currently employs 5179 persons, 983 of which are in senior managerial and junior executive positions including forty apprentices. Of the 4196 non-executives, 291 are employed in the marketing subsidiary, 2585 (including 207 trainees) are skilled workers and 1320 are semi-skilled labourers and clerical staff. All the executives and managers working in the holding company as well as in the subsidiaries are borne on a common cadre and are liable to transfer from one unit to another. However, the powers of direct recruitment or promotion to this cadre up to a certain level of officers have been delegated to the chief executives of the units who select and appoint officers in their companies but take care to make offers to the new recruits on behalf of NFC. It thus becomes possible to plan inter-unit transfers, common training and career planning of the executives on a centralised cadre basis. In order to provide the much needed technical manpower for its existing as well as new projects, NFC initiated a practical training programme for qualified engineers and technicians in 1976. More than 600 technicians and engineers have been trained in their respective fields. A batch of about fifty engineers is selected for practical training every year.

In the matter of compensation policy for its executives and managers, NFC has had to suffer from the consequences of certain restrictions imposed by the Government with the object of enforcing uniformity in the pay scales, perquisites and terms and conditions of employment of officers in the public sector industrial enterprises. The directives issued by the Government on these subjects have had to be followed scrupulously by the NFC Group with the result that freedom of action and flexibility required to deal quickly with problems arising out of a sudden change in conditions are lost, because it is not easy to get the concerned government authorities to agree to modify or withdraw such directives for fear of repercussions elsewhere. Some time ago there was a considerable increase in economic activity in the Middle East and a number of fertiliser plants were planned for installation there. The demand for qualified and experienced personnel for these projects grew and large numbers of such persons from the private sector and public sector organisations in Pakistan decided to avail themselves of the very attractive terms offered abroad. This in due course affected the NFC Group also whose officers/workers started resigning in large numbers in order to join the private sector organisations which had lost their personnel or find jobs directly in the Middle East. While it was recognised that it would not be possible for NFC to compete with the very lucrative terms offered by the employers abroad, it was felt that in order to retain its experienced and trained staff and to maintain its operations it should at least be in a position to match the terms and emoluments offered by similar private sector organisations within Pakistan. The development of a formula by which NFC could be given the necessary powers to increase the emoluments of its experienced technical staff without repercussions in other public sector organisations was a lengthy process and in the meantime the managerial effectiveness of NFC and its subsidiaries was greatly affected by a significant turn-over at all levels of its managerial and technical personnel. The impact of this exodus was most pronounced during the implementation and commissioning periods of NFC's major projects at PFL and PSFL. As mentioned above, the principal reason for the staffing problem was to be found in the low levels of remuneration admissible to NFC's technical and management staff; these levels were tied to government pay scales and historically had been well below those customary in comparable private sector industries. After long discussions, the Government finally agreed in 1979 to remove pay limitations of certain categories of executives in the two major NFC subsidiaries which were using sophisticated technology. These improvements have succeeded in reducing the turn-over significantly.

Further a scheme is being developed by NFC under which it will be possible to send promising engineers on deputation abroad for short periods. This will enable them to gain wider experience and also to benefit from the liberal terms of employment in the Middle East, at the same time retaining their links and lien with NFC to which they will return at the end of their tour of duty abroad.

NFC takes special care in broad-basing the management capabilities of its executives. It is a technically oriented Corporation where commercial and financial decisions are equally important. The decision-makers in NFC, by and large, come from an engineering background and thus it is necessary that they are exposed to commercial and financial management at appropriate stages in their career development. For this purpose, engineers are sent regularly to attend general management courses.

All sales of fertilisers from the manufacturing units are made through the National Fertilizer Marketing Limited (NFML). The sale of by-products such as acids, gases and other chemicals is the responsibility of the units themselves. The centralisation of marketing of products facilitates specialist concentration in the selling activities, advertising, and relationships with dealers, transporters, local

authorities and competitors. The technical managers of the manufacturing units are thus relieved of the need to deal with the problems of
the market and can give their undivided attention to maintaining
highest levels and quality of production. By having a common marketing organisation, which sells NFC products under the same brand
name, the subsidiaries avoid harmful competition with one another.

It could be argued that the isolation of factory managements from
the direct pressures and demands of their market creates a gap in the
comprehensiveness of their experience and in the full development
of their managerial skills. The importance of exposing middle and
senior management of manufacturing units to the intricacies of
marketing, distribution and selling operations is not denied but a
chronic shortage of adequately trained and experienced engineers for
staffing the units has contributed greatly to the evolution of the
present situation in which there is virtually no exchange of personnel
with the marketing subsidiary. However, it must be mentioned that
the top managements of the units are represented on the board of
directors of NFML and are thus aware of its marketing strategy and
problems. A more effective mechanism for ensuring a better appreciation of each other's problems at lower levels of management in the
manufacturing and marketing subsidiaries has yet to be developed.
The secondment to NFML of suitable executives who show an apti-
tude for marketing operations, has also to be arranged. It is proposed
to consider these for implementation as a part of NFC's management
development programme.

NFC completes ten years of its corporate life by 1983. During these
years it has had its share of set-backs and problems − slippage and
cost overruns in projects, strains on liquidity, under-utilisation of
installed capacity, piling up of losses, exodus of experienced staff,
accumulation of unsold stocks etc. − but it has been possible to deal
with them in an effective and timely manner. Its overall performance
has been rated amongst the best in the public sector in the country.
Its capability to tackle short-term and long-range problems points
towards the soundness of its organisational structure and operating
practices. Learning from the experience of PIDC days it has developed
its capacity to undertake activities with a minimum duplication of
effort, effect savings through centralisation of certain functions, and
provide leadership in presenting a common stand on issues affecting
the fertiliser industry in the public sector.

6. NFC AND THE GOVERNMENT

It is difficult to say whether the economics-of-scale argument can justify far larger expansions within the NFC apex. A move towards increasing the size of the holding company would imply the central- isation of many functions, which cuts across the desirability of dele- gation to, and assuring the autonomy of, the subsidiaries. The time taken in decision-making in day-to-day matters would be increased, without necessarily improving the quality of decisions. A large-sized holding company will sooner or later result in the movement of the scarce resource of competent and technically trained manpower to- wards the head office. This can have deleterious effects on the per- formance of the operating units. So long as co-ordination can be ensured effectively and the lines of communication kept open with (and among) the various units of the group, a small-sized holding corporation can reasonably be expected to combine the benefits of low overheads with greater flexibility in the matter of adaptation to changes in external conditions. The interface of the Group with the Government should be through the holding company only: otherwise unmanageable confusion will result. A recent proposal that the sub- sidiaries may send their periodical reports directly to the Expert Advisory Cell is under consideration.

Being the only Corporation responsible for all fertiliser units in the public sector, NFC has certain advantages as well as disadvantages. It has a fairly large share of the market and has, therefore, enjoyed a commanding position in the matter of allocation of funds for new projects. However, with the recent change in government policy which aims at encouraging the private sector for investment in the fertiliser industry, this advantage has been reduced considerably. At times the Government finds it convenient to get some aspects of its national fertiliser policy implemented through directions to NFC instead of to the entire fertiliser industry, e.g., the marketing of particular fertilisers in specified areas, publicity campaigns, conducting surveys and research. This development is not unique to NFC. Other public sector holding companies like the Cement and Chemical Corporations are also facing the same advantages and drawbacks because they were also created as the sole Corporations to manage all the public sector units in their respective fields. Public Sector Corporations have, therefore, to learn to live with and adapt themselves to changes in government policy and NFC has not yet found this to be a worrisome constraint.

During the last two or three years a significant change has taken place in the relationship between the NFC and the Ministry of Production/Government. The need for this change had been brewing for quite some time. Immediately after nationalisation, the Government was highly sensitive to critical reviews of the nationalised units, as these were interpreted to be a criticism of nationalisation itself. This, together with the emphasis on expansions in public sector investment, inter alia, led to greater emphasis on powers being exercised by the Ministry of Production. The organisational structure which had been adopted for the BIM enterprises was, in principle, based on a decentralised system in which similar units had been grouped under sector Corporations and the latter under BIM whose chairman was the Minister for Production himself. These Corporations were supposed to be autonomous with their chairmen having complete operating control. With the expansion in the role of the Ministry of Production, the organisational structure in effect had four tiers of management – the Ministry, the BIM, the sector corporations and the units. There was increasing evidence that this structure was not working very well because the functions of the different tiers of the structure had not been clearly defined and more and more powers were being appropriated at higher levels. After a careful examination of the state of affairs, it was decided in 1979 to abolish the Board of Industrial Management and to introduce measures and mechanisms which would enable performance to be evaluated at the unit level for prompt remedial measures at appropriate management levels. The number of sector corporations was reduced by re-grouping the units and emphasis was placed on allowing freedom to professional management and executives to run their organisations, with full accountability assured in the interest of the tax payers. In order to assist the Ministry in the performance of its functions, an Experts Advisory Cell (EAC) was created in December 1979 with the following duties and responsibilities:

(i)   collection of data from corporations/units regarding operational results and financial position and collation of information for the Ministry;
(ii) preparation of quarterly and annual performance reports;
(iii) appraisal and evaluation of cases referred to it by the Ministry;
(iv) performance review of any unit, company or corporation as required by the Ministry; and
(v)   special management and performance audits.

Since its inception, EAC has done useful work, conducted a number of studies, formulated proposals for financial restructuring/

reorganisation of some units and issued many reports. Most of all it has enabled the Ministry to permit the corporations and the units to function with a much greater degree of freedom than had been possible earlier when the Ministry did not have ready access to an authoritative and objective analysis of the actual performance of, and trends recorded by, the organisations sought to be controlled by it. The Cell is presently engaged in creating a computerised databank and a modern performance evaluation system with which a system of rewards is to be linked. Monthly results of operations are regularly fed to EAC by NFC and its units and the quarterly reports prepared by the former provide the basis for review sessions with the Ministry of Production when all the chairmen of the sector corporations meet the Minister, exchange views on common problems and seek guidance on current issues related to development and implementation of government policy in their respective sectors. The Minister and senior officers of the Ministry also meet the chief executives of the individual corporations along with the managing directors of their subsidiaries. These meetings provide a useful forum for thrashing out problems faced by the units and for outlining the direction in which future development should proceed.

7. ORGANISATIONAL CHANGES

NFC keeps under constant study its organisational structure, routines and procedures, relationships with the subsidiaries on the one hand and with the Government on the other. One such review was under-taken recently with the help of foreign consultants. This resulted in a number of recommendations for change. One of these observations was in favour of evolving a formally established administrative mechanism within the Group to ensure effective co-ordination of overall operation. The top management function involved mainly strategic planning and policy formulation to provide overall direction and guidance in the management and operation of the NFC Group. This function was being carried out mainly by the Chairman and the respective boards of directors of the subsidiary companies. Plans and policies laid down by them were then translated into concrete oper-ational plans and work programmes by the respective chief executives. This arrangement, suitable until the completion of large plants, is likely to be somewhat inadequate to meet the future needs. It was, therefore, recommended that a management committee should be established at the NFC level to serve as the formal administrative mechanism for overall planning and co-ordination of the operations within the group. The recommendation has been accepted and implemented. The committee comprises the chairman of NFC and the managing directors/general managers in charge of the individual companies in the group. Regular meetings are scheduled to discuss common problems and issues confronting the group as a whole. The decisions taken at the meetings are to be cleared with the board of directors concerned, before implementation.

Other recommendations of the study included:

(i)   provision by the Government of greater autonomy to the NFC Group on operational matters, particularly on the setting of compensation levels for its officers;
(ii) development of integrated training programmes for employees, with suitably improved systems for periodical appraisal and performance reviews; and
(iii) detailed review and revision of current management information systems, accounting manuals, etc.

Steps are in hand to implement these and other recommendations as early as possible.

In conclusion, it is fair to observe that NFC's organisational structure has proved itself workable and efficient and shown adequate sensitivity to the needs of change from time to time.

ANNEXE 1

The Pakistan Industrial Development Corporation

The Pakistan Industrial Development Corporation (PIDC) was established under the PIDC Act of 1950 — it actually came into existence in January 1952 — as an autonomous body with the object of accelerating the pace of industrial development in the country, particularly in those fields which the private enterprise found unattractive on account of technological complexity, or large size of initial investment required, or long gestation period involved or doubtful/inadequate profitability. (Subsequently, with the aim of transferring more activities from the central to the provincial spheres, this Corporation was bifurcated as between (the then) East Pakistan and West Pakistan provinces.)

The survey and investigation schemes for new projects were carried out by the Corporation out of a revolving credit with it. In case the expenditure was expected to go beyond certain specific limits, the Government's approval was obtained and funds were allocated out of its Annual Development Programme. When the results of preliminary surveys were found sound, 'feasibility reports' and 'project proposals' were prepared in collaboration with experienced technical experts and submitted to the Government for approval and allocation of funds. The foreign exchange requirements of the proposed projects were met through foreign aid/loans. If any private enterprises also participated in any of the schemes, part of the finances, of course, came from them. The annual budgetary grants provided by the Government up to 1964–65 were in the shape of investment funds, eligible for dividends and other income. However, from 1965–66 a revised pattern of financing was introduced and the investment funds were treated as 'developing loans' to the Corporation on which interest at specified rates was charged by the Government. On completion of a project, a 'completion report' was required to be prepared. The administrative overheads incurred during construction were transferred to each project's fixed assets account on a pro-rata basis. Immediately on start of production, operational accounts were introduced and a proper costing procedure was required to be laid down.

The schemes undertaken by the Corporation either continued to remain as 'projects' up to the stage of production or they were converted into joint stock companies under the Company's Act, due consideration being given to their individual capital structures. The share capital of such a company could either be wholly contributed by the Corporation out of the funds (equity investment or development loans) received from the Government for the 'project'; or there could be private sector participation in addition. There was a managing agency department in the Corporation's head office to take care of these formalities.

The policy of the Corporation was to promote and develop basic industries either on its own or in collaboration with private enterprises. In the initial stage all efforts were made to associate private capital with the projects sponsored by the Corporation. If such participation was not forthcoming, the projects were completed out of the funds provided/arranged by Government and thereafter the private enterprise was again offered the opportunity of participation in these projects. If there was no success even at this stage, then the projects on completion were converted into public limited companies and their shares offered for general public subscription with the Corporation acting as the managing agents of such companies. Even then the shareholding of the Corporation was available for disinvestment by offer to private enterprise. This disinvestment was, however, carried out with the Government's approval on terms and conditions mutually agreed; and the managing agency of the company was transferred to the party concerned, after the Corporation's disinvestment.

The general direction and administration of the Corporation and its affairs were vested in its board which comprised a chairman and two directors and which exercised all powers entrusted to it under its statute. The board was appointed by the Government and in discharging its functions it was required to act on commercial considerations, guided by such directions as the Government might give it from time to time. In case of failure to obey any such direction, the Government had the power to remove the directors and/or the chairman. One of the directors was to be the financial director, whose powers and duties included scrutinising and offering written comments to the board on such matters as schemes which were required to be submitted to the Government for approval, proposals regarding the sponsoring of public companies, annual budgets, reports and audited accounts of the Corporation, procedures for the purchase and sale of goods, immovable property and shares, suggestions and recommendations for the framing of rules concerning the terms and conditions of employment of officers, advisers and employees of the Corporation and cases relating to the grant of higher initial pay. If the board did not agree to the comments of the financial director in respect of any of these matters, the comments were to form part of the minutes of the meeting in which the matter was considered by the board. A statement incorporating the minutes of dissent recorded by the financial director from time to time was required to be submitted to the Government periodically. Every case involving interpretation of, or exemption from, any rule or regulation was required to be referred to the financial director who was also required to deal with all matters pertaining to insurance, foreign aid, loans, investments, economic evaluation of projects, accounts and audit. It was his responsibility to prescribe procedures for the exercise of financial control in the Corporation in respect of matters relating to receipts and expenditure.

The Government also prescribed that the accounting procedure for various activities of the Corporation should be laid down in consultation with the Auditor General of Pakistan. This was to include the system of internal financial control. A detailed procedure was also to be developed in consultation with the Auditor General regarding the manner in which audit should be carried out and a provision was to be made for 'special audits' on the direction of the Government. The pay scales for all categories of employees and their terms and conditions of service were to be laid down with the Government's prior approval. Rules regarding the delegation of financial powers to the managing directors of companies or to officers subordinate to them were also to have the prior approval of the Government.

In the case of limited companies sponsored by the Corporation to take over schemes and projects completed by it, the directors of the Corporation were represented on the boards of directors of such companies and the Corporation acted as the 'managing agent'.

The directors and chairman of the Corporation had a clear-cut allocation of industries and distribution of functions among themselves. A number of technical divisions had been set up in the head office to look after the responsibility for planning, promoting, organising and implementing programmes of new schemes and for managing the operational activities of the completed projects/companies. Fertiliser projects and companies fell under the Chemical Industries Division. A number of service divisions/departments were organised to cope with common problems. These included the secretariat (co-ordination, administration, legal affairs, and labour matters), divisions for sales and marketing, planning, finance, accounts, audit, purchase, medical and publicity divisions, and departments for managing agencies and civil engineering.

Each division of the Corporation was headed by a general manager. Administrative and financial powers of the board were delegated up to specified limits to the executives of the divisions, projects and companies in order to ensure efficient operations through on-the-spot decisions on day-to-day functions. Detailed rules were laid down for financial control in projects/companies and in the Corporation itself. These covered such aspects of working as procedures for accounting and reporting as prescribed in an accounting manual with a detailed chart of accounts; financial advice; budgeting including such features as production and sales targets, consumption of raw materials, stores and spares, salaries and wages, overheads etc.; pre-audit on receipts and payments through 'budgets and funds control', sanctions and competence of sanctioning authority, checks against rules and instructions, observance of financial propriety etc., and auditing. The Corporation had three types of audit, i.e., 'internal audit', 'external audit' and 'government commercial audit'. The first was undertaken by the Corporation's own audit division on a quarterly basis and its reports highlighted the state of accounts and contained suggestions for remedial action by the managements of projects, companies, divisions, etc. The external audit of the companies was undertaken under the Company's Law by firms of chartered accountants selected and appointed by the Corporation's audit division with the approval of the board. Normally, the audit was conducted on annual accounts on which a report was rendered to the directors and shareholders of the company concerned/Corporation. The government commercial audit was undertaken by an independent agency, viz., Director, Commercial Audit Department, on behalf of the Auditor General of Pakistan. This audit was taken up after the annual accounts had been approved by the board subsequent to their audit by the external auditors. The conclusions and observations of commercial audit were submitted in due course of time to the Public Accounts Committee of the legislature in the form of audit paras in the Auditor General's printed annual reports.

Within about twenty years of its establishment PIDC had developed or promoted sixty-two industrial projects involving a total cost of Rs. 1242.6 million, including projects in fertilisers, machine tools, gas production, heavy mechanical complex, ship building and engineering, sugar processing, cement and coal mining. About twenty of the industries or projects started by the Corporation and falling among its most profitable units have been disinvested from and sold to private shareholders during this period. It still has a number of projects in wool, sugar, gas, textiles, forest industries, refractories, iron ore, etc.

ANNEXE 2

Boards of Directors of NFC and Subsidiaries

National Fertilizer Corporation of Pakistan Limited
Chairman, NFC, Lahore
Additional Secretary, Ministry of Production, Islamabad
Additional Secretary, Ministry of Food & Agriculture, Islamabad
Managing Director, Bankers Equity Limited, Karachi
Chairman, Federal Chemical and Ceramics Limited, Karachi

Pakarab Fertilizers Limited
Chairman, NFC, Lahore
Managing Director, PFL, Multan
Managing Director, Bankers Equity Limited, Karachi
Vice Chancellor, University of Agriculture, Faisalabad
Joint Secretary, Ministry of Production, Islamabad
Four representing Abu Dhabi National Oil Company Limited, Abu Dhabi,
    UAE

Paksaudi Fertilizers Limited
Chairman, NFC, Lahore
Managing Director, PSFL, Mirpur Mathelo
Technical Advisor, National Development Finance Corp. Ltd., Karachi
Joint Secretary, Ministry of Food & Agriculture, Islamabad
Joint Secretary, Ministry of Production, Islamabad
Joint Secretary, Ministry of Industries, Islamabad
Joint Secretary (Investment), Ministry of Finance, Islamabad

Pak-American Fertilizers Limited
Chairman, NFC
General Manager, PAFL, Daudkhel
Secretary, Industries Department, Government of the Punjab, Lahore
Deputy Secretary, Ministry of Production, Islamabad
Managing Director, Punjab Agricultural Development and Supplies Cor-
    poration Limited, Lahore

Lyallpur Chemicals & Fertilizers Limited
Chairman, NFC, Lahore
General Manager, LC&FL, Faisalabad
General Manager, LC&FL, Jaranwala
Joint Secretary, Ministry of Food & Agriculture, Islamabad
Deputy Secretary, Ministry of Production, Islamabad
Two representing Central Chemicals Limited, Karachi

Pakchina Fertilizers Limited

Chairman, NFC, Lahore
General Manager, PCFL, Haripur
Joint Secretary, Ministry of Production, Islamabad
Joint Secretary, Ministry of Food and Agriculture, Islamabad
Secretary, Industries Department, Government of NWFP, Peshawar
Senior Vice-President, National Development Finance Corporation Ltd.,
    Karachi/Lahore
General Manager (Tech. and Plg.), NFC, Lahore

National Fertilizer Marketing Limited

Chairman, NFC, Lahore
Managing Director, NFML, Lahore
Managing Director, PFL, Multan
Managing Director, PSFL, Mirpur Mathelo
Joint Secretary, Ministry of Food & Agriculture, Islamabad
Deputy Secretary, Ministry of Production, Islamabad
National Logistics Cell, Rawalpindi
Secretary, Agriculture Department, Government of Punjab, Lahore
Secretary, Agriculture Department, Government of Sind, Karachi

ANNEXE 3

NATIONAL FERTILIZER CORPORATION OF PAKISTAN LIMITED
ORGANISATIONAL STRUCTURE

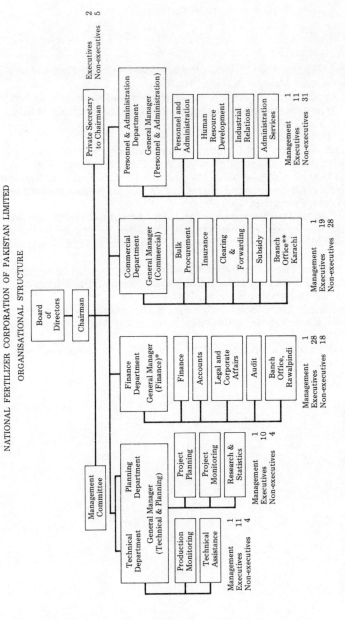

* General Manager (Finance), NFC acts as Secretary of the Company.
** Branch Office, Karachi in the process of being wound up.

ANNEXE 4

References

Ahmad, Shahid, *West Pakistan Industrial Development Corporation – Accounting Manuals* (Karachi, 1967).

V. V. Ramanadham, *Organization, Management and Supervision of Public Enterprises in Developing Countries* (United Nations Sale No. E 74 II.H.4, New York, 1974).

Ali, S. Babar, *Note on NFC* (Lahore, 1977).

Siddiqui, Dr. Anwar H., Editor, *Management of Public Enterprises in Pakistan* (Pakistan Administrative Staff College, Lahore, 1979).

Sycip, Gorres, Velayo & Co., Management Services Division, *National Fertilizer Corporation of Pakistan Ltd. Organization Management Study* (Manila, Philippines, 1981).

Mufti, Abdul Majid, *Experience of Public Enterprises in Pakistan with particular reference to manufacturing industry* (paper presented at the International Symposium on economic performance of Public Enterprises, Islamabad, 1981).

Twum, Gyasi, *Public Enterprises in Pakistan, background and issues* (paper presented at the International Symposium on economic performance of Public Enterprises, Islamabad, 1981).

Burmeister, H. Harald and Heath, Roger E. O., *Pakistan Fertilizer Industry Rehabilitation Project* (IBRD Report No. 3865-PAK, Washington DC., 1982).

National Fertilizer Corporation of Pakistan Ltd., various reports and annual accounts.

10

COAL INDIA LIMITED

B. L. Wadehra

The Indian coal industry, in the course of its development, evolved three main structural forms, viz., (i) captive collieries owned by consumer interests, e.g., railways and iron and steel industry; (ii) collieries controlled by managing agents who also financed and operated a number of other industries; and (iii) private collieries operating in small units representing individual enterprises.

The first represented vertical integration and is a global phenomenon in the coal industry. In the second structural form, there were a number of managing agents – reputed British houses – all of whom were members of the Indian Mining Association. The third structural form was represented by a large number of privately owned collieries, mostly of small size, with a very diffuse ownership structure. These small collieries were generally ill-equipped, had no scientific management structures and had been set up with the sole object of maximising profits for the owners without any regard for conservation and safety.

1. NATIONAL COAL DEVELOPMENT CORPORATION

National Coal Development Corporation (NCDC), the first central government enterprise in the coal sector in the country, was formed in October 1956 in pursuance of the Industrial Policy Resolutions in 1948 and 1956, with a nucleus of eleven state-owned erstwhile railway collieries. The NCDC started its operations with its headquarters at Ranchi and with a full-time Managing Director. The mines were spread over four states – Bihar, Crissa, Madhya Pradesh and Maharashtra. The collieries were organised into six Areas and each Area was placed under an Area General Manager.

The Government of India appointed a Committee under the chairmanship of Mr G. R. Kamath in July 1967 to make a comprehensive review of the performance of NCDC. Based on the recommendations of that Committee, submitted in August 1968, some basic changes were brought about in the management structure of the NCDC. The Committee recommended the appointment of functional directors in the following areas: (i) technical; (ii) finance, and (iii) administration.

The recommendation was accepted by the Government and Director (Finance), Director (Administration) and Director (Technical) were appointed in the early part of 1969. Subsequently, a post of Director (Marketing) was also created.

2. COAL NATIONALISATION MEASURES, BCCL AND CMAL

The question of conservation and scientific development of the coal resources of the country, including coking coal reserves, assumed importance in the context of the large scale development of the various sectors of the economy and also in view of the sudden and steep rise in the price of crude oil. A depleting asset like coal, especially coking coal, needed urgent attention and measures had to be taken immediately to stop unscientific mining and wastage. Thus the nationalisation of coal mines became a historical necessity. The coking coal mines were taken over on 16 October 1971 and subsequently nationalised in May 1972; and non-coking coal mines were taken over on 30 January 1973 and nationalised in May 1973. These major steps, entailing the take-over of the entire coal mining industry, marked the end of an era of unhealthy and unscientific mining as also of the exploitation of labour and other malpractices. Nationalisation heralded the beginning of a new phase of management of the coal mines in the overall interests of the nation. The takeover of the 214 coking coal mines of varying sizes, threw up the problems of reorganisation of these mines, augmenting the production of coking coal, opening up of new project management of personnel and industrial relations, integrating the management structure of the various groups of collieries into a single management stream, and so on. A company named Bharat Coking Coal Limited (BCCL) was formed and entrusted with the management of all coking coal mines. It operated as an independent unit for some time before it was made a subsidiary of Steel Authority of India Limited (SAIL). Subsequently, in November 1975, it became a subsidiary of Coal India Limited (CIL).

To manage the 711 non-coking coal mines taken over in January 1973, which were spread over seven states, unlike coking coal mines which were concentrated in the State of Bihar, Coal Mines Authority Limited (CMAL) was formed with its headquarters at Calcutta. In view of the geographical spread of these mines, CMAL had under it three Divisions:

- The Eastern Division – covering the collieries in the Raniganj and Mugma fields with its headquarters at Sanctoria;
- The Central Division – comprising the erstwhile NCDC collieries as well as the taken-over collieries in Bihar, Singrauli and Talcher, with its headquarters at Ranchi; and
- Western Division – comprising the collieries in Madhya Pradesh and Maharashtra, with its headquarters at Nagpur.

Each of these Divisions was headed by a Managing Director. The mines in Assam, due to their remoteness from the other Divisions, were kept as an Area directly under CMAL. A planning and design institute, under the name of Central Mine Planning and Design Institute (CMPDI) was also formed and placed under a Managing Director with its headquarters at Ranchi.

Under an agreement, the shares held by the Central Government in Singareni Collieries Co. Ltd. (SCCL) were transferred to CMAL. As per the agreement, it was stipulated that CMAL would hold 45% of the share capital of the company, the balance being held by the State Government of Andhra Pradesh. (SCCL came into existence in 1920 and covered all the coal mines in the Singareni area of Andhra Pradesh.)

The apex organisation at CMAL consisted of a Chairman and three functional Directors, looking after Finance, Personnel and Marketing, and was entrusted mainly with policy and co-ordination functions. The intention was to provide flexibility and autonomy to the Divisions in the production operations and allied activities. The apex provided co-ordination in respect of planning, marketing, transport, personnel, purchase and finance.

Thus CMAL had a five-tier organisation:

(i)   The apex body with its Board of Directors, Chairman and functional Directors;
(ii) Divisions under Managing Directors;
(iii) Areas in charge of Area General Managers;
(iv) Sub-Areas consisting of a group of collieries in charge of Sub-Area Managers; and
(v)   Projects/collieries in charge of Project Officers/Colliery Managers.

With CMAL and BCCL well established, the industry was able to achieve positive gains in terms of production and planning. In 1974/75 a record level of coal production was achieved at 88 million tonnes, thereby registering an increase of 10 million tonnes over the previous year.

During this period, a study was carried out by the Indian Institute of Management, Ahemadabad, on BCCL to evaluate the efficiency of the organisational structure in terms of the company's objectives. The study revealed that the tier of Sub-Area Manager was redundant in the management hierarchy, as its role and responsibilities overlapped with those of the tier below. A restructuring of the BCCL organisation was carried out eliminating the level of Sub-Area Manager.

Ultimately such a change was brought about in the other Divisions also. The three-tier organisation structure that emerged after this reorganisation was as follows:

Corporate management – MD and functional Directors;
Executive management – General Manager with specialised staff services;
Operating management – Colliery Manager/Project Officer with executive heads of various disciplines.

3. THE ESTABLISHMENT OF COAL INDIA LTD.

In October 1974, the Government of India created an independent Ministry for Energy headed by a Cabinet Minister with separate departments of coal and power under it. Subsequently, a decision was taken to bring all the coal mines under one umbrella and with this in view, Coal India Ltd. (CIL) was formed with headquarters at Calcutta on 1 November 1975; and BCCL, which was hitherto a subsidiary of SAIL, became a subsidiary of CIL. The three producing Divisions, viz., Central, Eastern and Western, and the Planning Division, CMPDI, were converted into independent subsidiaries of CIL, which in effect became a holding company with five subsidiary companies under it.

The holding company concept was applied to the nationalised coal industry for the sake of efficient governmental management of the industry. Its aim was essentially to bring the management structure of the operating enterprises in tune with the objectives of and demands upon the industry. The role of the holding company was to implement the basic policies of the Government, channel all investments in coal, stimulate growth in an industry where heavy investment was required, and where the gestation period of mine construction was long, and to oversee that the tasks were performed economically and speedily within the framework of the national plans.

The organisation of the holding company, Coal India Ltd., that emerged from all these measures, was as follows:

(a) Coal India Limited (CIL) with its headquarters at Calcutta;
(b) Eastern Coalfields Limited (ECL) with its headquarters at Sanctoria (comprising the erstwhile Eastern Division);
(c) Bharat Coking Coal Limited (BCCL) with its headquarters at Dhanbad (comprising the erstwhile BCCL mines; and Sudamdih and Monidih mines of NCDC, which are situated in Jharia Coal-fields);
(d) The Central Coalfields Limited (CCL) with headquarters at Ranchi (comprising the erstwhile Central Division of CMAL/ NCDC but excluding Sudamdih, Monidih and the other NCDC mines in the Western Division);
(e) The Western Coalfields Limited (WCL) with headquarters at Nagpur (comprising the Western Division of CMAL and in-cluding NCDC mines in the Western Division); and
(f) The North Eastern Coalfields with Area Headquarters at Mar-gherita being directly administered by Coal India headquarters.

The company headquarters was so selected that the collieries under it could be effectively managed.

The main tasks laid down by the Government for Coal India Limited were:

(a) to set overall corporate objectives and devise strategies for achieve-ment of these objectives;
(b) to establish policies regarding long-term planning, conservation, finance, recruitment, training, safety, industrial relations, wages, marketing, purchases and stores and utilisation of coal resources;
(c) to set targets in each area of its activities and monitor them;
(d) to approve budgets, determine standard cost and retention prices to evaluate performance;
(e) to co-ordinate the activities of the subsidiary companies;
(f) to lay down the overall policy regarding coal distribution;
(g) to establish broad linkages of consumers to different coalfields;
(h) to maintain liaison with major customers; and
(i) to advise the Government on formulating long-term policies on the above issues.

Thus Coal India Limited was given wide and comprehensive authority to co-ordinate and execute the programme and policies in respect of the nationalised coal industry in its various operating regions. The Board of Directors of CIL at the time of its formation, had fifteen members, consisting of a full-time Chairman and two functional Directors in Marketing and Technical, and twelve part-time members including the Managing Directors of the five subsidiary companies, four representatives from the Ministry of Energy, the Director of Central Fuel Research Institute, a labour representative and a representative of the State Government. This structure underwent slight modification subsequently in that the Board had only one functional Director in Marketing for some time and none for some time.

The Board of Directors is headed by a full-time Chairman, who is also the Chief Executive of the Company. At the beginning, the organisation did not envisage any functional Directors at Coal India headquarters; and the two Directors who were earlier on the CIL Board had these posts personal to them. However, the CIL Board presently has two posts of functional Directors – one in Finance and the other in Technical. The CIL headquarters has senior and experienced officers in various disciplines, who have been designated as Chiefs of the various divisions. They are the principal staff officers of the holding company and render specialist services.

The subsidiary companies have their own individual Board of Directors. Originally the Chairman of Coal India was also the Chairman of the Boards of Directors of the subsidiary companies and he provided the necessary co-ordination between the holding company and the subsidiaries. Each subsidiary company has a full-time Managing Director, who was the Chief Executive of the company.

The period 1975 to 1978 witnessed the production of CIL stagnating around 90 million tonnes. This was on account of various factors, related mainly to external environmental circumstances, over which the nationalised coal industry had little or no control, e.g., a slackening of demand, and infrastructural constraints.

4. ORGANISATIONAL DECENTRALISATION, 1977

This period saw yet another change in the organisational structure. In May 1977 the Government restructured the organisation of Coal India Limited whereby each subsidiary company was put under an independent Board of Directors headed by a Chairman-cum-Managing Director (CMD). The Chairman of the holding company ceased to be the Chairman of the subsidiary Board. This resulted in some dilution of the executive function and the co-ordination and control roles of CIL. The CMDs of the subsidiary companies were given wide powers to cover all those functions which were not the exclusive preserve of CIL.

The Government's decision to decentralise management at this juncture was a step in the right direction. The decentralisation connoted that each level of management spelt out the authority and responsibilities of the next tier, which might be exercised by it in unambiguous terms; and having done so, it gave the lower level the freedom to exercise those powers. But each level of management had to ensure that the policies which it laid down were punctiliously and effectively carried out by the management level below it.

It is to be noted that the nationalised coal industry started operations with a handful of experienced personnel. An industry which was radically different, in terms of technical and general management from other industries, needed clear, explicit and unambiguous guidelines on every facet of management for effective functioning. For several years and until such time as the basic pattern of organisation had become established and the management roles and techniques standardised, the management controls, by each level over the levels below it, had to be firm. This has been an inevitable corollary of the growth of a complex organisation evolved from a multiplicity of heterogeneous organisations with very different management cultures.

Delegation of authority has proved to be a complex variable, in respect of both the level at which decisions are authorised to be made and the degree of discretion decision-makers have. In a large organisation like CIL the organisation prevalent may be termed a 'centralised bureaucracy', where most operating decisions are made at lower levels, but these are restricted by written down policies, procedures and rules. A further complication is that the degree of delegation must be assessed at each level and within each division depending on the needs of the division concerned. Broad variations in patterns may co-exist in the same organisation, underlining the specific needs of each branch in each division.

The headquarters focuses on developing a general strategy for the common conditions facing the organisation, preparing an overall plan and maintaining consistency of direction. The headquarters operates away from pressure of day-to-day problems; it is primarily concerned with collection and analysis of information and planning the long-term development of the organisation. The operating unit is physically near to the scene of operations and is emotionally involved in the urgency of solutions. The thrust in the field is to solve the problems immediately as well as possible rather than delay solution for more information or on broader considerations. The headquarters emphasises the use of the formal structure while the thrust of the local management is upon forceful leadership and definite and on-the-spot decision making.

The appropriate degree of delegation depends upon the conditions existing in an organisation. In an organisation like CIL which is highly complex in terms of investment, size, nature of work-flow, nature of activities, complexity of task and spatial-physical barriers within and among groups, a prime pre-requisite for efficiency is to move decisions to the operating level while co-ordinating the parts. This is achieved by laying down formal policies, procedures and rules that serve as guidelines for the operating personnel. Top management concentrates upon long-term planning, policy formulations, major operational decisions, investment plans, personnel policy, marketing strategy, inter-industry co-ordination, industry–government relationships and other major issues; while the lower level personnel make operational decisions within this framework.

Based on this corporate strategy, the CIL Board has been entrusted with full powers in matters like borrowings for working capital, the starting of ancillary industries, budgetary matters like approval of capital budgets of subsidiaries, reallocation of capital funds and revenue budgets. The Board has also powers of capital expenditure up to Rs. 5 crores on ongoing projects and new projects included in the budget. It can authorise capital expenditure in excess of the sanctioned estimates up to 10% of cost or Rs. 5 crores, whichever amount is less and it can spend up to Rs. 1 crore in each project in anticipation of inclusion in the budget. On personnel matters, the CIL Board has full powers for administering recruitment, training, service, conduct and other rules and for the creation of all executive posts below the board level, the maximum salary of which does not exceed Rs. 2,750 per month.

Subsidiary company Boards have similar powers with the following exceptions: reallocation of capital expenditure within the budget approved by the CIL Board; funds earmarked for a new project cannot be diverted without the CIL Board's approval; and capital expenditure on new projects and on-going projects included in the budget is restricted up to Rs. 2 crores.

Similarly, subsidiary Boards have full powers for the creation of all posts below Board level, the maximum salary of which does not exceed Rs. 2500 per month, though recruitment for the executive cadre is done centrally for the subsidiaries by Coal India itself, while the subsidiaries are free to recruit non-executives. Area Management can recruit non-executives after obtaining prior approval of subsidiary headquarters.

The CMDs of subsidiary companies have been given adequate powers to cover all those functions which are not reserved for CIL. In turn, the CMDs have delegated powers right down to the Colliery Manager in keeping with the tasks assigned at each management level.

There is a constant review of the delegation of powers so that the powers delegated are commensurate with the requirements and the functional responsibilities at a particular level. An example of this is the enhanced power given to the General Manager of Singrauli Area of CCL. This coalfield is situated about 500 km from Ranchi and borders the States of Madhya Pradesh and Uttar Pradesh, with a reserve of some 10,000 million tonnes of coal ideally suited for thermal power generation. Owing to the strategic location of this coalfield vis-a-vis the industrialised states of Punjab, Haryana, Delhi, UP, etc., the Government has drawn up an ambitious plan for power stations on the periphery of this coalfield. The production performance of this relatively new coalfield in the past and the future production programme can be seen from the following figures:

Past performance   (figs. in million tonnes)

73/74	74/75	75/76	76/77	77/78	78/79	79/80	80/81	81/82
1.92	2.93	3.39	3.36	3.37	4.31	5.20	5.89	6.47

Future performance

82/83	83/84	84/85	89/90	94/95
7.95	9.00	10.45	28.40	48.35

To cope with the planned rapid development of Singrauli coalfield, the General Manager of the Area has been delegated powers equivalent to those of the functional Directors. This is with the objective that decision-making authority is kept close to the site of actual operations.

In the subsidiary companies, the functional Directors and the heads of departments at the corporate level have been delegated with requisite administrative and financial powers so that matters pertaining to their functional areas are disposed of speedily at their level.

The General Managers of the Areas and the Project Officers heading various collieries and washeries have been delegated with specific financial and administrative powers.

The existing organisational set-up of CIL is depicted in chart 1.1. The organisational set-up in subsidiary companies, at the headquarters, in the Areas and at the colliery/project, are illustrated in charts 1.2, 1.3 and 1.4 respectively at the end of this chapter.

5. THE COLLIERY LEVEL, LINE AND STAFF

In the existing organisational set-up, the cost and profit centre is the colliery. The colliery is modelled on the divisionalisation principle. At that level, people of different disciplines are brought together for coal production, coal processing and dispatch. The grouping of complementary, inter-dependent personnel at the colliery level has many advantages. It shortens the lines of communication among interdependent personnel. It makes production, planning and co-ordination of activities easy. The divisionalisation confers a great deal of autonomy in production activities on the head of the unit and motivates him to high performance, particularly because, in the corporate context, his unit is evaluated by its production, productivity and profitability. Divisionalisation also permits inter-colliery comparisons and brings in an element of competition among the various units. It enables the heads of these units to obtain valuable middle and top management training and experience in running, more or less, self-sufficient production units.

The divisionalised management structure at the colliery level is reinforced by an organisational structure with centralised staff functions at the Area level. The functional departmentalisation at the Area level, upon which is enjoined the task of overseeing and co-ordinating the various activities of the collieries under its administrative jurisdiction, permits of centralisation of staff services and utilisation of specialised expertise in dealing with various problems of colliery management. It permits of pooling of specialised personnel at the Area headquarters which can be made use of by the various collieries.

The management structure of the Area, therefore, combines the principle of functional and divisional tiers making the best use of both at different levels of management. It is found that there are two opposing views on the use of the functional channels, that is the channel of communication and personnel contact between a department at one level and the corresponding department at the next level below it. One view is that the functional channel should be used for exercising direction, management, advice and control; the other view is that, while there must be functional specialists, they must be only in an advisory capacity and should be approached by the lower levels only when the need for their advice is felt. It is further held that, if the advice of the specialists at the higher level is sought by the lower level, it need not be always acted upon, except at the discretion of line management. This dichotomy of viewpoints has been resolved, to a great extent, through constant interaction of personnel of various disciplines and by explicit guidelines issued by the top management on the issue.

As a matter of established policy, the functional head is empowered to issue instructions to the next level below him; but a copy must go direct to the line authority to keep him informed. The 'line' authority at each level of management establishes a system whereby his functional staff consult him before taking action on instructions issued departmentally. The higher functional level has to be satisfied that the work at the lower level is being carried out efficiently. This is achieved without interference in day-to-day line management's work.

The subsidiary companies are engaged in the production of coal, washed coal, soft coke and hard coke. WCL is a single product company, its product being only coal. ECL is a two-product company having coal and soft coke as the products. CCL is a three-product company producing coal, soft coke and washed coal. CCL also produces hard coke and some by-products on a very small scale at Giridih. BCCL is a multi-product company producing coal, washed coal, hard coke, soft coke, etc. In BCCL an adequate organisational set-up has been provided for coke-oven operations. There is an adviser (coke) at the corporate level. In each Area, a chemical engineer advises the general manager in matters of hard coke production. The by-product coke-oven plants are under a senior executive. The washeries in BCCL are owned by SAIL but are administered by BCCL, through a power of attorney, by a separate organisational set-up. In CCL, there is a separate organisation for the management of the four washeries which belong to the company.

The CMPDI has four Regional Institutes, one each at Asansol, Dhanbad, Ranchi and Nagpur to work in close collaboration with the producing subsidiaries in matters of prospecting, drilling, mining R&D and project formulation. Each of these institutes is placed under a Regional Director and controlled by the Chairman-cum-Managing Director, CMPDI. At the CMPDI headquarters at Ranchi, there is one Central Institute (HQRS) for co-ordinating the various planning and design activities, and the activities are organised under different departments created specifically for perspective planning, project preparation and appraisal, exploration, geology, coal preparation and utilisation technology, R&D, shaft sinking, blasting, etc.

6. COAL MARKETING

During the period 1979–81, a few more organisational changes were brought about in the structure of CIL. Central Coal Marketing Organisation (CCMO) was set up with the ultimate responsibility for the entire coal marketing functions. The objectives were:

(i) to ensure availability of desired quality and quantity of coal to meet all current and future demands within the country and also ensure equitable distribution of coal/coke;

(ii) to provide the relevant feedback to the government for the formulation of policy on coal transportation, distribution and pricing; and

(iii) to promote and expand the market for coal/coke and coal-based products within and outside the country in keeping with the total national policy on energy.

The formulation of CCMO was with the objective of enabling the producing subsidiaries to concentrate on production and project management functions. The reallocation of marketing and allied work, between CCMO and subsidiaries, is being carried out in a phased manner. The functions of CCMO, as spelled out, are that it will be responsible for overall policy matters regarding coal distribution; and that it will establish broad linkages of consumers to coalfields and maintain liaison with major consumers. It will be the responsibility of the concerned subsidiary companies to deliver the coal, maintain quality control, carry out after-sales service, arrange the realisation of sales proceeds, etc.

Since coal quality has been attracting considerable attention for some time, a separate department for quality control has been created in the subsidiaries of Coal India Ltd. for effective monitoring of the quality of coal dispatches and for establishing liaison with major consumers.

It is estimated that about 60% of our coal reserves consist of inferior grade coal containing over 25% ash. Further, the deployment of heavy earth moving machinery in opencast mines leads to pieces of over-sized coal and admixture with extraneous matter like stone and shale, etc. Coal India's largest consumers are the various thermal power stations situated in different parts of the country. Their complaints usually relate to oversize and presence of shale and stone, etc., in the supplies. With the establishment of the quality control organisation, steps have been taken to ensure the dispatch of proper quality coal to the different consumers. Remedial steps including erection of major and minor coal handling plants at pit-heads, improved blasting techniques and installation of crushers in opencast mines, intensive manual picking, etc., have been initiated. At present, there are 25 major coal handling plants (CHPs), 119 mini-CHPs and nine crushing arrangements. These are being augmented by 34 major CHPs and 66 mini-CHPs. For ensuring quality supplies to

steel plants, three major washeries are being put up besides modernising and modifying the existing eleven washeries.

7. CORPORATE PLANNING, PROJECT MONITORING AND EXPANSIONS

With the increase in the scale of activities of the holding company
and changing environmental conditions, three more departments,
viz., corporate planning, project monitoring and processed fuel
division, were set up in CIL. The projected growth of the company,
the long gestation period of projects, the technological innovations
and improvements sought to be brought about, the wide geographical
spread of its operations over a number of States, the large labour force
of over six lakh persons with differing skills, aptitudes and training,
etc., necessitate an integrated planning strategy for Coal India Ltd.
It has prepared a corporate plan for the period 1980–85 so as to
dovetail it into the objectives of the Sixth Five Year Plan of India.
Simultaneously perspective planning exercises for the next two
decades have been undertaken.

Further, large investments are being made in the current plan and
larger investments will be made in the Seventh Plan and beyond. The
number of projects having an investment of Rs. 5 crores and above
in Coal India total 74 with an investment of Rs. 1341 crores, creating
an additional production capacity of 97 million tonnes per annum.
The table below shows the companywise number of projects, ultimate
capacity and investment:

Company	Projects (no.)	Ultimate capacity (million tonnes/year)	Capacity investment (Rs. in crores)
Sanctioned Projects			
1. ECL	14	18.27	240.61
2. BCCL	10	9.76	160.80
	74		
3. CCL	21	35.42	474.77
4. WCL	29	33.34	463.74
Advanced action			
1. Mining projects	5	–	64.75
2. Washery projects	4		98.50
3. Other projects	4		94.18

Over and above these projects, there are 47 other projects which have a projected investment ranging between Rs. 2 and Rs. 5 crores, with a total outlay of Rs. 169 crores and slated to achieve an ultimate aggregate production capacity of 20 million tonnes/annum.

The monitoring of the progress of the numerous projects has necessitated the creation of a Project Monitoring Division at CIL. The functions of this cell include effective and timely monitoring performance evaluation and control of the major activities of the projects under construction in the different subsidiaries.

The performance profile of CIL over the years is delineated below:

	73/74	74/75	75/76	76/77	77/78	78/79	79/80	80/81	81/82
Raw Coal Production									
Opencast	69.96	20.77	23.77	23.65	24.91	28.91	32.32	39.96	46.34
Underground		58.22	65.21	65.83	64.05	61.14	59.12	60.99	63.27
TOTAL		78.99	88.98	89.48	88.96	90.05	91.44	100.95	109.61
Productivity (Output per manshift)		0.58	0.66	0.67	0.68	0.67	0.67	0.72	0.78
Washed coal production		6.88	7.70	8.68	8.79	8.23	7.62	8.29	8.97
Mechanised OBR (in Million Cubic Metre)		16.72	21.30	33.61	39.18	41.36	50.88	62.54	80.88

The expansion of production, however, was not uniform over the entire period since nationalisation, because of external constraints and inherited bottlenecks.

CIL is entrusted with the formidable task of increasing the production level from 114 million tonnes in 81/82 to 231 million tonnes by 1989–90 and to 358 million tonnes by 2000 AD. The production of an additional 250 million tonnes by the turn of the century will involve the expansion and reorganisation of the existing mines for higher production as well as the opening of new mines. On account of the long gestation periods involved in the attainment of capacity production – four to eight years for large mechanised opencast mines and six to ten years for underground mines – the last group of mines being planned to contribute to the production of 2000 AD will need to be opened by 1990–94, which implies that all geological exploration for the last group of contributing mines should be completed by 1987–88. The exploration programme has to take into account not only the need of geological data for preparation of feasibility and project reports but also drilling for production support, investigate drilling in geologically disturbed areas, etc. The exploration capacity has to match the requirements of planning for the preparation of a 'shelf of reports' to allow flexibility to the management in the selection of blocks/areas on techno-economic considerations and to provide some cushion to meet any unanticipated spurt in the demand for coal.

The scale of project construction activities will increase at a very rapid rate in the future. In particular the work relating to sinking, deepening and widening of shafts, drivages of inclines/drifts, installation of coal handling plants and beneficiation plants, sand gathering plants and surface power arrangements, etc., require special attention. In the next five years, about 120 shafts are projected to be sunk or deepened. There is a proposal to set up a Construction Division within Coal India Ltd. to effectively undertake the various mine construction activities. It will be entrusted with the task of shaft sinking, incline drivage, construction of CHPs, CPPs, designing, equipping and starting of longwall faces.

As per the corporate plan of Coal India Ltd., the investment outlay for the five year period 1980/81 to 84/85 would be Rs. 3100 crores against the actual investment of Rs. 1127 crores during the period 1973/74 to 1979/80. A major part of the increased outlay owes to the substantial rise in the prices of capital equipment, both imported and indigenous. Further a large share of the investment is for building up production capacity for coal production during the Seventh Plan period (i.e. beyond 1984/85). The bulk of the investment is on coal mining projects, followed by washeries, exploration, river diversion, fire control, sand gathering, LTC Plants, captive power plants, etc. Of the investment on mining projects, 46% will be on projects already approved and under execution. These projects will contribute the major share of production expansion during the Sixth Plan period. Another 32% of the investment will be on projects yet to be approved which will yield production in 1984/85 and beyond. The remaining 22% of the investment will be used for replacement of plant and machinery etc. in existing mines.

The investment in the coal sector will rise to a massive Rs. 7000 crores, Rs. 10,000 and Rs. 12,000 crores respectively in the successive Five Year Plans till the end of this century. Given the resources, Coal India Ltd. is confident that the country's coal requirements will be met so as to ensure steady economic growth through a stable energy policy.

There has been a progressive increase in the size of individual mines. In the pre-nationalisation days, there were about 800 mines, most of which were small units. After nationalisation, the number of mines was reduced to about 450 units through amalgamation, with emphasis on large capacity mines. The trend is towards planning larger capacity mines: underground mines up to 3.6 million tonnes and opencast mines up to 14.0 million tonnes have been planned and are under execution. For the management of mines of this size, new management organisation and strategies will have to be developed. The sequence of operations, the deployment of plant and equipment, construction schedules, face lay-out and other production problems will need a higher degree of co-ordination involving on-the-spot decisions, the lack of which will adversely affect the efficiency of the entire mining operations. Development of workshop facilities, procurement of stores and spares, etc. will be other areas where a high degree of management skills will be needed. The management information system has to be streamlined, covering all tiers of management. A massive human resources development programme, both for executives and non-executives, has been drawn up for meeting the challenging demands of output expansion.

Employees' welfare constitutes an important part of the corporate plan. Prior to nationalisation, very little had been done in the matter of amenities and welfare facilities by the private mine owners, except by some of the enlightened. The housing satisfaction at the time of nationalisation was around 20%, which has increased to over 35% at present. While considerable efforts have been made and massive investments have been allocated towards employees' welfare, much needs to be done. Coal mining is essentially fraught with hazards by the very nature of the industry. Coal mines are located mostly in rural and semi-urban areas where civic and other facilities for education, health, housing, water supply, transport, communication are yet to make a significant impact. In view of this, Coal India Ltd. has drawn up and is implementing a comprehensive welfare plan to provide housing for at least 55% of its employees in a decade's time; adequate supply of treated water to 100% of the colliery population by 1984/85; provision of colleges, schools; development of medical facilities; etc.

8. FURTHER ORGANISATIONAL RESTRUCTURING

On the basis of the actual working experience of the subsidiaries, it is felt that the span of control of each subsidiary has reached unmanageable proportions. Each subsidiary has a manpower varying from 115,000 to 180,000 persons; an annual production varying from 23 million tonnes to 32 million tonnes; an annual turnover between Rs. 400 and Rs. 500 crores; a projected annual investment between Rs. 200 and Rs. 400 crores; major reorganisation work of more than fifteen mines; construction of a large number of coal handling plants, coal preparation and coal beneficiation plants; an ambitious scheme for improving the quality of life of the employees involving crores of rupees; and opening of dozens of new projects with massive investments. Each subsidiary has been assigned a growth rate varying from 6% to 8% per annum. It is felt that such a mammoth task will require close superintendence and co-ordination in every conceivable sphere of activity. This is not likely to be possible for the existing subsidiary managements, and each subsidiary needs to be split up into more homogeneous and purposeful units so that it can exercise better control over the entire gamut of operations. In the light of this, the Government has already prepared a scheme for further restructuring of Coal India Limited and its subsidiaries. The scheme envisages the reorganisation of subsidiary companies into ten operating Divisions, each with an annual production of 10–15 million tonnes and each Division to be headed by an Executive Director.

These Divisions will function under the overall control of subsidiary company Boards to whom the Executive Director will be responsible and who will be vested with sufficient powers to take decisions for the day-to-day problems and will be responsible for the overall development of the Division under his management. The common facilities such as workshop, central stores, regional hospitals, etc., will be shared by the contiguous Divisions until independent facilities are developed in all the ten Divisions.

The delegation of powers to the subsidiary companies and the CMDs of the subsidiary companies are being redrawn on the basis of delegation by exception, whereas the delegation to the Executive Director is detailed delegation. The object behind the detailed delegation in the latter case is to delineate in clear terms his powers and responsibilities for fulfilling specific targets of production and development. The scheme also envisages enhancement of the powers of the CIL Board for sanction of projects, for expansion of existing facilities at mines and/or establishment of new mines and infrastructure costing over Rs. 5 crores.

The nationalisation of the erstwhile private mines brought in its wake a plethora of problems. The majority of those mines were decades old, developed in an unscientific and haphazard manner. Out of 711 non-coking coal and 214 coking coal mines that were nationalised, the bulk were small and unviable units. A survey found that out of 734 collieries, 259 produced less than 600 tonnes per month and another 475, less than 2500 tonnes per month. The mines had been worked with scant regard for conservation and safety, with the result that there were as many as 110 fires in the Jharia and Raniganj coalfields. The unscientific development rendered it well-nigh impossible to restructure the mine lay-out on scientific lines, introduce intensive mechanisation or rectify lay-out defects.

The main motivating factor of the private entrepreneurs was the maximisation of profits with minimal investment. Even the leading coal companies had made but small investments in the last one decade before nationalisation.

The coal companies had defaulted in royalty and other statutory dues to the tune of Rs. 30 crores. The financial viability of most collieries was bleak, with 40 out of 232 collieries in West Bengal closed and others on the verge of closure. No investment had been made in the mines for safety, for keeping up with improved technology, for mechanisation, for welfare amenities of employees, etc.

The Wage Board Award of 1967 had not been implemented even in 10% of the private mines by as late as 1972, in spite of the solemn assurances made by the industry. The private owners perpetuated a system of bonded labour. There were large scale deductions from workers' wages and other dues. And the default in remittances to Coal Mines Provident Fund alone exceeded Rs. 11 crores.

Most of the mine workers were on temporary roll, though they had worked for years. Records show that even mines employing more than 2000 persons had only a few on permanent roll. The miners lived in a twilight world dominated by mafia and musclemen, in a world dimmed by privation, penury and poverty, and without even the rudiments of a decent, human existence.

The nationalised coal industry had, therefore, many tasks to perform:

(i)   to reorganise and rehabilitate the erstwhile private sick mines;
(ii)   to conserve a scarce national resource through scientific mining;
(iii)   to bring about a synthesis of the heterogeneous management cultures of the various private companies and the then existing public sector, retaining the good features of both;

(iv)   to develop a common, dedicated management cadre;
(v)   to achieve targetted growth rates in production and productivity;
(vi)   to serve vital sectors of industry with adequate quantities of coal of proper quality;
(vii) to meet the 'rising tide of human expectations' of its employees, by providing housing, water supply, medical care, etc.; and
(viii) to develop and provide a principal source of energy to the nation in the overall framework of national plans.

The immediate need after nationalisation of the industry was, certainly, amalgamation of the large number of small holdings into economically viable and large units. The first two years of nationalisation were, therefore, devoted to tasks of consolidation. The restructuring of the nationalised coal industry into Divisions – Western, Eastern and Central – was based on considerations of geological continuity, administrative convenience, state boundaries, etc.

It was felt that for the tasks entrusted to the Divisions, a significant degree of autonomy was needed; and in the third year after the massive nationalisation Coal India Limited came into being and the Divisions were transformed into subsidiary companies. Bharat Coking Coal Ltd. was integrated into Coal India Limited for bringing about greater cohesiveness and better co-ordination for the entire coal industry. In due course it was realised that the Chairman of Coal India Limited who was the Chairman of the Boards of the subsidiary companies had a much wider span of control than was feasible for efficient management; so the subsidiary Boards were provided with independent Chairmen. The past few years have seen the growth of these subsidiaries with production peaking from 15 to as much as 32 million tonnes, with great increases in manpower, increased technological complexities, high investments, high projected rates of growth, immense problems of co-ordination, control and monitoring. We have thus reached yet another stage of restructuring, with the subsidiaries, whose span of control is expected to become too unwieldy, being split up into a number of Divisions – ten for the whole of Coal India Limited – for better co-ordination, control and management.

Organisational restructuring and management innovations are an ever-evolving process. Coal India Limited has been endeavouring to live up to this dictum.

CHART – 1.1

ORGANISATION STRUCTURE – COAL INDIA LIMITED

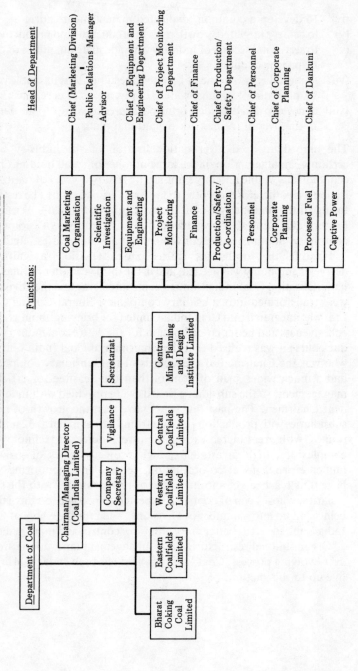

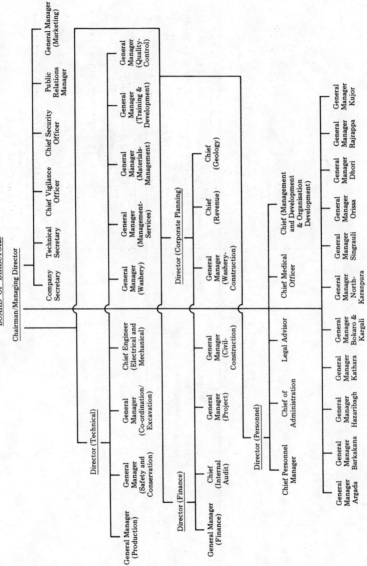

CHART — 1.2

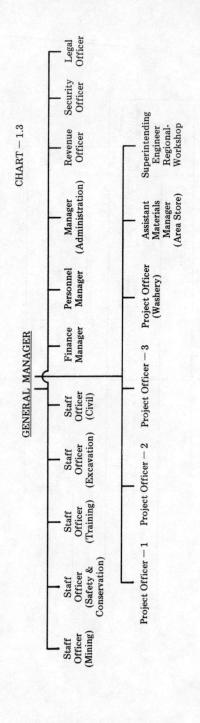

CHART — 1.3

GENERAL MANAGER

Staff Officer (Mining)

Staff Officer (Safety & Conservation)

Staff Officer (Training)

Staff Officer (Excavation)

Staff Officer (Civil)

Finance Manager

Personnel Manager

Manager (Administration)

Revenue Officer

Security Officer

Legal Officer

Project Officer — 1

Project Officer — 2

Project Officer — 3

Project Officer (Washery)

Assistant Materials Manager (Area Store)

Superintending Engineer Regional-Workshop

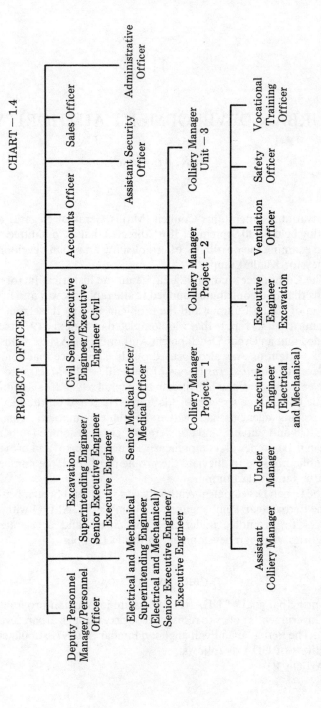

CHART – 1.4

PROJECT OFFICER

- Deputy Personnel Manager/Personnel Officer
- Excavation Superintending Engineer/Senior Executive Engineer/Executive Engineer
- Civil Senior Executive Engineer/Executive Engineer Civil
- Accounts Officer
- Sales Officer
- Administrative Officer

- Electrical and Mechanical Superintending Engineer (Electrical and Mechanical)/Senior Executive Engineer/Executive Engineer
- Senior Medical Officer/Medical Officer
- Assistant Security Officer

- Colliery Manager Project – 1
- Colliery Manager Project – 2
- Colliery Manager Unit – 3

- Assistant Colliery Manager
- Under Manager
- Executive Engineer (Electrical and Mechanical)
- Executive Engineer Excavation
- Ventilation Officer
- Safety Officer
- Vocational Training Officer

234.349

9300 6160
6140
5132
Malaysia

11

URBAN DEVELOPMENT AUTHORITY

A. K. M. Yusof

The National Operations Council (Majlis Gerakan Negara) at its meeting held on 30 September 1970, directed that a Committee be set up to examine the possibility of establishing an urban development agency for Kuala Lumpur.

The Committee studied in great detail the historical factors and trends that had contributed and led to the rapid growth and urbanisation of Kuala Lumpur and the problems arising therefrom. The Committee in its report that was completed in January 1971 recommended that an Urban Development Authority (UDA) be established. Special attention was also focused on the assistance that could be rendered to *bumiputeras* ('Sons of the soil' – the Malays) to help them engage in business activities in the capital city of Kuala Lumpur.

The Committee's recommendations were based on the fact that the existing agencies had neither adequate manpower, financial resources and suitable land nor were sufficiently equipped to participate in urban renewal, comprehensive redevelopment and provision of public housing to alleviate the problems of the large number of squatters in Kuala Lumpur.

The Urban Development Authority was set up on 1 September 1971 by the Perbadanan Pembangunan Bandar Act (UDA) 1971 with wide powers to promote, undertake, participate and accelerate all categories of urban development in Kuala Lumpur.

1. OBJECTIVES OF UDA

The principal goal of UDA is to translate into action programmes the Government's policy to restructure society through urban development. The Perbadanan Pembangunan Bandar Act 1971 stipulates the functions of UDA as follows:

'Article 3(1):

(a) To promote and carry out projects in urban development areas for:
  (i) development, redevelopment, settlement, resettlement and public housing; and
  (ii) improvement in environment, services, amenities, traffic circulation, vehicle parking, recreational and community facilities and other public improvements for the promotion of national unity, health, safety, convenience and welfare;
(b) to promote and carry out projects in urban development areas with a view to achieving the distribution of opportunities among the various races in the field of commerce and industries, housing and other activites; and
(c) to translate into action programmes the government policy to restructure society through development.'

At the official launching of UDA, the late Prime Minister, Y. A. B. Tun Abdul Razak directed the Authority to 'take steps to utilise available lands in the Central Commercial Areas of Kuala Lumpur and to prepare a scheme to help Malays and other *bumiputera* traders to purchase shophouses offered for sale'.[1]

UDA initially began its activities in Kuala Lumpur and later spread to the other state capitals and new townships. Although general statements of goals and objectives for UDA's participation were developed, no specific programmes or projects were spelled out. However, it was envisaged that UDA would initially operate in Kuala Lumpur and undertake programmes and activites that would assist and accelerate the creation of a *bumiputera* commercial community as envisaged in the New Economic Policy. With regard to this the Second Malaysia Plan states:

> In carrying out its functions of urban renewal and development, UDA will give priority consideration to the implementation of projects through which Malay and other indigenous business-men can operate in commercial buildings. It will also purchase or lease strategic private commercial buildings as and when they become available.
>
> As the main body responsible for urban development it will work closely with MARA[2] and SEDCs[3] in undertaking urban commercial and housing projects and with the co-operation of the State Governments ensure that suitable state and reserve lands are released for commercial development particularly for Malay and other indigenous businessmen. UDA will also provide such other assistance as is needed so that Malay and

other indigenous businessmen can rent premises, and make
optimum use of the facilities.[4]

2. ACTIVITIES AND PROGRAMMES OF UDA

UDA planned and devised an operational strategy and embarked on
five programmes of action to achieve its goals and objectives:

Programme A – Provision of Ready Premises;
Programme B – Developing New Premises;
Programme C – Participation in Business;
Programme D – Comprehensive Urban Development; and
Programme E – Early Land Purchase.

The action programmes of UDA were basically designed to provide
business premises and other facilities for *bumiputera* participation
in business, in the urban areas particularly in Kuala Lumpur. The
facilities in the form of loans to businessmen, provision of ready
premises at strategic locations and other specific strategies were
implemented with a view to increasing, expediting and facilitating
bumiputera participation in business and ownership of properties in
the urban areas.

UDA's activities were focused initially in Kuala Lumpur and
extended to the urban centres in other States with increased demand
for UDA's participation.

A. *Provision of ready premises*

This programme was aimed at providing premises for *bumiputera*
entrepreneurs at strategic locations in urban areas, thereby increasing
bumiputera participation in commerce and industry. It is divided into
three sub-programmes.

Sub-Programme AI

Purchase of Business Premises From Private Development. Premises
are provided through bulk purchase (to secure maximum discount) of
shoplots, shophouses and the office premises from private developers.
These premises are either rented or sold to businessmen by UDA.
From its establishment till 31 December 1982 UDA purchased 974
units to the value of $157,556,000 in several urban centres like Kuala
Lumpur, Petaling Jaya, Klang, Ipoh, Penang, Johore Bharu, etc.
through this programme.

Sub-Programme AII

Leasing of Premises Through Private Owners. Under this programme UDA leased premises from private owners at strategic locations on private leasing terms and then sublet to businessmen on easy terms of one month deposit and one month rental in advance.

This sub-programme was designed as a 'crash programme' to increase UDA's property stock in urban areas to meet the demand for business premises in urban areas, since UDA's own development projects were then in the early stages of development and most of the premises bought by UDA from private developers were still under construction.

Between 1972 and 1974 UDA leased 292 units of business premises. In 1978 this programme was stopped due to several problems encountered in the implementation of this programme. Thus in 1981 the number of premises leased through private owners was reduced to only 9 units and by 1982 the leases on all these units expired.

Rental And Sale of Premises Built/Bought By UDA. UDA rented out all the 580 units of business premises built through its own development projects until 31 December 1982. Of the 974 units bought from private developers UDA leased 235 units to *bumiputera* businessmen and sold 512 units; the rest of the units were in the various stages of construction.

The premises were sold by way of hire-purchase or cash payments. Reasonable hire-purchase terms are offered whereby the purchaser is required to pay 10% of the sale price of the building as deposit and the balance in monthly instalments over a period of 10 to 15 years, at a reasonable interest rate.

Sub-Programme AIII

Renovation and Equipment Loans. Loans were provided to finance the purchase of equipment and renovation of premises which were leased or bought by the businessmen from UDA. The objective of this programme was to assist the businessmen to utilise fully whatever capital they had for working capital. Repayment period for such loans was from three to five years.

As a result of several problems which were encountered through the implementation of this programme, sub-programme AII on leasing from private owners and sub-programme AIII of renovation and equipment loans were stopped from as early as 1978.

It was also decided that UDA would increase new purchase of properties in the designated towns,[5] particularly where the demand from *bumiputera* businessmen for premises is high. Purchases would also be done in bulk for easy management and supervision. Provision of bulk premises in designated towns would also be effective in increasing *bumiputera* participation in business in the designated areas.

B. *Developing new premises*

The objective of this programme is to increase *bumiputera* participation in land development, property ownership and participation in commerce and industry in urban areas. This programme is divided into two sub-programmes.

Sub-Programme BI

Shares In Land Development: Joint-Venture Companies. UDA established joint-venture companies with private developers and government agencies in the field of land development in urban areas. Under this programme UDA was able to venture into strategic areas which were owned by the partners and UDA was able to influence the appointment of consultants, increase the number of *bumiputera* employees, purchase premises at a discount and at the same time secure high profit as well as to provide training for UDA personnel.

UDA established forty-eight joint-venture companies with private developers in land development. Through this programme UDA developed sixteen shopping cum office complexes, ten projects of shophouses, nineteen housing schemes and three hotels. It must be mentioned here that 25.7% of the 974 units of business premises were purchased under this programme.

Joint-venture companies were also established with State Development Corporations during the period 1975–78 to undertake land development projects. However this programme was terminated in 1979, in line with the general directive to review the role of all UDA joint-venture companies.

In August 1979, UDA reviewed under its rationalisation programme its land development joint-venture companies and the following decisions were made:

(a) Selling of UDA's equity to its partners;
(b) Transfer of UDA shares to a holding company called PEREMBA Berhad;
(c) Winding up of a few companies.

Only five out of forty-eight land development joint-venture companies were retained by UDA.

Sub-Programme BII

Loans To Develop Bumiputera *Land.* The objective of this programme was to develop *bumiputera* lands in order to increase ownership in terms of number and value. UDA's study showed that there were lands owned by *bumiputeras* in urban areas left idle and this programme assisted these individual owners to develop their properties. UDA provided financial, technical, and management assistance to these land owners.

Through this programme UDA assisted in developing eighty-three land projects which formed 46.4% of the total number of projects implemented by UDA.

C. *Participation in business*

The objective of this programme is to encourage and assist *bumiputeras* in the business sector by providing capital, management and advisory services. This programme was implemented with *bumiputera* businessmen as UDA's partners in business joint-venture companies. UDA held a certain percentage of equity in the companies for a period after which UDA would sell these shares to its *bumiputera* partners or other *bumiputera*. Since 1973 UDA established forty-six business joint-venture companies. However, no new companies were formed since 1977 as most of the business joint ventures were not performing profitably.

D. *Comprehensive urban development*

The objective of this programme is to undertake urban redevelopment and urban renewal with a view to restructuring society, as encompassed in the UDA's Act. In the Fourth Malaysia Plan, UDA has been directed to concentrate on comprehensive urban development. Projects under this programme include the urban renewal project in the areas bounded by Jalan Pudu, Jalan Tun Perak, Jalan Sultan/Jalan Silang comprising the Hentian Puduraya project (Pudu Bus Terminal project), Cahaya Suria, Sinar Kota and the Petaling Street projects. The other projects under this programme include the Dayabumi complex, Lot 81, Jalan Bangsar and the Tampoi New Township in Johor.

Through this programme, UDA is able to:

(a) Provide business premises at strategic locations in the urban areas where participation of *bumiputera* businessmen had been very low or negligible. Prewar shophouses which were in a dilapidated condition were demolished and complexes were built with the necessary amenities and facilities.
(b) Increase *bumiputera* property ownership;
(c) Plan urban development in an organised and systematic manner which would give a new image to the Federal Capital with improved traffic flow condition; and
(d) Provide social amenities including bus and taxi terminals, ample car parks, organised and planned traffic system.

E. *Early land purchase (landbank)*

This programme is aimed at purchasing land in strategic areas in urban centres for future development. It is based on the rationale that early land purchase will in the long run provide sufficient stock of land for future development.

3. ORGANISATION

Since early 1979 several studies have been undertaken in order to get the right picture and perspective and ascertain UDA's position at the time.

The study on 'organisation review' incorporated the identification of the strengths and weaknesses in UDA's activities and programmes, strategies and operation policies, organisational structure, delegation of duties and functions and manpower positions. As a result of the reorganisation study, several positive measures were taken to strengthen UDA's position.

UDA is managed by a Board which is responsible to the Minister of Public Enterprises.

Board composition

In accordance with Part II Article 4 (1) of the UDA Act, the Perbadanan (Authority) shall consist of the following members:

(a) A Chairman
(b) A Deputy Chairman
(c) Not less than five or more than nine other members of whom not less than three shall be Public Officers.
(d) The Director General of UDA.

ORGANISATIONAL STRUCTURE

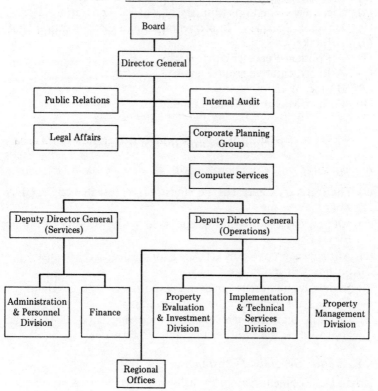

In accordance with the Act, currently the Board Composition is as follows:

(1) The Chairman (who is also the Chairman of the Board)
(2) The Director General of UDA
(3) Secretary General of Ministry of Public Enterprise
(4) Secretary General of Ministry of Federal Territory
(5) Director General of Implementation and Co-ordination Unit
(6) A Banker
(7) A Political Representative
(8) A Representative from Treasury
(9) Businessman
(10) Former Mayor of Kuala Lumpur

Relationships with the government

(i) *The Ministry of Public Enterprises*

(a) The Secretary General of the Ministry is represented on the UDA Board.
(b) All Board decisions must be endorsed by the Minister of Public Enterprises.
(c) All reports prepared by UDA are forwarded to the Ministry for purposes of monitoring.
(d) Budget requirements for both administrative and development budgets are forwarded through the Ministry.
(e) Decisions on financial involvement exceeding $5,000,000 must be approved by the Minister of Public Enterprises.

(ii) *Auditor General's Department*

Urban Development Authority, being a government agency, is subjected to Government auditing regulations and procedures.

(iii) *Ministry of Finance*

(a) All budget allocations are made by the Treasury.
(b) UDA's short term and long range plans are forwarded to the Treasury for purposes of budget allocation and monitoring.

(iv) *Economic Planning Unit*

The relationship with the Economic Planning Unit, Prime Minister's Department, is more or less similar to that with the Ministry of Finance.

(v) *Implementation and Co-ordination Unit (Prime Minister's Office)*

UDA submits quarterly performance reports − physical and financial performance for monitoring.

The Chief Executive Officer of the organisation is the Director General assisted by a Deputy Director General (Operations) and a Deputy Director General (Services); the latter position is yet to be filled.

The organisation is divided into five major Divisions, two of which perform service functions and the other three are involved in operations. The five units, namely Public Relations, Internal Audit, Legal Affairs, Corporate Planning Group and Computer Services are directly responsible to the Director General.

The functions of the five major Divisions are as follows:

Administration and Personnel Division

(i)   Provides general administrative services throughout UDA;
(ii)   Provides maintenance services for UDA's main office building and its assets;
(iii)   Purchases supplies and equipments for UDA's office needs;
(iv)   Handles central filing and records, including strong room;
(v)   Maintains the upkeep of UDA's library;
(vi)   Undertakes manpower planning on the needs of personnel in UDA by co-ordinating the requests from all Divisions and administers personnel welfare services and benefits;
(vii)   Ensures harmonious employee relations;
(viii) Recruits and employs personnel;
(ix)   Caters for the training and development of UDA's personnel;
(x)   Provides personnel welfare services; and
(xi)   Administers personnel welfare services and benefits.

Finance Division

(i)   Formulates, recommends and implements policies, plans and programmes for the Controllership and Treasury functions of UDA;
(ii)   Ensures proper administration of financial resources in terms of utilisation and mobilisations;
(iii)   Ensures sufficient funding for UDA's development and administrative expenditures;
(iv)   Maintains and controls UDA's books of accounts to conform to the requirements of relevant government agencies;
(v)   Is responsible for UDA's accounting systems and procedures;

(vi)   Prepares prescribed periodic financial reports so as to provide the management with information to enable them to plan, control and co-ordinate more efficiently its component divisions in particular;

(vii)   Assists Corporate Planning in all budgetary preparation; and

(viii) Provides financial monitoring services for all projects undertaken by UDA.

Property evaluation and development Division

(i)   Undertakes research studies on the property market at macro level for comprehensive urban development and for investment purposes;

(ii)   Formulates conceptual plans and design layout plans on land to be purchased by the Authority;

(iii)   Recommends the land-use pattern on land identified;

(iv)   Provides independent valuation on land and premises;

(v)   Purchases land either for development or land bank and purchases premises for sale/rental;

(vi)   Advises Management on appointment of external consultants and vets their work;

(vii)   Prepares annual divisional budget as part of the Authority's development expenditures based on corporate guidelines;

(viii) Provides property development consultancy services for small landowners to develop their land; and

(ix)   Provides the overall project administration for property development from initiation to completion.

Implementation and Technical Division

(i)   Implements land development projects;

(ii)   Provides technical services in architecture, engineering and quantity surveying;

(iii)   Supervises, monitors and co-ordinates projects from initial stage of construction to completion;

(iv)   Reports on the progress of projects during construction;

(v)   Advises Management on consultants' work and vets their designs; and

(vi)   Prepares annual divisional budget for the Authority's development expenditures based on corporate guidelines.

Property management and marketings

(i)   Develops and implements property management and marketing plans and strategies for the Authority's properties and premises;

(ii)   Determines the prevailing market price for sale and rental of UDA's premises within specific locality by undertaking periodic surveys and analyses;
(iii) Recommends appropriate rates for the Authority's premises;
(iv)   Acts as custodian of the Authority's developed and purchased properties which are not sold;
(v)   Ensures the proper maintenance of UDA's premises, oversees all repair and renovation works;
(vi)   Provides facilities for upkeep of records and the physical maintenance of UDA's premises;
(vii) Supervises and monitors the functions of the Regional Offices pertaining to property management and marketing; and
(viii) Prepares annual budgets for property management and marketing activities using corporate guidelines as a basis and monitors Division's plans based upon the approved budgets.

Staff

The following table gives a picture of the staff strength of the Urban Development Authority as at January, 1983:

	Category	Number	%
A	Managerial & Professional	177	22.6
B	Sub-Managerial & Professional	130	16.6
C	Technical & Clerical	301	38.4
D	Subordinate	175	22.4
	Total:	783	100

The total number of staff include those in the three regional offices.

4. FINANCIAL MATTERS

There is provision in the Urban Development Authority Act, Clause 19 (2), which allows UDA to secure funds through grants and loans from government, loans from other financial institutions, income or profits received from development projects.

In order to facilitate identification and control of activities and financial needs of its administration and development UDA created

PE-I

two funds namely: (i) Administration Fund; and (ii) Development Fund.

Administration Fund

Sources of funds for the Administration Fund include government grants, income from management and professional fees imposed on projects, interest on loans given to staff, interest on short term and fixed deposits, fees imposed on legal documents, loan processing fees, etc.

The allocation from this fund is used for staff salaries and other expenditures (medical, travel, etc.), rental of office and all other administrative expenditures.

Development Fund

Sources of income for the Development Fund include:

(i)   Income from interest on loans to UDA's subsidiary companies and joint-ventures, *bumiputera* businessmen and *bumiputera* developers;
(ii)   Income from rental of UDA's premises;
(iii) Income from dividends received from UDA's subsidiary and joint-venture companies; and
(iv)   Income from profits on investment e.g. sales of UDA's premises and sale of UDA's shares.

The application of this fund covers:

(i)   Lease of premises by UDA from other developers, to be sublet to *bumiputera* businessmen;
(ii)   Repayments of Treasury loans, bank overdrafts and loans from other institutions;
(iii) Provision for doubtful debts, drop in value of shares, losses on guarantees, etc.; and
(iv)   Other development expenditures on UDA's bill, for example, quit rent assessment, maintenance and repairs, insurance payments, etc.

5. UDA IN THE FUTURE

As a result of the efforts undertaken to review UDA's programmes various changes were implemented from the Fourth Malaysia Plan period.

New strategies and direction of UDA were formulated and implemented with the view to improving the performance of UDA.

Implementation strategies are as follows:

Emphasis On Development In Fourteen Towns

UDA will concentrate its activities in designated areas only. The designated areas for concentration of development were based on two criteria, namely growth trend in towns and the poverty profile.

The fourteen towns were identified from a comprehensive study on growth trends of forty-five towns (in West Malaysia) with a population of 10,000 and above, covering the years 1960 to 1980.

The fourteen towns identified were Alor Star, Georgetown, Tanjong Tokong, Butterworth, Ipoh, Klang, Petaling Jaya, Shah Alam, Kuala Lumpur, Seremban, Malacca, Johor Bahru, Kuantan and Kota Bharu.

UDA's programmes

In the Fourth Malaysia Plan and thereafter UDA would pay special attention to two programmes, namely Purchase of Business Premises and Comprehensive Urban Development together with Early Land Purchase Programme. UDA in future would also implement projects through its Consultancy Services programme to develop *bumiputera* lands.

One-stop agency

Since UDA was directed to stop all forms of loans including loans for development of *bumiputera* lands, UDA established the Consultancy Services Unit with the view to assist *bumiputeras* to develop their lands.

This Unit acts as a 'One Stop Agency' whereby individual *bumiputera* landowners would seek the advice of the Unit which would study the needs of the landowner, suggest suitable development and advise on the necessary steps to be taken in order to develop their lands either by leasing their lands to UDA, through bank financing to develop their lands on their own or appoint UDA as a development agent. UDA also assists applicants by providing technical and management advisory services.

UDA as developer

This concept is based on the landowner appointing UDA as his developer.

The concept is being implemented to assist *bumiputera* landowners to develop their lands and to prevent *bumiputera* lands from being sold or mortgaged. Through this concept UDA is able to increase the number and value of *bumiputera* properties and at the same time provide an increased number of premises for *bumiputera* businessmen.

Provision of Premises

In the Fourth Malaysia Plan, UDA has decided to purchase 500 units of business premises to increase the facilities for *bumiputera* businessmen in urban areas.

Spin-offs

Since the establishment of UDA up to the end of 1982, a total of 386 contracts to the value of $718,731,000 have been awarded to the contractors.

In terms of consultancy services, UDA had awarded 277 jobs to the value of $110,383,000 to consultants including architects, quantity surveyors, engineers, valuers and surveyors.

Subsidies

Resulting from the review of UDA's activities and programmes, it was found that a number of programmes implemented provided subsidies to *bumiputera* entrepreneurs. A conservative estimate for the subsidies through rental of premises, sales of premises, sales of land and other projects showed that UDA has provided a subsidy of $75,293,532 since its establishment up to 31 December 1981.

Establishment of Peremba Ltd.

In 1979 UDA was directed to transfer its shares in 26 joint-venture companies dealing in property development to a subsidiary company, PEREMBA Ltd.

Joint-ventures in land development

UDA decided to revive the concept of joint-ventures in land development although in 1979 it was directed to stop all joint-ventures, to
allow for a period of review. The strategy of joint-ventures was found
to be very beneficial to UDA and had the advantage that UDA was
able to participate in land development projects with those who owned
lands at strategic locations.

UDA would evaluate and review its financial position and formulate a financial plan in order to ensure that self-sufficiency would
be achieved as from the Fifth Malaysia Plan, i.e. from the year 1986
onwards.

NOTES

1. *UDA Annual Report 1975.*
2. MARA or Majlis Amanah Rakyat is a Federal statutory body.
3. SEDCs or State Economic Development Corporations established in each State
   to undertake development.
4. *Second Malaysia Plan (1971–75).*
5. Designated towns: UDA decided to concentrate its development activities within
   the fourteen designated towns identified after a study on the various towns of
   Peninsular Malaysia.

250·260   6140 8332

12

THE YUGOSLAV ENTERPRISE

V. V. Ramanadham

Enterprises in Yugoslavia are characterised by 'self-management'. They are a class by themselves. They differ from public enterprises elsewhere in the world. The 'self-management' transcends all forms of joint consultation, workers' participation, and worker directors on the board, with which we are familiar in other countries.

This paper seeks to present the essential nature of self-management underlying every Yugoslav enterprise. The pattern is so common to all enterprises that a delineation of its structural implications would be of value. Apart from this, a comparison is made between certain elements of the Yugoslav enterprise organisation and the corresponding position with the generality of public enterprises elsewhere. This, incidentally, renders unnecessary references to the Yugoslav enterprise in the last chapter of this volume containing a comparative review.

1. THE ORGANISATIONAL STRUCTURE

The crucial element in the Yugoslav enterprise is the Basic Organisation of Associated Labour (BOAL). This is composed of workers who are mutually inter-dependent in their work and give rise to joint results of labour. The emphasis of the Associated Labour Act of 1976 is on the formation of the smallest BOAL possible. The statute lays down the methods of distribution of resources and rights and obligations among the BOALs.

The level above the BOALs is the 'work organisation'. This is comprised of BOALs that are inter-linked by common interests concerning labour, production or business.

Several work organisations can come together to form a 'composite organisation'. The binding factor is some common interest − in production, marketing, technology or finance. It is possible for a work organisation to associate itself with more than one composite organisation, on the criterion of functional commonness.

The central theme of the self-management agreements that bring about a BOAL, work organisation or composite organisation, is that it is the *workers* that have the power to make or change rules. For instance, at the level of the work organisation they jointly plan the business and the mutual relationships and determine the nature of distribution of income and allocations for 'personal incomes'.

From the above description of how workers come together to form an enterprise, let us proceed to discuss the organisational framework of the enterprise. This can be analysed under the heads: the decisional framework, the business-management framework, and the supervisory framework.

A.   The Decisional Framework

The agency that law designates as responsible for managing the work of a BOAL is the Workers' Council. Every BOAL with 30 workers or more has to form it in such a way that all processes and categories of workers in the BOAL are represented on it. The members have a two-year term. The functions of the BOAL are as follows:

(i)   to determine the draft by-laws, etc.;
(ii)   to determine the draft guidelines for the plan of the BOAL;
(iii)   to determine the draft elements of self-management agreements and social compacts to be concluded;
(iv)   to formulate the business policy, adopt the BOAL's plan and determine measures of implementation;
(v)   to determine questions of credit;
(vi)   to draw up periodical and annual balance sheets;
(vii)   to elect and relieve the executive organs of BOAL;
(viii) to ensure that workers are informed on matters relevant to their decision-making and supervision;
(ix)   to issue guidelines to, and supervise, the executive organs;
(x)   to determine programmes, and ensure implementation, regarding total national defence and social self-protection as related to the BOAL.

Though the Workers' Council is the important organisational level, the rights of the workers are fundamental. On several questions they are empowered by referendum to take decisions. This right is of supreme value in relation to such items as the allocation of resources for workers' incomes and for collective consumption.

The Workers' Council can set up 'executive' organs to which the Council elects members on a two-year basis. None can stay on a given organ for more than two consecutive terms. The executive organs are intended to assist the Workers' Council in its functions and in the implementation of decisions.

At the level of the work organisation there is again a Worker's Council, composed of delegates from BOALs in such a way that every BOAL is represented. The functions of the Council at this level are as follows:

(i)   to determine the draft by-laws;
(ii)   to adopt self-management enactments;
(iii) to determine the draft of the self-management agreement on the plan of the work organisation, and to adopt the plan;
(iv)   to adopt plans and programmes concerning total national defence and social protection;
(v)   to formulate business policy and measures of implementation;
(vi)   to elect and relieve executive organs in the work organisation;
(vii) to issue guidelines to, and supervise, the executive organs.

The importance of the BOALs is reflected in the arrangement under which the decisions of a Workers' Council are only valid with the consent of every BOAL.

There is, finally, a Workers' Council at the level of the composite organisation. Its constitution and functions are parallel to those of the other levels.

B. The Business-Management Framework

This refers to the actual management function. Every BOAL has a business manager (or a managing board) appointed by the Workers' Council on proposals received from an appointments panel. The sole manager or a member of the board is appointed for a period not longer than four years; re-appointments are possible. The functions of the business manager (or board) are:

(i)   to manage the BOAL's business;
(ii)   to organise and co-ordinate its labour processes;
(iii) to propose business policies and implementation measures, execute the Workers' Council's decisions, and consider draft plans and offer his views thereon;
(iv)   He is responsible for his work and is accountable to the Workers' Council of the BOAL.

Similar arrangements exist for the establishment of a business manager or board at the level of the work organisation and of the composite organisation. True to the principle of self-management, the mutual relations among the business management organs at different levels are governed by self-management agreements among them.

C. *The Supervisory Framework*

A unique feature of the Yugoslav enterprise is that the statute provides for direct supervision of the entire business process – both decisional and management – by workers. Every worker has the right to inspect documents (other than those termed 'secret') and inspect the work of the Workers' Council or the business management organ. This right is formalised through an organ of self-management workers' supervision in every BOAL, and then at the levels of the work organisation and the composite organisation. Among the items supervised are the implementation of self-management agreements, appropriate use of social resources, income distribution, and the allocation of resources for personal incomes. The supervisory organs can take the help of outside experts, where necessary, for establishing facts.

The preceding description brings out the uniqueness of the Yugoslav enterprise. It will be useful to draw certain points of contrast between its organisational structure and that of public enterprises elsewhere in the world.

First, there is a clear decisional hierarchy here; and the Workers' Council at the lowest (BOAL) level is not inferior, in any way, to that at a higher level, though the nature of subjects covered gets broader at the latter levels. On the other hand, in enterprises elsewhere there is one board of directors at the top, which is the formally entitled decisional agency for the entire enterprise, though assistance is taken from management committees (or regional or product-wise advisory bodies) in several cases.

Second, the decisional and the business management organs (and hierarchies) are distinct in the Yugoslav enterprise, whereas in the cross-section of enterprises elsewhere there are overlaps, in the sense that certain board members are simultaneously engaged in management (as heads of departments). This practice is growing progressively. The term we have for it is 'functional directors'. The U.K. enterprises covered in this volume evidence this feature.

Third, there is an intrinsic difference in respect of supervision. In the Yugoslav enterprise, there is a distinct supervisory organ (and hierarchy). In enterprises elsewhere this function is discharged, in varying degrees, by the board of directors, O & M units, internal auditors, specialist committees, and external auditors. Besides, the focus of all these is on the management processes and rarely extends to the decisional framework itself.

Fourth, the entire approach of the Yugoslav enterprise is to derive the sine qua non of decision and management from the bottom level, the workers. There are several issues of basic significance which can only be decided by the workers by referendum; and no managing body can act contrarily. In enterprises elsewhere the approach is from top downwards, despite progressive participation of workers in the management and, in some cases, in the decisional process.

Two broad comments on the structure of the Yugoslav enterprise are in order at this stage. One is that it can tend to be very elaborate and cause delays in decision making. To some extent the enterprise is bound to experience this problem. It is also true that, as experience is gained, the business management wing of the enterprise and the decisional wing begin to develop mutual trust in such a way that the formal routes that can make for delays and frictions are successfully abridged.

The other comment concerns the real connotation of 'self-management'. Apparently the entire process of management is by the workers inside a BOAL or a works organisation or a composite organisation. Apparently – to cite an illustration – the proportion of income that can be allotted as personal incomes – i.e., wages – is strictly under the workers' own decisional powers. External influence on the working of the enterprise, apparently, has little place.

2. THE EXTERNAL INFLUENCES

But is this so? Let us examine this question at some length. This question broadly resembles the enterprise–government relationships that are discussed in the other papers.

It may be noted at the outset that the external influences on the Yugoslav enterprise are 'social' rather than merely government-derived. In fact direct governmental relationships are far too minimal as the following passages indicate.

The external influences on the Yugoslav enterprise may be examined under eight heads:

(a) statutory stipulations;
(b) self-management agreements;
(c) social compacts;

(d) socio-political communities;
(e) trade unions;
(f) consumers of goods and services;
(g) conceptual stipulations;
(h) special agencies.

A. The Statute

The simplest of qualifications to worker's self-management comes from the statute which lays down certain financial obligations of the enterprise or BOAL prior to the distribution of personal income. These are ten-fold:

(i)   obligations toward BOALs performing activities in the spheres of education, science, culture, health, social welfare etc.;
(ii)   obligations ensuring workers' social security;
(iii)   obligations concerning general social needs;
(iv)   conservation and environment;
(v)   national defence and social self-protection;
(vi)   insurance premia for social property;
(vii)   contributions to chambers of economy etc.;
(viii) obligations towards work communities;
(ix)   depreciation beyond minimum rates;
(x)   fines etc.

The balance of net income is to be allocated among:

(i)   personal incomes;
(ii)   collective consumption;
(iii)   expansion of the material base of labour and
(iv)   reserves.

As regards reserves the stipulation is that 2.5% of the income (i.e total revenue minus materials and depreciation) should be set aside, under law, until the reserve fund equals 25% of the average income of the previous three years.

One may get the impression that, subject to these provisions, a BOAL or enterprise is entitled to distribute as personal income to workers (which is analogous to the total wage) any amount that the Workers' Council determines. In fact there are subtle, but serious, limitations emanating from self-management agreements and social compacts.

B. Self-Management Agreements

These are defined as 'self-management acts adopted, on equal terms
by workers in organisations of associated labour and by workers in
work communities, communities of interest and other self-managing
organisations, with a view to regulating and co-ordinating their
interest for purposes of a more efficient specialisation of production,
the pooling of labour and resources, and the formation of work and
other organisations of associated labour' (The Associated Labour
Act, p. 412).

These govern the inter-relationships among workers in a BOAL,
among BOALs in a work organisation, and among the BOAL or work
organisation and outside communities. These, in a sense, reduce 'outside' pressures on the enterprise on an *ad hoc* basis, since the areas
of inter-relationship get clearly defined in the agreements. Terms
relating to personal incomes are among the important components
of the self-management agreements. For example, they may stipulate,
in the interest of minimum personal income, that under the 'solidarity
principle' the 'able' BOALs offer to the 'needy' BOALs a grant or
a loan to meet occasional difficulties in providing the guaranteed
personal incomes. Likewise an occasional grant or loan is also possible
from special reserve funds at the Commune or Republic level.

C. Social Compacts

These are concluded among the labour organisations, socio-political
communities, chambers of commerce, communities of interest, local
communities, trade unions and socio-political organisations. These
contain provisions that qualify the workers' autonomous decisions
in a BOAL or enterprise in such a way as to accommodate broader
socio-economic interests. The most significant of such provisions
concern personal incomes. They enunciate, Republic-wise, the extent
to which a given increase in net income may justify an increase in
personal incomes in a given year. The general theme is that increases
in personal incomes are at lower rates than those in net incomes.
Herein lies a subtle external injunction in favour of reserve or business
fund building.

D. Socio-Political Communities

These bodies are endowed with certain rights and obligations vis-à-
vis the BOALs. We noted earlier that the business-managing personnel

are appointed by Workers' Councils on the recommendations of the appointments commission. The socio-political communities have representatives on that commission. Besides, they can require a BOAL to adopt measures of remedy when it does not secure enough for personal incomes or minimum reserve building. They are also required to offer assistance to BOALs, if necessary. Finally, they are empowered to exert ameliorative measures when a BOAL or enterprise violates proper principles of income distribution, or when it uses social resources in a 'socio-economically inappropriate way', or when a decision is taken to launch an activity without certainty of resources for completing it, or when the business causes harm to the community. The measures can include changes in the business-managing organ and dissolution of the Workers' Council. They can even appoint a temporary organ in a BOAL in extreme cases.

E. Trade Unions

They have powers of participating in the formulation of the self-management agreements, of being represented on the appointments commission, of being heard before the Workers' Council relieves a business-managing organ and of being provided with the information sent to workers from time to time. They have a weighty role in the formation of the organs of supervision; and they have to be informed by the latter of any failures of a BOAL or of any harm caused to social property.

True, some of the personalities are the same in the socio-political communities and trade unions on the one side and the BOALs on the other. Yet their roles in the respective agencies are different and the influence of the former vis-à-vis the BOALs should be considered as external, in the institutional sense.

F. Consumers

They have the right to enter into self-management agreements with a BOAL or enterprise concerning mutual relations, outputs, prices and consumers' sharing in the incomes raised.

G. & H. Conceptual Stipulations and Special Agencies

Finally we may refer to the Court of Appeal and the Social Attorney of self-management who have functions of enforcing the law and taking preventive and remedial steps in certain situations. And the statute bristles with such exhortations as that workers can 'freely' dispose of net income but 'under conditions of responsibility ... to society as a whole'. One can understand the force of such stipulations in the self-management-oriented administrative system of Yugoslavia.

It would be useful to present a brief comparative review of the external influences on the enterprise in Yugoslavia and those elsewhere. There is far less direct relationship with the Federal Government in Yugoslavia than most public enterprises have in other countries. There is hardly any 'control' as such from the Government, either.

The external influences are rather local in orientation than national or country-wide. In fact they can give us the impression of being too diffuse.

It is important to note that, even where external influences touch on important aspects of enterprise decisions, they are determined *ex ante*, and also usually form part of a self-management agreement. There is little chance, as in other countries, of the Government or any external authority jumping in with a control decision in an *ex post* or *ad hoc* manner.

Basically enterprise decisions of most public enterprises other than in Yugoslavia are not strictly decisions of insiders. Government representatives and many other outsiders usually sit on the boards. We are not debating the relative merits of the arrangement here. The point on hand is simply that in the case of the Yugoslav enterprise the decisions are, technically, those of the insiders of the Workers' Council or the workers. They are, of course, subject to the impact of external influences delineated in the preceding passages; but then they are derived through self-management agreements, involving the workers (BOAL or enterprise) themselves.

A final point of conceptual interest. In the parlance of the Yugoslav enterprise organisation the issue is not one of what authority to confer on the enterprise management; it is really one of BOAL or enterprise 'sovereignty'; and one has to think if any element of it is to be taken away in favour of an external agency. This is all that the external influences discussed above aim to achieve.

3. CAPITAL STRUCTURE

The Yugoslav enterprise is claimed to be under 'social ownership'. It is not under government ownership. Nor is it 'owned' by the workers or the bankers who offer loans.

This is a point of more than semantic interest. In the absence of an 'owner' there is no question of owners' rights in management or directoral policy. The use of the resources is under the direction and decision of the workers. And the profits or net incomes of the BOAL or enterprise do not go to an outside agency wholly or partly, apart from the payments that have to be made to the Commune, Republic or Federal agencies under statutory obligations and taxes, or under self-management agreements. These payments are, however, not linked with the profits as such but constitute, in most cases, a cost item.

Mention may be made of the statutory obligation of a BOAL to offer 'loans' for the development of under-developed regions. These, in some cases, can be larger than the contributions to the business fund and the reserve fund of the BOAL or enterprise itself. It is not certain that these loans get repaid.

The absence of 'equity' in the capitalisation ensures that the enterprise does not begin to treat its capital as costless; for, the loans that constitute the capitalisation have to be remunerated with interest payments. Thus the enterprise is under a healthy stress to earn enough. This situation is in contrast with that of many public enterprises in the rest of the world where equity is openly or covertly wielded as a nearly permanent cost relief to the enterprise.

This brings us to the questions of profit accumulation and losses.

One of the lacunae in the Yugoslav enterprise organisation is that there has not been sufficiently effective emphasis on the accumulation of the business fund. This really represents the major element of plough-back or re-investible internal resources, unlike the 'reserve fund' which is set up to meet losses and the 'common consumption fund' set up for a specific purpose in the workers' interest. The autonomy of workers in deciding on personal incomes, coupled with any external insistence on the building of the business fund seems to have led to inadequate re-investments, on the whole. The enterprise 'plan' is expected to attend to this question, no doubt; and there are external influences in favour of curbs on excessive personal incomes and of business-fund building. But these are not enough; and the absence of a more positive spur to re-investment has begun to be felt over the years. And a law has recently been passed that a specified percentage of a proposed investment has to be found from the business fund – higher if in buildings than in production factories. It is not clear that this kind of statutory formulation is adequate to achieve the basic purpose of ensuring that BOALs or enterprises 'retain profits' substantially in business – to use non-Yugoslav phraseology – and to regulate the saving targets of the self-managed institutions upwards, consistently with the national needs or targets of saving.

As to losses incurred by a Yugoslav BOAL or enterprise, the remedy of external assistance is limited. Some help can come from other gainful BOALs or from the solidarity funds of the Commune or Republic, earmarked for this purpose. These are very temporary and small in size. The BOAL or enterprise gradually drives itself into a mandatory obligation to explore and implement remedial measures. These, in the extreme, can involve a merger with other BOALs or enterprises or even liquidation. External agencies also can get involved in effectuating such compulsory remedial processes. Thus the pressure to earn enough is continuously felt by the Yugoslav enterprise. This is not so in the case of the cross-section of public enterprises elsewhere; there the wage remunerations are a 'cost' and governments step in, in devious ways, to meet the situation of losses, liquidation being a rather rare incident.

(For a fuller treatment on the Yugoslav enterprise, please see: V. V. Ramanadham, *The Yugoslav Enterprise*, published by International Center for Public Enterprises in Developing Countries, Ljubljana, 1981.)

CONCLUDING REVIEW

V. V. Ramanadham

We shall attempt an overall review of the material presented in the preceding chapters, introducing the comparative angle to the extent possible. At the outset it may be noted that total uniformity in presentation has not been their aim. An obvious reason for differences in coverage is that the enterprises belong to different countries and to different sectors and have evolved themselves in the public sector in different contexts of national strategies of development. While some of these will come out in this chapter, our focus is on aspects intrinsic to public enterprise organisation and on the differences in practical approach to the problems of apparent commonality.

1. DISTINCTIVE ASPECTS OF COVERAGE

Considering the diversities in coverage, we may find it helpful to start with a brief account of the major aspects emphasised in each paper. *British Steel Corporation* contains rich material on the evolution of the organisational structure within the Corporation and brings out the impact of a variety of economic factors on it. The trend towards organisational decentralisation and the limits to it in the circumstances of a large enterprise are presented.

The Post Office records the rationale and gradualness of the institutional change from departmental status to the public corporation form − a process that began in 1932 and ended in 1969. It suggests, besides, the logicality of disintegrating strictly non-homogeneous lines of business − posts and telecommunications.

Electricité de France emphasises the dual role of EDF as an enterprise and as a public enterprise and discusses the intricacies in the use of the financial powers of the government with serious consequences for the autonomy of the managers. It comments on the features of the unique French device of 'contrat de programme'.

Istituto Ricostruzione Industriale throws out valuable material

on the nature of IRI's size and holding complex and the devices of
co-ordination between the holding apex and the sub-holding units,
on the complexities of the non-commercial functions imposed on it
and the related issues of governmental guidelines thereon, and on the
capital structure designed to be appropriate both to the commercial
environment in which it works and to the fulfilment of certain macro-
economic obligations.

Salzgitter AG brings out the German experience in the organisational aspects of a diversified group and indicates the techniques
of holding company control over, and co-ordination among, the
constituent units. Of special interest is the functional involvement of
the members of the top board in the directoral conduct of the Group's
business.

The Port Authority of New York and New Jersey emphasises the
bi-statal nature of the enterprise and examines directoral methodology
under conditions of a totally non-functional board. Of special interest
is the delineation of the internal organisation structure suited to
changes in size and nature of its business and of the precise patterns
of applying principles of management to changing needs.

Corporación Venezolana de Guayana contains useful material on
its characteristic as a regional development agency. It shows how, in
course of time, it has found itself significantly deflected from the basic
concept of its purposes, having been unable to resist the development
of organisational dualism in the conduct of its business functions as
a result of FIV's progressively growing financial participation in the
CVG firms.

National Fertilizer Corporation of Pakistan Ltd. makes relevant
references to the origins of public enterprise in Pakistan, which had
an impact on its own organisational structure and deals extensively
with its techniques of fulfilling holding-complex obligations consistently with considerations of autonomy of subsidiaries. Aspects of
capital structure pertaining to NFC merit notice, too; so does the
conscious decision to concentrate all selling in an exclusive subsidiary.

Coal India Ltd. brings out the influences on enterprise organisation
traceable to the circumstances of the nationalisation measure and
describes the meticulous efforts constantly made with the object of
rationalising the relative power-and-function structures within the
organisation. The eventual emphasis on the colliery as the profit
centre, and the description of the factors determining the economics
of size at different levels within the organisation are among the other
aspects of interest covered in the chapter.

Urban Development Authority highlights the distinctiveness of its non-commercial objective of restructuring society and developing a commercial community among the 'sons of the soil'. The distinction between the Administration Fund and the Development Fund is an interesting facet of its financial organisation; and the changes of policy towards the strategy of joint ventures with UDA participation are indicative of a non-doctrinaire approach in deciding the organisational framework for its functions in the most efficient and economical manner.

The above is a statement of the particular issues raised in the different papers and is exclusive of several such commonalities as internal organisation and structures, techniques of managerial control, and formal enterprise–government relationships. It will be our purpose next to present a comparative review of organisational facets ranging over form, boards, size and sub-unitisation, financial structure, structure of objectives, basic directions of internal organisation and interface with external agencies.

2. COMPARATIVE REVIEW

A. *The Form*

Seven of the enterprises covered in the volume are in the form of a public corporation, while the other three, Salzgitter AG, National Fertilizer Corporation of Pakistan Ltd., and Coal India Ltd. are joint stock companies. It is doubtful if the choice of form has resulted from any distinctive considerations. Does it result from sectoral differences? No, even as British Steel Corporation and Salzgitter AG evidence. Does it depend on the spatial coverage of the enterprise? No, as Electricité de France and Coal India Ltd. – both national in jurisdiction – illustrate. Has it close connection with sectoral coverage? No; while British Steel Corporation covering a whole sector is a corporation, Coal India Ltd. covering a whole sector is a company. Has a measure of nationalisation had any bias for the corporation form? Not necessarily; by and large, yes in the UK but not so in India and Pakistan, as the enterprises covered in the volume suggest.

It is by now familiar that the distinction between the corporation and the company forms has not been very significant in practice, except in certain de jure senses. For instance, a Corporation Act might contain provisions regarding the organisational form to be evolved within the enterprise, as the paper on British Steel Corporation suggests. Even in this case the 1981 Act has nearly freed it to consider changes at will in respect of internal organisation. Corporation Acts generally have provisions regarding the number and nature of board memberships, whereas company boards are governed by the Companies Act which applies to both public and private sectors. One of the main implications of a Corporation Act is that it may codify, though not necessarily, the outlines of government relationships with the enterprise; and these could be tailor-made, as in the case of the UK Post Office – in respect of its international relations, work for the government and telecommunications licensing. The Act might, in some cases, have specific clauses on the capital structure, vide the Iron and Steel Act 1968 under which British Steel Corporation, unlike the majority of the British public corporations, was accorded 'public dividend capital', analogous to equity capital.

The company form, it may be deduced, offers greater flexibility in such areas as were cited above. It is, on the whole, not certain that this is an advantage. Experience suggests that what is desirable is an enunciation of government – enterprise relationships independently of the form of organisation.

B. *The Board*

The statutory board directing the affairs of the enterprise, by whatever name it is designated – e.g., Corporation, Conseil d'Administration or Commissioners – is generally appointed by the government, either by the minister concerned, as in British Steel Corporation and Post Office, or by the President, as in CVG and IRI, with reference to the Chairman and the Vice-Chairman, or by the State Governors as in the Port Authority of NY and NJ.

The size of the board varies greatly from one to another among the enterprises covered in the volume. CVG has a rather small board of six, while Salzgitter AG, with twenty-one, and British Steel Corporation with seventeen at one time, come at the other end.

Of greater interest are the practices as regards the composition of the board. By and large there is a bias for functional membership in the British corporations, Steel and Post Office, and to a relatively small extent in a major Indian public enterprise like Coal India Ltd. (Actually there were times when this complex had no functional member on the board, apart from the Chairman, and when the two functional members held the posts in their personal names. The latest position is one in which three of the twelve board members are full-time headquarters officers, viz., the Chairman and Managing Director,

Director (Technical) and Director (Finance); and four Chairmen and Managing Directors of the subsidiaries (Western Coalfields, Eastern Coalfields, Central Coalfields and the Central Mine Planning and Design Institute) are also on the board. The Port Authority of NY and NJ has no functional member. All, including the Chairman, are honorary commissioners. CVG has no full-time director, apart from the Chairman; similar is the case of the National Fertilizer Corporation of Pakistan Ltd.

While it would be hazardous to pronounce judgements on what could be considered as the best practice, the case for a competent functional core would be strong indeed. For one thing, it adequately professionalises the directoral level; for another, it correspondingly restricts the unpredictable freedom of the appointing authority in the choice of board members. In countries with relatively limited 'outside' sources for board members, this should be particularly commendable.

Two points suggest themselves on a close study of the papers. First, where the board is relatively, if not wholly, part-time and non-functional, there is a subtle organisational device that bridges the 'gap'. The Port Authority of NY and NJ has an extremely powerful Executive Director and standing committee structure, each commissioner serving on one or two committees. The committees bristle with executive competence. IRI has an Executive Committee, formed by the Chairman, Vice-Chairman and the three 'expert' directors, though part-timers, appointed by the Minister of State Holdings. To this committee are delegated most directoral matters. Over time it accumulates a high degree of competence which one might associate with a functional core.

The other point is that the law stipulates, in some cases, a composition that weakens the functional proportion on the board. This is illustrated by Electricité de France which has a tri-partite board constitution characteristic of French public enterprise: five from government, five from employees and five from business, local authorities, etc. The UK Post Office is another instance. The Post Office Act was amended in 1978 to accommodate − for two years − seven employee representatives. British Steel Corporation likewise had six employees added to the board in 1978 as a sequel to the Labour Government's policy towards industrial democracy.

Governmental preference for civil servants on boards has on the whole been slight in the UK. British Steel Corporation is one of the few public corporations on which two civil servants began to be appointed in 1978. Elsewhere the practice is quite common. IRI has nine civil servants on a board of twelve; the National Fertilizer

Corporation of Pakistan Ltd. has two civil servants and two public enterprise executives in a board of five; the Coal India board has a sizable official element — four out of twelve. Three of these are from the Department of Coal; and UDA has eight officials in a board of ten. Two of them are the Secretaries General of Ministries — a practice deliberately avoided in Indian Central Government enterprises.

Civil servant memberships probably result from the notion of co-ordination of public enterprise operations with government policies and of adequate interface between the two sides. But two problems arise: conflicts of interest on the part of the civil servants as directors and as government officials; and subtle, restrictive impacts on the managerial autonomy of the enterprises. At the extreme these may culminate in apparently managerial decisions owing really to 'external' influences, though the government as such escapes formal responsibility.

One other facet of board composition worth notice is the worker involvement. Some degree of it has long been introduced in the British Steel Corporation; but worker representation as such was introduced only in 1978 through government action. Similar was the Post Office experiment during 1977—79. It was given up as unsuccessful. In some other countries specific representation — even if very minor — has been a matter of policy. Salzgitter AG has two employee representatives in a board of twenty-one; Electricité de France has five out of fifteen; and CVG has one out of six. Some others like the Port Authority of NY and NJ, the National Fertilizer Corporation of Pakistan Ltd. and UDA have no worker representation on the board. The problem of conflict of interests is particularly weighty in the case of the worker-directors.

If one should speak of an ideal board composition, it should be such as provides for homogeneity in directoral approach on grounds of well set criteria, supported by adequate functional expertise and fertilised by outside expertise. We may add that it would be preferable not to aim, through board composition, at internalising externalities that ought to be transmitted in a transparent manner. This is one of the great dangers of an official-dominated board.

C. Size

The enterprises covered here are all large in size, in terms of investment, employment and output. This observation rests on the following grounds:

(a) In most cases the sizes are large in absolute terms. For example,

IRI, with assets valued at $30 billion (in 1982), employees numbering 525,000 and value added at $13 billion, is easily the largest enterprise (group) in Italy. It is twice as large as the next one in that country, viz., ENI.

(b) In almost all cases the sizes are larger than were formerly common in the private sector in the given sectors of activity. The British Steel Corporation illustrates a massive statutory merger (of about 210 companies in 1966, with £1409 million of capital employed, 270,000 in labour force, and turnover around £1000 million). This was at once the largest steel enterprise in Western Europe. Similar has been Coal India Ltd. which is an amalgam of eleven railway collieries (to start with), 214 coking mines and 711 non-coking mines. Electricité de France and the National Fertilizer Corporation of Pakistan Ltd. illustrate similar features of gigantic creations at the stroke of the nationalising pen – too large and too sudden.

The teeth of the finding that the sizes are large really lie in the question: are they uneconomical? We cannot offer a statistical answer. However, there is room for conjecture.

The hectic efforts made constantly by the top managements of the large enterprises, e.g. British Steel Corporation and Coal India Ltd., in streamlining the organisational structure, suggest that the size-setting is problematic from the angle of efficient management, another term for cost economy. Comments on such efforts will be made in a following section. Suffice it to note at this point that the 'commercial case' for decentralisation – to quote from the Roseveare paper – is realised in strong terms, even if being in the public sector might hinder the full extent of reform measures in many cases.

It is in the Bokhari paper that we come across the nearest direct comment on the size question; and that is doubtful of the merits of enlarging the present size of the National Fertilizer Corporation of Pakistan Ltd. For that would involve centralisation of many functions, delay in decision-making without any improvement in the quality of decisions, and a shift of scarce human resources to the 'head office'.

The papers give us reasonable scope, at the minimum, to call for a pause on size expansions in public enterprises and for insisting on a rigorous enquiry into the diseconomies already traceable to size (and its complexity, as in a holding structure or in a nation-wide structure), with a view to streamlining the organisational structure. This may be two-pronged, selectively: break the over-large unit into a few less large units, and/or make the organisational structure below the apex far more autonomous not only as operating units but as decisional entities.

Two kinds of largeness may be inferred from the papers. Some enterprises are statutorily monolithic, like British Steel Corporation and Electricité de France. Arrangements below the top level are non-statutory; and the extent of autonomy on the part of the constituent sub-units is a function, strictly, of internal decision. The other type is the holding complex, where the subsidiaries have statutory autonomy in de jure terms. De facto, it is subject to limits; and this is the problem of largeness-cum-complexity.

Reading between the lines, one can infer from the papers that a major influence in the direction of large size in public enterprise is generally 'external' in origin. That is, it is independent of the scale economies (or diseconomies), though in a few cases and within limits (as in the UK electricity distribution) economies may have been co-extensive with the external preference for large size. This is often the product of a standardised pattern of thought on national-isation, favouring total unification. British Steel Corporation and the National Fertilizer Corporation of Pakistan Ltd. illustrate this. In Pakistan, for instance, the background was one of creating sectoral holding complexes right through the public sector; and the method of a 'holding' apex was more or less forgone in the case of the National Fertilizer Corporation of Pakistan Ltd. The genesis of IRI reveals another external shade: it had to take over industrial assets from distressed banks; and it was soon realised (in 1936) that there was no prospect of disposing of them. Thus not only bigness but a highly diversified structure came to stay. In a few cases, as suggested by the Coal India Ltd. experience, the case for total unification appeared to be overwhelming, since an efficient pattern of exploitation and management had to replace the positively unscientific situation of the erstwhile private sector and massive investments in expansion had to be formulated and implemented. An all-industry approach was indeed imperative. Two questions seem to remain unanswered, though: how far has Coal India Ltd. internalised external decisions in the process, and what would have been the economies of scale under alternative options as against a single holding complex? Its 'main tasks', as laid down by the govern-ment, lend weight to the first question, and its unceasing efforts at internal organisational reform, to the second.

D. *Internal Organisation Structure*

We now turn to the structure of internal organisation which, in the case of the large and complex public enterprises, holds the key to exorcising the demerits and diseconomies of size. All the papers contain detailed material on this subject.

The papers suggest that it would be helpful to our analysis to distinguish between two broad categories; the unitary or monolithic type and the 'holding' type. The former comprises the British Steel Corporation, the Post Office, Electricité de France and the Port Authority of New York and New Jersey, and the Urban Development Authority. Their major business is organised under what the statute recognises as one unit or board, though gradually some subsidiaries have come into being, for example, as joint ventures in the case of the non-main stream businesses of the British Steel Corporation and of a specific activity – land development – in the case of UDA. The other enterprises covered in the volume may be placed in the 'holding type'. Here the statute conceives of legally autonomous units within the top unit or board. One may deduce that, at least in theory, this can provide an environment in which the major organisational issue concerns the choice of the extent and modalities of centralisation in a situation of legal subsidiaries; whereas in the unitary case the major anxiety should be how and how far to decentralise. To put it simply, unless the holding apex makes a positively restrictive move, the subsidiaries can look for an autonomous status, whereas, in the case of the unitary apex, unless it makes a positively permissive move, the constituent units cannot wield a high degree of autonomy.

The papers provide ample evidence on the distinctive approaches in the two cases. Let us review the experiences in some detail.

In so far as the unitary category is concerned, the objective has been progressive decentralisation and the modalities may be classified under the following heads.

(a) *The constitution of management committees*

British Steel Corporation has these at two levels. The Chief Operating Officer (substantively analogous to the position of a chief executive) has a high-level Operations Committee, which meets every month before the board meets. Besides, the managing directors of all 'Businesses' (see later paragraphs for the connotation of this term) are themselves advised by management committees. In the Port Authority of NY and NJ great reliance is placed on the committee system. Four important committees have stood the test of time for forty years now. They concern themselves with port planning, finance, construction, and operations. And a fifth (the audit committee) was added in 1983.

(b) *Organisational relief to top level*

British Steel Corporation illustrates this in several ways at different times. First it had three Deputy Chairmen, though the Chairman was also the chief executive. Then the two posts of Chairman and Chief Executive were separated. Recently, though the Chairman has again been designated as the Chief Executive, there has been an effective shift in the latter functions to the chief operating officer. In the Port Authority of NY and NJ the apparently long span of control on the part of the Executive Director is relieved, in practice, by effective delegation of substantial authority to three assistant executive directors. Below the board level in the UK Post Office headquarters directors and regional directors exist, with wide delegated and devolved powers.

(c) *The creation of sub-boards*

Regional, product-wise or functional boards may be set up with non-statutory but effective status. The best example is provided by the British Steel Corporation which had 'Group Boards' to advise the Group managing directors. Electricité de France's experience suggests a contrast. The prescription of the Act in favour of entrusting distribution to local enterprises has not yet been followed; so much so that each Technical Division of the headquarters has evolved its own regional and local units. Urban Development Authority has pursued the formation of smaller joint ventures with 'bumiputeras', the intended beneficiaries of its activities.

(d) *The evolution of profit centres*

Apparently a conceptual method, this has an effective impact of decentralisation. Each Division within the British Steel Corporation was designated as a profit centre during 1970–76, though constraints did exist on its autonomy on grounds of overall optimisation. Then came a change (during 1976–80) in favour of geographical manufacturing Divisions acting as 'cost or performance' centres and not profit centres. This was followed, in 1980, by a complete move towards highly decentralised product-based profit centres or 'businesses'. The latter, no doubt, do not have 'complete' profit centre autonomy, since the corporation has to be managed as a 'total' corporate entity.

Similar has been the trend in the Port Authority of NY and NJ. The term used has been 'net revenue responsibility', clearly delegated to levels below the Executive Director. This has been considered as the principal device to ensure the accountability of line departments for financial returns on investments.

Developments went a step further in the case of the UK Post Office, in that it has been set distinct financial targets for its main lines of business: posts, giro and (formerly) telecommunications. Such a financial arrangement naturally entailed measures of departmentation that sheltered a high degree of decentralisation.

Turning to the holding type of enterprises, the case for centralisation rests on the economies of scale obtained from bringing the subsidiaries within co-ordination, control or monitoring by the apex. The aim of treating the total complex as an optimisable entity has greater justification when the subsidiaries are all in a given sector, as in the case of the National Fertilizer Corporation of Pakistan Ltd., than when they are in diversified sectors, as evidenced conspicuously by IRI. In the latter case such an aim reduces itself to financial maximisation in an overall sense. This may be somewhat uncontested when the apex has full or dominant ownership of the subsidiaries. When its ownership is minor, the interests of the other shareholders become vocal enough to resist any financial aims of the apex level that cost certain subsidiary profits, dividends, share values, growth rates and managerial autonomy.

The 'holding' cases covered in this volume are heterogeneous. IRI has a widely diversified structure. Hence, right away, a strong system of principal sub-holding companies has been devised, under which many similar – though not necessarily identical – activities have been grouped together: e.g., ship-yards under Fincontiori and iron and steel, industrial plant and engineering and cement under Finsider. The National Fertilizer Corporation of Pakistan Ltd., on the other hand, is wholly in the single sector of fertilisers. So is Coal India Ltd., concentrating on coal. Salzgitter AG is moderately diversified, for the sake of efficiency. Steel, shipbuilding and trade are among its activities today, the slant being towards steel, of course. CVG's diversified structure owes to its character as a regional development agency.

IRI's Group Policy and Co-ordination Committee is a major innovation as a point of continuous contact and co-ordination at the management level among the Group constituents. It consists of the General Manager, the Chairman and Managing Directors of the sectoral sub-holdings and other directly controlled subsidiaries and, meeting once in three months, deals with problems of common interest.

While there is no information on the existence of such a formal

committee in the other holding enterprises covered in the volume,
there is some uniformity in the relationship contacts as between the
apex and the subsidiaries. IRI has two crucial procedures: one relating
to the annual review of multi-year investment programmes and the
other to approval of draft report and accounts. The Executive
Committee of IRI comes directly into the picture, aided by the
Planning Department. A broadly similar mechanism obtains in the
National Fertilizer Corporation of Pakistan Ltd. Monthly review
meetings are held, over which the Chairman of the holding apex
presides; and the top levels of managers of subsidiaries participate
in it and have full opportunities of discussions with the staff officers
of the apex. Likewise, quarterly meetings are held for reviewing the
budget performance of the subsidiaries.

A basic determinant of the apex's organisational impacts on the
subsidiaries lies in the board constitution of the latter. Here practices
are diverse; and in some enterprises they have varied from time to
time. In the case of IRI the Chairman selects the members of the
subsidiary boards – both executive and non-executive members –
and the Executive Committee checks their qualifications and suit-
ability in conformity with the board's guidelines on the subject. The
subsidiary boards also include some of the heads of departments in
IRI, especially those responsible for planning and liaison functions.
They sometimes sit on the executive committees too in so far as the
first-level subsidiaries are concerned. In the case of the second-level
subsidiaries such memberships are drawn from the junior staff of IRI
headquarters.

The directoral inter-relations are more direct in Salzgitter AG. The
board members act as Chairmen of the supervisory and advisory
boards of its subsidiaries. This arrangement is tied with the functional
division characteristic of the apex board in Salzgitter AG, viz., that
a board member has control of two business lines. Besides, the
Directors of Finance, Labour Relations etc. are, in addition, responsible for designated subsidiaries.

The most integral tie-up is presented by the National Fertilizer
Corporation of Pakistan Ltd. Its Chairman is the Chairman of every
subsidiary – a point which gains in significance in that there is no
full-timer on its board, apart from its Managing Director.

The Chairman of Coal India Ltd. used to be the Chairman of all
subsidiary boards originally, but a change occurred in 1977 when others
were appointed as Chairman and Managing Directors. (Today there
is an interesting relationship, in reverse. Four Chairmen of subsidiaries
and the Chairman of Singareni Colliers Ltd. sit on the apex board.)

The directors of the CVG subsidiaries are generally managers in CVG headquarters of related organisations.

Two other modalities, fairly common with most of the holding enterprises, need mention at this stage. It is in fact on the precise way in which these manifest themselves that the degree of abridgement of subsidiary autonomy depends. The first is the provision of staff services from the head-quarters; and the second is the provision of guidelines, targets and procedures of action.

The case for staff services in a 'holding' complex derives essentially from the concept of economies of scale. As mentioned in the Bokhari paper these can lead to the 'minimum deployment' of scarce technical resources, the more significantly in a developing country. It is often implicit in the objectives laid down by the government for a holding apex that it should maintain proper staff services. For instance, Coal India Ltd. is expected to approve budgets, determine standard costs and evaluate performance, co-ordinate the subsidiaries' activities, establish broad linkages of customers to different coalfields, etc.

The National Fertilizer Corporation of Pakistan Ltd. maintains four major Departments at the head-quarters: Planning, Finance, Commercial, and Personnel and Administration. As a response to specific needs of massive expansions, Coal India Ltd. has established three new Departments: corporate planning, project monitoring and processed fuel; it is likely to set up a Construction Division because of huge mine construction activities in the offing. In fact the anxiety of the enterprise is to bring about effective decentralisation even below the level of the subsidiary companies, by reorganising them into ten operating divisions, each under an Executive Director. Salzgitter AG offers direct assistance to the group of companies in R&D, financing and tax and legal matters.

It is difficult to judge exactly how heavy the influence of the head-quarters over the subsidiaries is in practice, through the framework of staff services. But there is sufficient indication in most papers, of watchfulness against involvement in direct management and in favour of keeping the apex staff at a minimum. Where certain sectoral planning functions devolve on the enterprise, as in the case of Coal India Ltd. and the National Fertilizer Corporation of Pakistan Ltd., the headquarters is bound to be rather circumspect in relaxing the staff service input in total performance.

And there is another reason too, which applies even in the case of IRI and Salzgitter, which have less sectoral planning responsibilities and do not face dearth of human resources at the subsidiary levels. As public enterprises, they have special responsibilities. For instance, the government's control interface is with IRI and not with the subsidiaries. Being in the intermediary position of ensuring account-ability of its empire, the IRI headquarters has to maintain adequate closeness with the subsidiaries, which does involve some limits to decentralisation. Likewise, Salzgitter is obliged to bear responsibility for certain audit desiderata applicable to German public enterprises and for the submission of the audit reports to the Federal Ministry of Finance.

The other common modality of apex–subsidiary relationships consists of issuing criteria, guidelines and norms. If well set and based on a fully participatory exchange of views, these can substantially limit the need for control interferences by the headquarters with the managerial operations of the subsidiaries. Almost all the papers speak of this technique: e.g., guidelines by IRI for the investment and production programmes of group companies; inter-company direc-tives by Salzgitter AG for uniform practices among the companies; targets and detailed guidelines formulated by the National Fertilizer Corporation of Pakistan Ltd. for the projects or companies; and formal policies, procedures and rules laid down by Coal India Ltd., in each area of activities.

The papers leave us enough room to suspect that in the field of selling the bias for centralisation is heavy, though it is sought to be justified on grounds of economy and benefits of overall planning. Coal India Ltd. centralised the sales function by setting up a Central Coal Marketing Organisation, and has found some justification in the fact that it would enable the producing subsidiaries to concentrate on production and project management. The experience of the National Fertilizer Corporation of Pakistan Ltd., another one-product enterprise, is similar. The sales activity has been detatched into an exclusive subsidiary, National Fertilizer Marketing Ltd. The experience of the British Steel Corporation has varied over time; there was some centralisation of commercial organisation before 1980, but then the need for decentralisation asserted itself. Even in the somewhat diversified Salzgitter one of the board members has charge of sales co-ordination for the 'whole group', though we cannot deduce from this the degree of centralisation that actually exists. The Virole paper does not suggest that any significant decentralisation in electricity distribution exists within Electricité de France, unlike in the UK.

The point about inadequate decentralisation in the marketing function gains significance on two grounds. For one thing, this is a relatively weak function in many public enterprises; for another, the evils of largeness in public enterprise organisation can be kept under check if a reasonable degree of competition within the constituent units exists. Besides, a sub-level has a chance of being a profit centre in a meaningful, even if limited, sense only when it enjoys some competitive selling autonomy.

E. *External Impacts*

Let us proceed to examine the impacts of governmental interface with public enterprises on their organisational structure. (It is not our intention to delve into the whole problem of 'government and public enterprise', on which there has been a recent global review under that title.)[1]

First, there is the impact on board composition. Though the basic logic of governmental relationships with public enterprises is nearly the same in all countries, practices have greatly varied not only among countries but among enterprises in the same country also. In the British Steel Corporation, for instance, two civil servants have been added to the board, whereas the Post Office board does not include any civil servant. The majority of the IRI board is official; most of the UDA board members are officials; and so on.

Analytically a major demerit of officialdom on the board of a public enterprise is that the influence that the government wishes to exert on its decisions and operations comes through the board room; whereas it would be more correct to transmit it in a transparent manner. The proposition gains strength in the case of an enterprise whose objective mix significantly covers non-commercial obligations, though one might be tempted to take a contrary view, namely, that here is a case for dominant official memberships on the board. It is on this ground that the institutional framework devised in the case of IRI, other than through board constitution, merits commendation. The Council of Ministers lays down the general guidelines that IRI should follow in 'the public interest'. The Interministerial Committee and the Ministry of State Holdings have the powers of direction and control. The sponsor ministry, the non-sponsor ministries, the Planning Cabinet and the Ministry of State Holdings all have their respective roles to play in the context of the policy objectives of the government. There is an interesting statutory provision for the specification of non-commercial obligations in the enterprise's pro- grammes submitted to the Interministerial Committee. What is more, there is a Joint Committee of Parliament (which is the counterpart of the Interministerial Committee) whose views must be obtained by the government as regards the endowment fund, the extra costs of political origin, and the government's proposals for the appointment of IRI's Chairman and Vice-Chairman.

Less elaborate but clear interventions from the government side exist in the case of Salzgitter AG. The Ministry of Finance exerts control over personnel and other managerial matters; while the Minister of Economic Affairs has control in so far as the politico-economic interests of the government are concerned. An interesting facet of governmental interface consists of ministry officials attending supervisory meetings in all major subsidiaries. This can be a channel of direct influence; whether a more open transmission of influence would be commendable is an open question.

Several of the enterprises covered in the volume have institutional innovations integrating government officials with enterprise management at certain strategic levels, other than the board level. The two British enterprises are nearly free from such innovations. Electricité de France has two civil service institutions supplementary to the board: the Commissionnaire du Gouvernement and the Mission de Contrôle économique et financier. The former ensures compliance with government policies; and the latter particularly ensures compliance with financial policies and regulations of the government. He is supposed to keep the Ministry of Economy and Finance informed of the financial position of EDF. That the powers of these two institutions are weighty, in conception, may be seen from the fact that both of them can exercise 'suspensory veto' on the decisions of the board and the Director-General.

IRI is one of the enterprises whose accounting organisation bears an institutional impact from the side of the government. A board of auditors is appointed by the Ministry of State Holdings. A Magistrate of the State Court of Accounts attends all meetings of IRI's administrative bodies with a view to ensuring the economic viability of investments provided by the government. The focus is on the correct application of the decisional rules, as contrasted with the intrinsic justifiability of an investment. There is an analytically commendable connection between this institutional device and the non-commercial segment of IRI's objectives. The latter entail 'extra costs of political origin', in evaluating which the Magistrate's role can have crucial importance.

No 'hierarchical' control points are set up by the government in CVG. Only the Controlaria General has an office at CVG headquarters to exercise control over its activities. An interesting facet of CVG is that, being vested with functions of regional development, it virtually operates as the office of CORDIPLAN in so far as the region of Guyana is concerned.

There is no evidence of government agencies implanted in public enterprise organisations in the many other papers covered in the volume. This does not imply the absence of government control relationships. These are derived, sometimes very seriously, from the ordinary routines of departmental scrutiny and, on occasions, from guidelines and directions. The latter, apart from any informal interventions, are transparent and reflect the positive thinking of the government in the context of a given enterprise. The scrutiny function, as illustrated by UK experience, though apparently of a routine nature, is not necessarily less control-triggered than the institutional devices cited above. Mark what the Industry and Trade Committee of Parliament said about the departmental control over the Post Office in the UK:

> We are left with the impression that since the separation of the Post Office and British Telecommunications there has been a return to a form of financial and managerial control in the Post Office similar to that exercised when the Corporation was a Government Department.

> Our view is that the scrutiny by the Department of Industry of the Post Office's activities is detailed and too intrusive for a body which is supposed to be a commercial enterprise.[2]

The other type of government intervention which is more purposeful than direct institutional infiltration in enterprise organisation at different levels takes the form of meaningful target-setting or formal agreement on mutual relationships. The former has been the British method — applicable, among the cases in this volume, to the British Steel Corporation and the Post Office. The financial targets can have the effect of providing organisational clarity to the enterprise managements and, hopefully, a reasonable degree of autonomy. There is a subtle point. Where the target is overall, the organisation is not inhibited in policies of cross-subsidisation and in over-working the 'total entity' concept. The Port Authority of NY and NJ, for example, follows the statutory principle of pooling revenues and implements deficit financing of the railway (passenger) services it operates. Where the targets are set activity by activity as in the case of the UK Post Office, there can be an organisational urge for adequate financial decentralisation.

In the case of enterprises which have neither governmental agencies sitting within them nor financial targets set for them, the impacts of government relations on organisational behaviour are highly indeterminate. An extreme possibility, perhaps valid in several cases, is over-centralisation in the fancy that the top level of management can then be in a satisfactory position to meet governmental control incursions.

We may sum up the organisational impacts of non-commercial objectives. These are fairly material in most cases, though in the case of the British Steel Corporation and Salzgitter AG the latest position is one of nominal or no exclusively public enterprise 'duties'. The 'Rowland Hill' principle of uniform prices (in the case of the Post Office), 'missions of general economic interest' and regional development (Electricité de France), investment and employment in the backward South (IRI), employment in distressed border areas and training (Salzgitter), instrumentality as a regional development agency (CVG), promotion and protection of the commerce and economy of the Port District (Port Authority of NY and NJ), and 'the restructuring of society' in the interests of the 'bumiputeras' (sons of the soil) (UDA) – all these amply evidence the ubiquity of the non-commercial segment of functions shouldered by public enterprises. However, their organisational structures do not reflect due attention to this fact; nor are institutional links properly evolved for the impact of such objectives on the enterprises.

F. *Capital Structure*

The enterprises covered in this volume present diversities as regards the composition of the capital outlay. Some have exclusively loan capital, e.g., the Post Office, the Port Authority of NY and NJ, and Electricité de France; and some others have both loan and share capital, e.g., the National Fertilizer Corporation of Pakistan Ltd., and Coal India Ltd. The long-standing British practice of bonded debt constituting the capitalisation of the public corporations has undergone a change in respect of a few enterprises in recent years. The British Steel Corporation is one of them and has received 'public dividend capital'. The reason for the change is that an enterprise which faces competition and business fluctuations ought not to be saddled with the burden of interest on capital in the years of low net revenues.

The equity segment in the capital structure has no doubt a purpose in providing the enterprise with the convenience of not having to find the cash from which to pay the cost of capital employed in a period of poor net revenue or loss. The device becomes particularly valid if the enterprise operates in competition with others and if the latter enjoy the convenience of equity capital.

It appears, however, that equity has been employed with two other purposes as well. The first is that an enterprise subjected to social obligations and 'extra political costs' ought to be given the benefit of a soft capital structure: soft in the sense that resources are available for use in relatively non-commercial directions and yet without involving it in the full recovery of costs of capital. Endowment capital is the designation given to that part of the capital that approximates to the non-economical functions of IRI. Comment has been made in the Marsan paper that this has not maintained its functional parallelism in recent years, so much so that IRI has been obliged to go in for borrowings in the market, both local and international. The endowment device stands justified if the amount is correctly determined so that it measures exactly the capital and continuing costs of non-commercial functions; and if Parliament, in full knowledge, approves of it.

The other situation of capitalisation with a high equity segment is less justifiable, viz., when it is used as a disguised cost relief under conditions of losses. The Bokhari paper illustrates the use of the method in the case of the National Fertilizer Corporation of Pakistan Ltd. It would be preferable, in the long run, to so design the capital structure as to show up the full costs of capital; and if need be, the right quantum of aid should be devised from the government in an open manner. Or, the end should be an organisational restructuring, involving not simply a capital reduction but probably a capacity contraction or a change in the product mix or readjustments in managerial organisation.

One last point on the capital structures of large public enterprises, which the papers bring out. It is the unitary or apex level that is obliged to show overall financial balance. Certain parts of its activities or certain of the subsidiaries – as amply illustrated by IRI – have very poor net returns; and perhaps there is justification for effecting suitable contractions in their activities. Yet the overall arrangements with the government as investor lead to subsidisation of the unprofitable parts of the organisation and conceal the intrinsic need for reviewing the investment, size, and returns questions on an appropriately disaggregated basis. (At the minimum the credit-worthiness of the apex on the whole can be a channel of subsidy to a part of it whose credit-rating is poor.)

3. CONCLUSION

Two concluding observations would be in order at the end of a close review of experience narrated in the enterprise papers.

First, it is clear that top managements have not only upheld the principle of decentralisation but exerted measures continuously towards intensifying it, subject to constraints of public sector organisation. For instance, Roseveare speaks of 'a complete move to a highly decentralised system'; the Port Authority of NY and NJ follows the fundamental principle of 'delegation of authority'; Bokhari refers to the imperative of 'a large measure of decentralisation'; and the Wadehra paper bristles with the continuum of experiments towards 'a significant degree of autonomy' at below-apex levels (Divisions, in fact) and of dissatisfaction with the 'unmanageable proportions' that the 'span of control' of each subsidiary has been reaching. Great significance attaches to effective programmes of decentralisation within the enterprise; for they represent a major − in some cases, the only practicable − method of dealing with the diseconomies of large-sized (public) enterprises. Not only internal enlightenment − at the managerial level − but external permissiveness if not persuasion − from the government level − are essential to the success of such programmes. The lack of the latter can, in fact, be determinative in keeping the organisational structure uneconomically large and complex.

Second, organisational structure is a basic parameter in determining the success of an enterprise. Good men, good markets, and good technologies go a long way and for a while; but all these are constrained, fundamentally, by the organisational setting. The latter, in the long run, conditions the optimal integration of men, materials and markets through the enterprise. True, it is not a sufficient condition for its well-being; but it is a necessary condition. And in the public sector where disincentives are inherently heavy, the creation of an appropriate organisational structure is of particular significance. In the words of the Executive Director of the Port Authority of NY and NJ (in 1952):

> The form of organisation is not an end unto itself, it is the means by which the work and efforts of individuals are directed to an end result. The effectiveness of a staff ... depends, therefore, not only upon the competence and ability of the individual but also upon the manner in which individual efforts are coordinated through the form of staff organisation.

NOTES

1. G. Ram Reddy (Ed.), *Government and Public Enterprise (Essays in honour of Professor V. V. Ramanadham)* (India, N. M. Tripathi and London, Frank Cass, 1983).
2. Fifth Report from the Industry and Trade Committee (Session 1981–82), *The Post Office* (London, 1982), p. ix.

INDEX

Salzgitter AG (continued)
    processing business line, 118–19
    regional interests and policies, 127,
        128–9
    Research and Development, 122
    shipbuilding business line, 116,
        117–18
    steel, 114–16, 117
    structure and functions, 120–4, 264,
        266, 272
    training policy, 128–9
    unions, 126
    mentioned, 262
Salzgitter Consult GmbH, 119
Salzgitter Güterverwaltung GmbH, 123
Salzgitter Industriebau GmbH, 119
Salzgitter Maschinen und Anlagen AG,
    119, 127
Salzgitter Stahl GmbH, 117
Salzgitter Versicherungsdienst GmbH,
    123
Salzgitter Wirtschaftsbetriebe GmbH,
    123
Salzgitter Wohnungs-AG, 123
SAPAR (*Société anonyme de
    Participations*), 71
Saraceno, Professor, 97, 99, 111n
Scheremetjewo II air terminal,
    Moscow, 128
sectorally dominant public enterprises,
    9–11
    consumer councils, 11
    government concern, 9–10, 11
    subdivisions of, 10–11
    ways of dealing with organisational
        problems, 10
shareholder interest, 16–17
shipbuilding, German, 116, 117–18
SIDOR, 170, 179
Singapore, public enterprise in, 2
Singareni Collieries Co. Ltd. (SCCL),
    213
Singrauli Area coalfield, 219
SIP, 88
Size of public enterprise, 1–11, 266–8
    comparative review, 266–8
    excess capacity, 6–9
    largeness, 3–6, 266–7
    sectoral dominance, 9–11
    types of enterprise discussed, 1–3
SME, 109n, 110n
SNCF, 80, 81
Social content in public enterprise

functions, 12–13
Stahlwerke Peine-Salzgitter AG, 116,
    117, 127
Steel Authority of India Ltd. (SAIL),
    2, 5, 212, 214, 221
Steel industry
    Britain *see* British Steel Corporation
    Germany, 114–6, 117
    Italy, 84, 85, 86, 90, 92, 93, 108
    Venezuela, 165, 170
    see also Steel Authority of India
STET, 110n
Stewarts & Lloyds Ltd., 28
Subsidiaries, comparative review of
    organisation of, 269, 271–4

Tanzania, public enterprise in, 2, 5, 7,
    20n
Taranto steel plant, 85, 86, 111n
Telecommunication
    Italy, 85, 87, 88, 90, 92, 93, 94
    U.K., 52, 53, 54, 55, 56, 57, 58
Temasek, 2
Tinajones Project, 119
Tirrenia, 111n
Trade Unions
    in British Steel Corporation, 30, 40,
        46
    in Corporación Venezolana de
        Guayana, 172, 176
    in Electricité de France, 68
    in Istituto per la Ricostruzione
        Industriale, 106, 107
    in Post Office, 53, 55, 56, 60
    in Yugoslavia, 257
Trinidad and Tobago, public enterprise
    in, 19n
Types of public enterprise, 1–2

UDA *see* Urban Development Authority
U.K. *see* Britain, public enterprises in
Union of Communication Workers, 60
Unions *see* Trade Unions
Unitary type of public enterprise,
    internal organisation structure
    of, 268–71
    constitution of management
        committees, 269
    creation of sub-boards, 270
    description of, 269
    evolution of profit centres, 270–1
    organisational relief to top level, 270
    see also names of enterprises